Functional Integration for Success:
Preschool Intervention

Functional Integration for Success: Preschool Intervention

• • •

SEBASTIAN STRIEFEL

JOHN KILLORAN

MARIA QUINTERO

pro·ed

8700 Shoal Creek Boulevard
Austin, Texas 78758

© 1991 by PRO-ED, Inc.

All rights reserved. No part of this book may be reproduced in any form or by any means without the prior written permission of the publisher.

Printed in the United States of America

Library of Congress Cataloging-in-Publication Data

Striefel, Sebastian, 1941–
    Functional integration for success / Sebastian Striefel, John Killoran, Maria Quintero.
        p.   cm.
    Includes bibliographical references and indexes.
    ISBN 0-89079-416-2
    1. Handicapped children—Education (Preschool)—United States. 2. Mainstreaming in education—United States.   3. Individualized instruction.   I. Killoran, John.   II. Quintero, Maria.   III. Title.
    LC4019.2.S76   1990
    371.9′046—dc20   90-15565
                                                                                    CIP

pro·ed

8700 Shoal Creek Boulevard
Austin, Texas 78758

1   2   3   4   5   6   7   8   9   10   95   94   93   92   91

Contents

Preface

An increasing demand for integrated preschool services was created by Public Law 99-457, which was passed to develop comprehensive statewide early intervention services. The law guarantees a free, appropriate public education in the least restrictive environment for children 3 to 5 years of age who have handicaps. For many, if not all, 3- to 5-year-olds, this means an education in an integrated preschool program.

Most administrators, teachers, and related services personnel (e.g., speech and language therapists, occupational and physical therapists, and school psychologists) have not been prepared by education or experience to educate preschoolers who have handicaps in integrated settings. This book is based on over 5 years of experience in educating preschoolers in integrated settings.

The purpose of this book is to provide administrators, teachers, school psychologists, speech and language therapists, occupational and physical therapists, other school personnel, and, to a more limited degree, parents with the information needed to establish and operate an integrated preschool program. This book is intended as both a preservice and an inservice reference. It would be particularly well suited for use as an undergraduate text in the education of regular and special education preschool teachers and by school personnel in desegregating existing self-contained classrooms.

The functional integration model consists of 10 tasks. The first five tasks focus on general planning, which must occur before the initiation of integrated placements, and include (a) obtaining administrators' involvement, (b) staff preparation, (c) modifying the service delivery program, (d) parent preparation, and (e) peer preparation. The second five tasks are child-specific and are completed after integration has been initiated. These tasks include (a) child identification, (b) IEP decision-making, (c) integrated service delivery, (d) evaluation, and (e) transition to other environments. Specific development and implementation procedures and materials are provided within the chapters relevant to these 10 tasks. Relevant definitions and examples are also provided.

A reader who has mastered the information provided within this book should feel very comfortable in implementing a functionally integrated preschool program and should be successful in this process, as verified by child progress and parent, administrator, teacher, and related staff satisfaction.

Most of the procedures and materials included in this book were developed during the course of two concurrent, federally funded mainstreaming projects. The Functional Mainstreaming for Success (FMS) project was a model demonstration program funded by the Handicapped Children's Early Education Program in the U.S. Office of Education. The project focused on children 3 to 5 years of age. The Validated Strategies for School-Age Mainstreaming (VSSM) project was a field-initiated project funded by the U.S. Office of Education. This project focused on children 6 to 13 years of age. Both projects included the word *mainstreaming* in their title; yet in retrospect, the primary goal of both projects was integration. Several of the materials developed also include the term *mainstreaming*, but would be better served if the word *integration* were used. These titles have been reworded where practical (e.g., the title of this book includes the term *integration*, and the focus of this book is on integration).

The authors wish to acknowledge the assistance of many people in developing the procedures and materials in this book. We wish to thank Ellen Frede-Barnett, Patti Bodine, Steve Campbell, Brooki Sexton, Gary Percival, Todd Braeger, LeAnn Hyer, Trenly Yanito, Stacy Mott, Afsaneh Ahooraiyan, Paul Adams, Connie Nelke, Jane Schultz, Brady Phelps, Mark Thornburg, Robin Korones, Nancy Yonk, Diane Thornburg, Connie Morgan, Nancy Drown, Larry Jacobsen, Prent Klag, Rose Newman, Dick Mecham, Mary Cadez, Ann Miller, Larry Neves, Scott Spencer, Ellyn White, Mary Hardy, Nan Gutshall, Nancy Bartelt, Teresa Larsen, Sandra Legaard, Kimberly Snow, Karen Sampson, and everyone else who helped, but whose names we have forgotten to list.

Chapter 1

• • •

Integration and
the FMS Model

The passage of P.L. 99-457 (Education of Handicapped Children Act Amendments of 1986) is a legislative recognition that young children who have handicaps can benefit from early intervention. Section 619 of P.L. 99-457 mandates a free, appropriate public education in the least restrictive environment in which the needs of the preschool-age child with handicaps can be met. The legislative intent is to educate children, with and without handicaps, in the same classrooms whenever possible. Such an education is based on the philosophy of providing equal educational opportunities to all 3- to 5-year-olds who have handicaps through Individualized Education Programs (IEPs) that are developed to promote learning, achievement, and social interaction. Current research supports the conclusion that children with handicaps benefit from educational programs in integrated settings (Odom & McEvoy, 1988).

Interactions with other children, particularly those who demonstrate behaviors that are developmentally age-appropriate, are critical to the development of a child who has handicaps. Young children acquire skills primarily through play and social interactions (Hanson & Hanline, 1989). If children play and interact with others who lack skills or who demonstrate inappropriate behaviors, appropriate learning can easily be delayed or can be difficult to achieve. Appropriate models facilitate appropriate social, emotional, and language development. Such learning can be greatly enhanced through the use of systematic instructional and social interventions that group children with and

1

without handicaps. Programs that segregate children who have handicaps generally lack access to appropriate nonhandicapped models, thus development and social interaction are not maximized. Integrated settings are essential to the maximal enhancement of learning for children who have handicaps. In addition, since most activities for preschoolers (3- to 5-year-olds) are of short duration, do not require sitting in a chair for hours, and are conducted within a play or fun context, there is no reason why children with and without handicaps cannot be served together in the same setting. In fact, federal law mandates that if a nonintegrated placement is to be used, documentation should be attached to the IEP to explain why an integrated placement could not be used, including the specific services that were tried before a segregated placement was selected (McClean & Odom, 1988). The integration needs of young children are different from those of school-age children developmentally, educationally, and in terms of family involvment. The difficulty in establishing integrated programs is often in locating or creating appropriate settings in which integration can occur. However, since many states now fund services for children who are not handicapped, the dilemma of identifying school-based programs for children without handicaps is decreasing.

Mainstreaming and Integration Defined

Presently, there are no agreed-on definitions for the terms *mainstreaming* and *integration* (Odom & McEvoy, 1988). In addition, overlaps in definitions that do exist make it difficult to determine when mainstreaming versus integration has occurred. For purposes of this book, a distinction is needed between the terms *mainstreaming* and *integration*. Mainstreaming refers to the process of placing or grouping children, with and without handicaps, in the same setting (e.g., classroom) *without* planned/structured involvement in common social and instructional activities. Integration refers to the process of placing or grouping children, with and without handicaps, in the same setting (e.g., classroom) *with* planned/structured involvement in common social and instructional activities. As such, the focus of the term *mainstreaming*, as used herein, is on physical placement; for integration the focus is on active involvment in common social and/or instructional activities. Mainstreaming and integration can be total or partial. Total refers to full-time (day) placement or involvement, and partial refers to part-time (day) placement or involvement. Reverse integration is when children without handicaps are taught with children who have handicaps in a setting that has traditionally been a segregated special education environment (e.g., self-contained classroom).

Integration of Children with Handicaps

A number of factors must be considered in planning integration for children who have handicaps.

1. All activities in regular preschool classrooms do not occur in groups; thus, the integrated preschool classroom does not require that 100% of activities be in groups. In fact, children do many activities by themselves or even in isolation (e.g., working alone at a table, going to the bathroom alone).

2. The percentages of time normal preschoolers spend in social interaction activities vary widely. The percentage should be higher for a class of 3-year-olds than for a class of 5-year-olds. Five-year-olds should be participating in more activities designed to develop the skills needed in kindergarten (e.g., sitting still in a chair or raising one's hand and waiting to be called on before speaking). By age 6, children spend at least half of their school day engaged in academic activities by themselves.

3. Participation in integrated activities does not require social interaction between children 100% of the time. Rather, involvement in a common activity with periodic interaction occurring once per 15 minutes is sufficient for the activity to be considered integrated (Horner, 1989).

The goal of integration is to help children develop social networks that include a sufficient number of children, both with and without handicaps, to assure that they have the social support they need to function in daily environments including school, home, and the community (Striefel, Killoran, & Quintero, 1984, 1985b). A social network consists of people with whom a person has engaged in common activities within a specific interval (Horner, 1989). Social support consists of any of a variety of social functions delivered to one person by another including, but not limited to, companionship, feedback, or assistance.

Components of Successful Integration

Successful integration is a continuing process, rather than a discrete event. It includes the maximal age-appropriate, instructional, and social acccommodation of children who have handicaps into educational and community environments with children who do not have handicaps (Johnson & Johnson, 1981; Kaufman, Gottlieb, Agard, & Kukic, 1975; Nash & Boileau, 1980; Pasanella & Volkmor, 1981; Peterson, 1983; Reynolds & Birch, 1982; Stremel-Campbell, Moore, Johnson-Dorn, Clark, & Toews, 1983; Turnbull & Schultz, 1979; Weisenstein & Pelz, 1986; Zigmond & Sansone, 1981). Successful integration must:

1. Require the IEP team to identify the skills the child should achieve through integration.

2. Provide alternative integration activities that range from brief to longer periods of interactions and from dyads to large groups.

3. Specify the responsibility of students, parents, regular and special education teachers, administrators, and support personnel (Cansler & Winton, 1983; Hughes & Hurth, 1984; Johnson & Johnson, 1986; Pasanella & Volkmor, 1981; Peterson, 1983; Powers, 1983; Taylor, 1982; Weisenstein & Pelz, 1986; Zigmond & Sansone, 1981).

4. Include preplacement preparation, postplacement support, and continued training for students with and without handicaps, their parents, teachers, administrators, and support personnel (Cansler & Winton, 1983; Donaldson, 1980; Guralnick, 1983; Hughes & Hurth, 1984; Larrivee, 1981; Nash & Boileau, 1980; Peterson, 1983; Powers, 1983; Reynolds & Birch, 1982; Schwartz, 1984; Taylor, 1982; Thomason & Arkell, 1980; Zigmond & Sansone, 1981).

5. Maximize appropriate interactions between children with and without handicaps through structured activities (e.g., peer tutoring or buddy systems) and social skills training, as appropriate to specific situations and abilities (Arick, Almond, Young, & Krug, 1983; Gresham, 1982; Hughes & Hurth, 1984; Johnson & Johnson, 1981; Madden & Slavin, 1983; Reynolds & Birch, 1982; Schwartz, 1984; Stainback & Stainback, 1981; Stainback, Stainback, & Jaben, 1981; Taylor, 1982; Voeltz, Keshi, Brown, & Kube, 1980; Walker, 1983; Weisenstein & Pelz, 1986).

6. Provide functional, age-appropriate activities that prepare the child with handicaps to function in current and future community environments (Brown, Nietupski, & Hamre-Nieupski, 1976; Wilcox & Bellamy, 1982; Wilcox, McDonnell, Rose, & Bellamy, 1985).

7. Occur without major long-term disruption of ongoing developmental activities or other detriments to children with and without handicaps in the integrated setting (Cooke, Ruskus, Appolloni, & Peck, 1981; Hanline, 1985; Price & Weinberg, 1982; Vergon & Ross, 1981).

Rationale for Integration

Increasingly, children with handicaps are placed (mainstreamed) into self-contained classrooms located within regular schools. These children often have little access to, or interaction with, their nonhandicapped peers outside the self-contained classroom. Though they are physically present in the same school, they may be physically, socially, and instructionally isolated from their peers who are not handicapped. This isolation is the result of obstacles such as (a) a lack of valid procedures for making placement decisions and selecting the integration activities appropriate for each child (Hamre-Nietupski, Nietupski, Stainback, & Stainback, 1984; Schrag, 1984; Stremel-Campbell, Moore, Johnson-Dorn, Clark, & Toews, 1983; Taylor, 1982); (b) a lack of valid procedures and activities for productively grouping children with and without handicaps (Nietupski, Hamre-Nietupski, Schultz, & Oakwood, 1980; Rule, Killoran, Stowitschek, Innocenti, Striefel, & Boswell, 1985; Salend & Johns, 1983; Schwartz, 1984; Taylor, 1982); (c) a lack of validated procedures for preparing school staff, children without handicaps, and their parents for the integration of children with handicaps (Donaldson, 1980; Gresham, 1982; Turnbull, Winton, Blacher, & Salkind, 1982; Voeltz et al., 1980; Walker, 1983); (d) a lack of validated procedures for preparing children with handicaps and their parents for integration (Turnbull et al., 1982; Walker, 1983); (e) a lack of validated procedures for determining and providing the necessary support services for regular teachers when children with handicaps are integrated into their classrooms (Hannah & Pliner, 1983; Larrivee, 1981; Lombardi, Meadowcroft, & Strasburger, 1982); and (f) ideological and economic barriers (Berres & Knoblock, 1987).

Integration may be difficult to achieve because children who have handicaps often require (a) a greater number of trials to learn a skill, (b) smaller groups and individualized attention during training, and (c) specific procedures for generalizing learned skills across different settings and trainers (Brown, Nisbet, Ford, Sweet, Shiraga, York, & Loomis, 1983; Stokes & Baer, 1977).

Traditional teaching techniques used in normal preschool programs often lack the intensity and systematic components needed to teach a child who has handicaps. These components—assessment, individualization, and progress monitoring—have been demonstrated to increase the effectiveness of instruction (DeWulf, Biery, & Stowitschek, 1987). Teachers report their perceived lack of preparation and training for teaching children with handicaps (Stainback & Stainback, 1983). An innovative alternate model of service delivery is needed that accommodates training to meet an individual child's needs while still addressing the needs of the group. The Functional Mainstreaming for Success (FMS) model was developed to address these needs.

Integration is a desirable goal. Frequently cited reasons for integration include:

1. Preparation for functioning in society requires exposure to normal environments (Brown, Ford, Nisbet, Sweet, Donnellan, & Gruenewald, 1983; Masat & Schack, 1981; Weintraub, 1979).

2. Addressing the individual needs of children who have handicaps requires a range of alternatives (Beery, 1977; Birch, 1974; Karnes & Lee, 1978).

3. The costs for educating some children are lower when integrated (Redden, 1976; Schultz & Turnbull, 1983).

4. Children who have handicaps benefit from integration opportunities (Carlberg & Kavale, 1980; Madden & Slavin, 1983).

5. Individuals who have handicaps have the same rights to life, liberty, and the pursuit of happiness as everyone else (Ballard, Ramirez, & Zantal-Wiener, 1987).

6. Society is directly affected by its treatment of those with handicaps (e.g., productive vs. nonproductive members of society).

7. Exposure to more advanced peers can result in imitation of language, social, and other skills (Gresham, 1982; Schultz & Turnbull, 1983).

8. Integration challenges students who have handicaps by creating a more complex and demanding environment (Johnson & Johnson, 1981; Kaufman et al., 1975; Reynolds & Birch, 1982).

9. Integration may create a more positive attitude toward persons who have handicaps (Mott, Striefel, & Quintero, 1986; Striefel & Killoran, 1984a, 1984b; Walker, 1983).

10. Integration can result in increased self-esteem for the child with and the child without handicaps, if appropriate planning has occurred (Scruggs, Mastropieri, & Richter, 1981; Taylor, 1982; Walker, 1983).

Assumptions Supporting Preschool Intervention

Intensive intervention efforts in the preschool years are important because:

1. The major foundations of development, including language and motor skills, are generally completed by age 5. Social interaction is no exception. In fact, difficulties in establishing peer relationships are predictive of later adjustment problems (Guralnick & Bennett, 1987).

2. Intervention during the preschool years has repeatedly been shown to produce consistent, positive changes in development (Guralnick & Bennett, 1987).

3. Some early experiences may have a disproportionate positive or negative effect on later development (Guralnick & Bennett, 1987).

4. The effect of some, or lack of some, early experiences may not be canceled by later experiences (Guralnick & Bennett, 1987).

5. The preschool years may be more critical for those with handicaps because the ability to cope, adapt, and reorient may be more limited and fragile (Guralnick & Bennett, 1987).

6. Environmental factors during preschool years, as in later life, influence development greatly; thus, the impact of integrated settings is critical.

Activities for Preschool Integration

Preschool education can be defined as a series of systematic, planned education activities focused on promoting development through environmental and experiential change initiated during the preschool years (age 3 to 5 years). Briefly, activities that must be considered when integrating preschools include:

1. A clearly specified mission and goals for the program.

2. A philosophy that facilitates maximum child development.

3. A stable funding base, preferably one that is adequate for achieving the program's mission and goals.

4. Policies and procedures to guide program staff activities.

5. Established formal linkages with other community agencies and professionals (e.g., the health department, Head Start, schools, and pediatricians).

6. Community involvement and advocacy.

7. A community awareness program.

8. A child find and referral system.

9. A parent information manual that describes the program, rights, and grievance procedures and includes copies of the necessary forms for parent consent.

10. A local neighborhood school that is accessible, and that meets health and safety standards.

11. A transportation system for getting children to and from the program.

12. A wide range of age-appropriate curriculum materials.

13. Adaptive and assistive equipment appropriate to the needs of those served.

14. A range of integration activities within or available to the program (e.g., peer buddies and peer tutors).

15. A transdisciplinary staff competent in the skills needed to serve families and preschoolers, those both with and without handicaps.

16. A comprehensive system for personnel development to provide staff inservice training and support. .

17. A clear specification of who will be served, for example, those with clearly established disabilities and delays, those at risk, and children without handicaps and delays.

18. A specification of the type, quality, duration, and intensity of program to be provided (IEP process)

19. A comprehensive transdisciplinary assessment to develop a comprehensive developmental profile of each child's strengths and deficits. Such an assessment includes, but is not limited to, social, motor, language, self-help, cognitive skills, and physical and social environmental characteristics. A variety of standardized and criterion-referenced tests, rating forms and checklists, and direct observation measures can be used. Assessment must be ongoing.

20. A comprehensive range of normal development, special education, and related services that can be accessed to meet the unique needs

of each child served. These services are guided by an assessment-based IEP developed for each child.

21. A formal process for transitioning 3-year-olds from infant programs (Part H of P.L. 99-457) to preschool and 5-year-olds from preschool to kindergarten (Part B of P.L. 99-457).

22. A mechanism for evaluating all aspects of the program, including a corrective mechanism for improving the quality of the program.

Exemplary Preschool Special Education

Since the passage of P.L. 99-457, an increased emphasis has also been placed on identifying best practices in preschool special education, and in examining the implications of these practices for model development, implementation, and evaluation (McDonnell & Hardman, 1988). While the concept of early intervention may be widely accepted by policymakers and practitioners alike, the need for further investigation of the efficacy of integrated preschools is highly debated among researchers (Casto & Mastropieri, 1986; Killoran, 1988a; Strain & Smith, 1986; White & Mott, 1987). Despite this empirical debate, teachers and intervenors face the immediate reality of providing preschool special education. Practitioners must teach with the best available technology while ensuring the inclusion of new best practices as they are identified (White & Mott, 1987).

McDonnell and Hardman (1988) have identified six characteristics of exemplary preschool special education classrooms as follows:

1. Integrated service delivery

2. Comprehensive services

3. Normalized services and settings

4. Adaptable services

5. Peer- and family-referenced services

6. Services that are outcome-based

Admittedly, these six characteristics are broad concepts which, in themselves, synthesize many effective practices. However, they presently represent the best guide for developing exemplary models of service delivery that incorporate today's technology, yet are adaptable to tomorrow's.

Integrated Service Delivery

The argument for integrated service delivery is no longer purely philosophical. Recently, federally funded model demonstration projects (Handicapped Children's Early Education Program) have demonstrated integrated services that have (a) increased skill acquisition in preschoolers both with and without handicaps, (b) increased parent and staff satisfaction, and (c) increased cost effectiveness when compared to self-contained placements (Rule et al., 1987; Striefel, Killoran, & Quintero, 1987).

Comprehensive Services

To comprehensively meet the needs of students and families, services must be coordinated across a variety of administrative and funding agencies including health, education, and social service agencies. Agencies must strive for the development of theoretically and procedurally well-defined models that rely on transdisciplinary and consultative service delivery. In addition, service delivery must include the intensity and systematic components of instruction needed to effectively teach children with handicaps, including:

1. Individual criterion-referenced assessment
2. Individual education programs
3. Integrated (least restrictive) instruction
4. Direct instruction
5. Ongoing process monitoring (Killoran, 1988a; McDonnell & Hardman, 1988)

Normalized Services

If adults who have handicaps are expected to function and contribute to normal settings, they must first learn to function as children in normal settings (Donder & York, 1984). However, exposure to a normal environment alone will not guarantee successful interaction in that environment (Brown, Branston, Hamre-Nietupski, Johnson, Wilcox, & Gruenewald, 1979). In contrast, placing students with handicaps in physical proximity of (nonhandicapped) peers without planned and systematic social intervention (integration) increases the likelihood of negative social interactions occurring between the students. Normalizing preschool special education must include:

1. Providing support for the roles of parents.

2. Using age-appropriate instructional strategies and teaching age-appropriate skills.

3. Ensuring concurrent skills training across skill areas.

4. Distributing practice of skills across settings.

5. Establishing spontaneous responding (McDonnell & Hardman, 1988).

6. Avoiding artificial reinforcement and aversive control techniques (Killoran, 1988a).

Adaptable Services

To be successful, services must be adaptable. Adaptability in preschool special education programs should include (a) the use of flexible, noncategorical models, (b) increased family support and involvement, (c) emphasis on functionality and age-appropriate programming, and (d) ongoing program modification based on individual evaluation (McDonnell & Hardman, 1988).

Peer- and Family-Referenced Services

Four guidelines are presented by McDonnell and Hardman (1988) for providing peer- and family-referenced services. These guidelines are based on the premise that natural environments should generate curricular objectives and be the location for teaching children with severe handicaps. For preschool-age children these natural settings include family, school, peer, and community settings. Their guidelines call for (a) referencing curricula to families, peers, and communities; (b) including parents in active planning and decision-making;

(c) systematically communicating between school and home; and (d) generalization programming for training and transferring skills to the student's home and community.

Outcome-Based Services

Student-centered outcomes for early childhood special education programs address (a) preparation for future settings, (b) skill aquisition for demands presented in present and future environments, and (c) planned systematic transition (Killoran, 1988b; McDonnell & Hardman, 1988). By concentrating model development around these student-centered outcomes, practitioners increase the likelihood of successful functioning in normal family, school, and community settings.

Service Delivery Philosophy

The Functional Mainstreaming for Success (FMS) project (Striefel et al., 1987) developed a model for preschool mainstreaming that is committed to the philosophy of providing services to preschoolers with handicaps in totally integrated settings. This philosophy is based on the premise that adults with handicaps who are expected to function within, and contribute to, normal community settings must learn as children to function within normal environments (Donder & York, 1984). However, exposure to a normal environment alone will not guarantee successful interaction in that environment (Brown, Branston, Hamre-Nietupski, Johnson, Wilcox, & Gruenewald, 1979; Gresham, 1982). Integration must go beyond physical integration to the incorporation of instructional and social integration as major goals of a program (Nash & Boileau, 1980; Striefel & Killoran, 1984a, 1984b; Zigmond & Sansone, 1981). In fact, McClean and Odom (1988) point out that it is not the presence of normally developing children per se that determines how well children with handicaps do in mainstreamed programs, but rather the quality of the education program.

Goals of the FMS Model

Numerous integrated preschools abound and have proven to be a successful education option throughout the United States. However, the need for integrated preschool services is greater than the number of presently available options. This need will only become greater as P.L. 99-457 is fully implemented. The law requires services for preschool children who have handicaps in the least restrictive setting. Since services are not mandated in many states for children who are not handicapped, it is likely that many programs will initially be housed in self-contained classrooms or centers. The model of totally or partially integrating children should have tremendous appeal, since the model was developed for precisely these types of settings. As a Handicapped Children's Early Education Program model demonstration project (1984–87) and component of a statewide outreach project (1988–91), the Functional Mainstreaming for Success (FMS) project focused on developing a model for providing preschool-age children who have handicaps with age-appropriate experiences and systematic intervention services in environments with normal preschoolers. To accomplish the social and instructional integration of preschoolers with and without handicaps, the FMS project identified a need for developing effective, replicable procedures to accomplish the following five goals:

1. Determining the type of integration activities appropriate for each child served and for selecting the most appropriate integration alternative.

2. Developing alternative activities that promote meaningful integration of children with and without handicaps.

3. Preparing staff, normal children, and their parents for the integration of children who have handicaps into a specific school or classroom.

4. Preparing children who have handicaps and their families for integration of the child into activities with peers who are not handicapped.

5. Determining and providing the support services needed by a regular teacher when children who have handicaps are integrated into regular classrooom activities.

Factors Affecting Replication of the Model

To effectively replicate the FMS project's five goals, the following seven factors must be considered:

1. The program provides services to children who have handicaps in what were traditionally self-contained classrooms (in either a self-contained training center, a regular school, or the community). The same model can be used in a regular developmental classroom to bring children with handicaps into that setting. Doing so would require evaluating the accessibility to program facilities and the need for specialized equipment.

2. The costs for start-up and normal operation of the program are covered by an existing program budget, or extramural funding is available for start-up costs. The budget could be supplemented via enrollment fees for children who are not handicapped, donations, or other contracts and sources of funds. These are costs above those necessary for implementing the existing self-contained programs. These costs are discussed in Chapter 11.

3. Staff include the specific disciplines needed to meet the individual needs of the children served. This means that transdisciplinary personnel must be available on staff or as consultants (e.g., speech and language therapists, occupational and physical therapists) for direct services.

4. Staff have minimal to moderate levels of knowledge about integration and/or are willing to learn more about integration. Staff with extensive experience and knowledge concerning integration will find the model easier to implement than will those with less knowledge and experience in integration.

5. The program and facility meet the existing state and federal health and safety codes and educational regulations concerning preschool-age children.

6. Some person with sufficient formal (school board, administrator) or informal (staff member or parent) power is committed to integrating children. Someone must be willing to put in the effort required for the model to be implemented.

7. Children without handicaps who are of preschool age are readily available in the immediate vicinity where the program is operating.

Completion of the Self-Evaluation Checklist of Factors Affecting Replication (Figure 1.1) will help you determine which of these seven givens are available at your site and what resources must be obtained.

Initially, the implementation of the FMS model can seem overwhelming in terms of the number of instructions to read and forms to complete. Users have found that going through the process of

Figure 1.1. Self-Evaluation Checklist of Factors Affecting Replication of the FMS Model

---

Circle the number for each question for which the correct response is yes.

Questions

1. Is a classroom (self-contained or normal) available that has enough space to serve up to 16 children at one time?

2. Is a program budget available for adequately implementing the existing program?

   a. Are start-up and maintenance funds available?

   b. If not, can they be obtained?

3. Is an appropriate transdisciplinary staff available?

   a. If not, can such a staff be hired on a regular or consultive basis?

4. Do existing staff have limited experience and/or knowledge concerning integration?

5. Does the program and facility meet existing federal and state regulations?

   a. If not, can the program and/or facility be brought into compliance?

6. Is some person with sufficient power to implement the program committed to integrating preschool-age children who have handicaps?

7. Are preschool-age children who are not handicapped readily available in the immediate vicinity of the program?

   a. If not, is appropriate transportation available for transporting such children to the integration site?

   b. If not, can the program's location be moved elsewhere so that normal peers are available?

---

reading instructions and completing forms provides them with extensive knowledge and experience about integrating children who have handicaps into settings with children who do not have handicaps. Moreover, a learning set occurs with repetition, so that by the time teachers have used a form 3 to 5 times (or less) they no longer need the instructions and, in some cases, reach the point where the process is so ingrained that not even the forms are needed.

FMS Total and Partial Integration Approaches

The preschool-age student in a special education self-contained classroom generally has limited contact with nonhandicapped peers. Yet, this same student rarely, if ever, needs to be in a self-contained classroom at all, much less for the entire day. Preschool-age children are in self-contained classrooms for any number of reasons, including (a) a historical placement based on what has been done for many years with children who have handicaps; (b) a placement utilized because funding for preschool-age children who do not have handicaps is not available, thus self-contained classrooms are seen as the only logical choice; (c) a lack of familiarity with appropriate integration models because few such models are available; and (d) administrative ease.

In response to this situation, the FMS total and partial integration approaches were developed. Authors of the FMS total integration model recommend use of classrooms that are noncategorical. That is, children with mild to severe and profound handicaps and children aged 3 to 5 years without handicaps attend the same classes. In the integrated classrooms, eight of the children have handicaps and eight of the children do not. Student enrollments larger than this are difficult to manage and enrollments that are smaller are not cost-efficient. In fact, it is most efficient if each classroom is used for one group in the morning and one in the afternoon and if there are two or more classrooms. Any proportion of 50% or more of children who are not handicapped per classroom is desirable.

Children are taught in large and small groups. IEP goals for children with handicaps are addressed within these groups unless a child's progress indicates that more intensive intervention is needed. One-to-one sessions are kept at a minimum so that the child can still participate in other activities where language, social, and group attending skills can be developed and practiced. Within groups, FMS staff assist in training teaching personnel to use effective prompting and praising procedures, strategic grouping of children in the classroom for learning groups, and peer interaction systems to facilitate social interactions (see Chapters 8 and 9). Parents are encouraged to be active in the classrooms and to express their concerns about integration. Parents are provided written materials on opportunities for informal exchanges of information to answer their questions about the integration process (see Chapter 5 for information on parent involvement).

The total integration classrooms are staffed by a teacher and two aides. Children who need one-to-one therapy may need a speech and language pathologist, a behavior specialist, a motor therapist, and/or other specialists on a consultative or direct service basis. Individual programs vary according to each child's needs, and are delivered through professionals, paraprofessionals, and volunteers (e.g., college students and parents) who are solicited to conduct programs under the supervision of specialists and/or the classroom teacher. Additional aides can be hired if volunteers are not available. In a classroom where the handicapping conditions of the children range from mild to moderate, few one-to-one sessions are needed and the need for additional personnel is minimal. In the classroom where eight or more children with moderate-to-severe handicapping conditions are being served, the number of intervenors needed will vary depending on how many sessions are necessary, the length of the sessions, and when one-to-one sessions are conducted.

Children who are deemed by the IEP team as not yet ready for total integration are involved in partial integration as appropriate to the needs of the individual child. School staff not experienced or trained in the skills needed to implement an integrated program are more likely to consider some children not yet ready for total integration. Figure 1.2 illustrates the process of placing children into partial and/or total integration based on the IEP process.

An Overview of the 10 Tasks of the FMS Model

The intent of the model developed by the FMS project was to desegregate existing self-contained special education preschool programs—that is, those programs that have traditionally taught children with handicaps in totally segregated settings. The model has been used by state and local educational agencies, state and local social service agencies, and private preschool programs providing services to children with handicaps. The model comprises 10 tasks, beginning with the demonstration of administrative commitment to the philosophy of integrated service delivery systems, and ending with the transition of students from the preschool program to the public schools. The 10 tasks that represent the model are shown in Figure 1.3. Tasks 1

Figure 1.2. Flowchart of Children's Total or Partial Integration

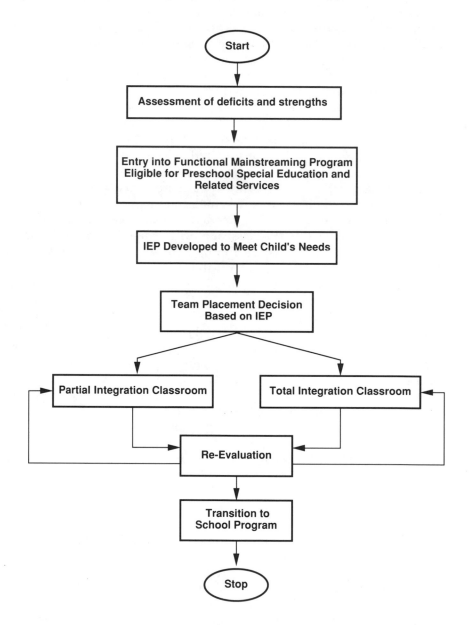

Figure 1.3. The Ten Tasks of the FMS Model

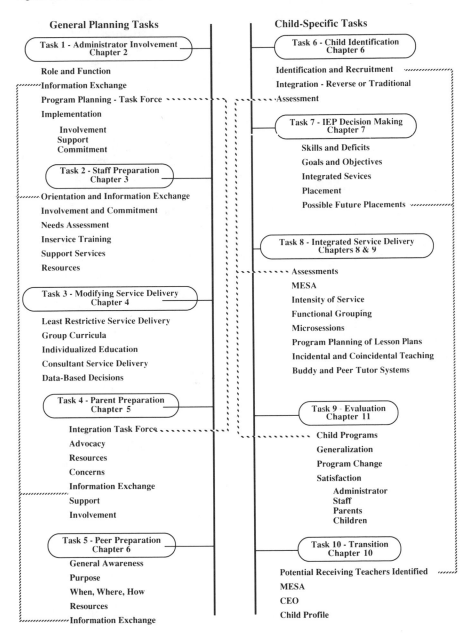

General Planning Tasks

Task 1 - Administrator Involvement
Chapter 2

Role and Function

Information Exchange

Program Planning - Task Force

Implementation

    Involvement
    Support
    Commitment

Task 2 - Staff Preparation
Chapter 3

Orientation and Information Exchange

Involvement and Commitment

Needs Assessment

Inservice Training

Support Services

Resources

Task 3 - Modifying Service Delivery
Chapter 4

Least Restrictive Service Delivery

Group Curricula

Individualized Education

Consultant Service Delivery

Data-Based Decisions

Task 4 - Parent Preparation
Chapter 5

    Integration Task Force

    Advocacy

    Resources

    Concerns

    Information Exchange

    Support

    Involvement

Task 5 - Peer Preparation
Chapter 6

    General Awareness

    Purpose

    When, Where, How

    Resources

Information Exchange

Child-Specific Tasks

Task 6 - Child Identification
Chapter 6

Identification and Recruitment

Integration - Reverse or Traditional

Assessment

Task 7 - IEP Decision Making
Chapter 7

    Skills and Deficits

    Goals and Objectives

    Integrated Sevices

    Placement

    Possible Future Placements

Task 8 - Integrated Service Delivery
Chapters 8 & 9

Assessments

MESA

Intensity of Service

Functional Grouping

Microsessions

Program Planning of Lesson Plans

Incidental and Coincidental Teaching

Buddy and Peer Tutor Systems

Task 9 - Evaluation
Chapter 11

    Child Programs

    Generalization

    Program Change

    Satisfaction

        Administrator
        Staff
        Parents
        Children

Task 10 - Transition
Chapter 10

Potential Receiving Teachers Identified

MESA

CEO

Child Profile

through 5 are general planning tasks that occur prior to or at the initiation of integrated placements. Tasks 6 through 10 are child-specific tasks to be completed after the initiation of integrated placement. The remaining chapters of this manual discuss tasks 1 through 10 in detail, as well as the products developed by the FMS staff for accomplishing each task. Tasks 5 and 6 are combined into one chapter.

Effectiveness Data

The results of progress evaluations conducted on children in totally versus partially integrated classrooms indicated that children with mild to severe handicaps who were enrolled in the FMS total integration classes achieved IEP goals and objectives as well as, or better than, comparable peers in partially integrated classes. On standardized testing, totally integrated children with handicaps showed greater developmental gains than did those who were partially integrated. Children in totally integrated classes also demonstrated higher levels of appropriate social and language interactions than their partially integrated counterparts. Futhermore, they had opportunities to develop classroom behaviors (sitting in a group, waiting their turn, and working next to peers) and independence (asking for assistance when needed and being assertive), which are almost nonexistent in traditional self-contained classes. These skills enhance the likelihood for successful transition to less restrictive environments upon reaching school age. In light of these and other experimental findings, it appears that children with handicaps receive a higher quality early experience if they are enrolled in totally integrated programs that provide systematic intervention for children with handicaps. Even for children whose teachers believe that their behaviors may be too extreme for total integration (e.g., a child who aggresses toward others), partial integration for short periods with teacher supervision is a goal to designate, address, and implement as a first step toward total integration.

A complete summary and details of project effectiveness data can be found in the FMS final report (Striefel et al., 1987). A brief summary follows (also see Table 1.1):

1. Both totally and partially integrated children made gains in most areas measured.

2. Gains were generally larger for totally integrated children.

3. The levels of social interactions were higher for totally versus partially integrated children.

Table 1.1. Summary of Mean Gains on All Tests and Measures for All Subjects in All Three Groups from September to May

Areas Assessed	Partially Integrated N = 18	Totally Integrated N = 21	Control N = 20
% Objectives Achieved	35.67	42.00	*
Number of Microsessions	13.31	6.36	*
% Reciprocal Social Interactions	6.24	18.22	32.49
% Group Play Interactions	4.36	11.32	20.77
Gain in Months on Battelle	6.22	10.15	12.23
Gain DPIYC	9.06	10.05	4.56
PAPG Social	49.54	16.00	19.80
PAPG Language	22.92	23.44	25.00
MESA-PK	59.25	41.92	24.25
Peabody Gross Motor	5.17	12.94	*
Peabody Fine Motor	9.74	21.05	*

* Measure not applicable/administered to children without handicaps.

N	= Number of Children
Battelle	= Battelle Developmental Inventory
DPIYC	= Developmental Programming for Infants and Young Children
PAPG	= Program Assessment and Planning Guide
MESA-PK	= Mainstreaming Expectations and Skills Assessment - Preschool and Kindergarten

4. Parents and staff were very pleased with the integration program and the progress of the children served.

5. Children without handicaps also made age-appropriate gains in most areas measured.

6. The children without handicaps generally enjoyed being in the program and did not discriminate against children on the basis of handicaps.

Chapter 2

* * *

Administrator Involvement as a Key to Integration

The success of an integrated preschool program depends on many factors. These include, but are not limited to, the availability and allocation of resources, the success of the initial implementation of the program, and the commitment of its administrators to the program. Effective programs are managed by effective administrators. The resources and support for the implementation and maintenance of integrated preschools are controlled by its administrators. Thus the key to effective, integrated preschool programs is the commitment of administrators. Commitment is also needed by parents, educators, and policymakers (Reynolds, 1988). Commitment is demonstrated by leadership and proactive actions, and varying levels of commitment impact the success and durability of programs. Some administrators actively support integration, while others assign a staff member to be responsible for integration and support that person's efforts. Others make integration a part of the school service system by assigning a task force consisting of several people including staff and parents; unfortunately, others still actively oppose integration efforts. Unless the integration effort becomes ingrained in the formal service system, it will last only as long as those who are spearheading integration are available, will not be totally effective, nor will it be available to all children. Successful integration requires progressive inclusion and acceptance of children with handicaps in all school and community activities (Reynolds, 1988).

Local education agencies and administrators have an obligation under P.L. 99-457 to provide a free appropriate education in individually determined least restrictive environments. Moreover, most administrators are motivated by a desire to do a good job, and their behavior is maintained by its consequences. If an administrator receives positive consequences and support for efforts at enhancing integration, such efforts will continue. If negative consequences are forthcoming, it will require a very committed administrator to continue to press for integration in spite of opposition.

A school district has many levels of administration, ranging from the board of education and superintendent to the school principal. Depending on the size of the district, there may be few or many intervening levels of administration. It would be expected that with total implementation of P.L. 99-457 (i.e., 1991) all administrators would be committed to mainstreaming and to integration. That is not the case. As Berres and Knoblock (1987) have pointed out, most school administrators are not trained in the implementation of special education. Thus, their lack of commitment to integration is not surprising. Moreover, those who are interested often lack the skills needed to plan and/or implement an integrated preschool program and are hesitant to publicly acknowledge this lack of skills.

Knowledge is the essential component for establishing and/or maintaining integrated preschool programs (McCormack, 1984). A well-informed administrator is in the key position for disseminating information to others. Administrator commitment to integration requires that he or she have the knowledge needed. The Monitoring and Planning Checklist for Integration (Figure 2.1) provides an overview of the primary areas concerning integration with which an administrator must be familiar (each area is discussed in this book). The task then becomes one of determining the administrator's level of knowledge and commitment to integration so that resistance and hesitation can be replaced by enthusiasm and leadership.

The sooner administrators are involved in the process of planning and implementing an integrated preschool program, the more likely it is that commitment will be obtained. Involvement and commitment to integration can be initiated by other administrators and teachers in the district, at the state level, or by parents, teachers, or as a special university-based project such as the Functional Mainstreaming for Success project. Common areas of needed information include the barriers to successful integration and reasons for supporting integration.

Barriers to Successful Integration

In addition to a lack of knowledge about integration, other common barriers to implementation include (Berres & Knoblock, 1987):

Figure 2.1. Monitoring and Planning Checklist for Integration

	Projected Date	Date Started	Date Completed	Comments or Priority
Administrator Commitment				
Introduction to FMS Model				
Administrator Checklist				
Task Force Appointed (Adm. Option)				
List of Goals and Activities that Demonstrate Commitment to Integration				
Directory of Local Training Resources				
Staff Preparation and Commitment				
Inservice to Discuss Integration Options				
Questions Teachers Often Raise About Mainstreaming and Integration (Brochure)				
General Parent Preparation				
PTA Meetings				
Newsletters				
Fliers				
Parent Integration Opinionnaire Facts about Mainstreaming and Integration: Answers for Parents (Brochure)				
School-wide Peer Preparation				
Puppet Shows				
Child Identification				
Special Educator fills out MESA				
Special Educator fills out Child Profile				
Regular Educator fills out MESA				
Identify potential receiving teachers by evaluating completed MESAs				
Determine options available for the student (See IEP)				
Plan for addressing				
Teacher needs				
Training child needs				
Parent concerns				
Environmental adaptions				
Peer Prep				
Peer interventions				
Plan for follow-up				

Figure 2.1. (continued)

	Projected Date	Date Started	Date Completed	Comments or Priority
Implementation				
Use of Buddies and Tutors				
Communication system between regular and special educators				
IEP				
Specific Parent Preparation				
Special educator fills out Continuum of Parent Involvement				
During IEP, parents need:				
Understanding and support				
Information and facts				
To be active participants				
To have identity				
Realistic expectations				
Child-Specific Preparation				
Determine options available for the student:				
Reverse Integration				
Tutors, Buddies				
Lunch, Recess, Reading Groups, Library				
Math, Reading, Science, Soc. Studies				
Teacher-Specific Preparation				
Analyze MESAs from teachers				
Discuss integration options with teacher				
Sending teacher fills out CEO				
Provide technical assistance				
Send Child Profile to receiving teacher				
Placement of Child into Integration				
Classroom preparation activities				
Peers				
Facilities (where applicable)				
Evaluate the Implementation of Plan and Revise as Needed				
Special educator completes appropriate standardized assessments				
Special educator completes appropriate criterion-referenced assessments				
Staff fills out Satisfaction Surveys				
Parents fill out Satisfaction Surveys				

1. Expectations concerning integration are often unknown or are set at minimal levels by state and local education agencies. There are few if any payoffs for exceeding expectation levels.

2. Many state funding patterns provide a strong disincentive for integrating or mainstreaming students since more dollars are generated if a child remains in an intensive self-contained program with a low teacher-to-student ratio.

3. Administrators, teachers, related services staff, parents, and other community members often believe there are no benefits to integrated programs.

4. Putting services on a continuum from least to most restrictive often precludes children from moving to a placement that best meets their needs, because staff require them to move through the continuum one step at a time and perceive this movement as sequential.

5. A lack of leadership and direction often exists within education agencies in the area of preschool integration.

6. A lack of staff trained in the skills needed to develop and/or implement an integrated preschool program often exists.

7. A lack of administrator commitment to integration often exists.

8. A lack of clear, local data on the cost efficiency of integrated preschools and their instructional benefit is common.

Common Reasons for Supporting Integration

Many administrators are convinced as to the benefits of integrated programs and are committed to implementing such programs. Common reasons for their commitment include:

1. Having relevant knowledge on the benefits of integration.

2. Being familiar with the mandates of P.L. 99-457 and P.L. 94-142.

3. Being motivated to do the best job possible.

4. Working with colleagues who are committed to integration.

The Roles of the Administrator

The major roles of the administrator in fostering the development and continued implementation of integrated preschool programs include:

1. Providing leadership (e.g., modeling acceptance of all students with and without handicaps).

2. Allocating the necessary financial, staff, and space resources needed.

3. Establishing and facilitating two-way communication with all relevant groups including regular and special education teachers, related services personnel, parents, children with and without handicaps, volunteers, other agencies, and others as appropriate.

4. Obtaining input and involvement by representatives from each relevant group.

5. Establishing a system for ongoing self-evaluation.

6. Maintaining a flexible administrative style.

7. Modifying the service pattern as needed.

8. Incorporating sound ideas from all sources of input.

9. Maintaining a child-centered program.

10. Assuring that staff are competent in the skills needed to implement an integrated preschool program.

A listing of all activities in which an administrator could engage to demonstrate commitment and leadership could be endless. The FMS project focused on three main activity areas: Activity 1—Obtaining and Disseminating Information, Activity 2—Program Planning, and Activity 3—Implementation.

Activity 1–Obtaining and Disseminating Information

One of the first activities for an administrator is to do a self-evaluation to determine his or her level of knowledge and commitment to integration. One way to do this is to complete the Integration Self-Evaluation Checklist for Administrators (see Appendix 2.A). Completion of the checklist will help an administrator identify activities that should be occurring in a functionally integrated preschool program. The checklist items require a yes answer or a corrective action plan, since each question is worded to identify activities that should be occurring in an integrated preschool. The end result is that the Self-Evaluation Checklist can serve as a planning tool for program improvement.

Other methods for obtaining and disseminating information include the development of a topic-specific annotated bibliography, the distribution of this information to all relevant persons (e.g., staff and parents), the determination of staff and parents' reactions to the information, and the use of content experts to make presentations to staff, the PTA, and other parent groups (Gaylord-Ross, 1988; Wilson, 1988). Some samples of information that can be used for dissemination are (a) the 10 tasks of the FMS model, which provide an overview of the FMS project tasks and materials (see Figure 1.3 in Chapter 1); (b) the Monitoring and Planning Checklist for Integration (Figure 2.1); (c) the List of Goals and Activities That Demonstrate Commitment to Integration (see Appendix 2.B), which provides an extensive list of goals, activities, obstacles, and areas of support relevant to establishing and maintaining an integrated preschool program; and (d) additional items in the form of checklists and appendices which can be found in other chapters of this book (e.g., appendices 3.A, 3.E, 5.A, and 5.C).

Activity 2 – Program Planning

Careful planning is essential for the development and implementation of an integrated preschool program. Planning activities include (Gaylord-Ross, 1988; Knoll & Meyer, 1986):

1. Appoint an integration task force with a clearly established role, goals, and time lines. Members should be chosen carefully to be representative of all concerned groups, including administrators, regular and special education teachers, related services staff, aides, principals, parents of children with and without handicaps, and a neutral facilitator from outside the school district. The facilitator should have content knowledge concerning integration, be experienced in group dynamics, and have excellent social and communication skills. The typical role of an integration task force is to educate, to plan, to advocate, and to monitor program progress. Appendix 2.C includes the Integration Task Force Overview, which consists of questions and answers related to the integration task force, and the Integration Task Force Evaluation Questionnaire for evaluating the function and organization of the task force. The Integration Task Force Organization Flowchart and Potential Roles is shown in Figure 2.2.

2. Designate someone with the appropriate skills and background to take primary responsibility for coordinating integration activities. This person can be a teacher, principal, administrator, or external consultant.

Figure 2.2. Integration Task Force Organization Flowchart and Potential Roles

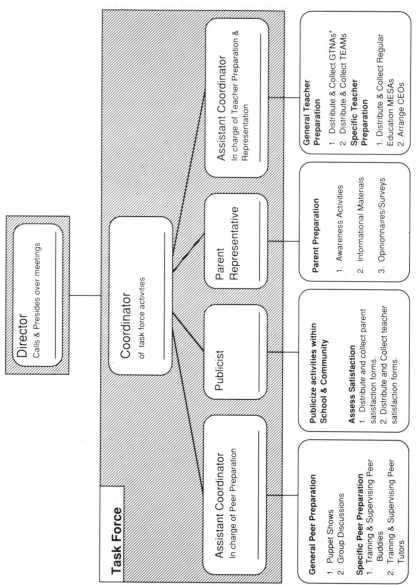

Task Force

Director
Calls & Presides over meetings

Coordinator
of task force activities

Assistant Coordinator
In charge of Peer Preparation

Publicist

Parent Representative

Assistant Coordinator
In charge of Teacher Preparation & Representation

General Peer Preparation
1. Puppet Shows
2. Group Discussions

Specific Peer Preparation
1. Training & Supervising Peer Buddies
2. Training & Supervising Peer Tutors

Publicize activities within School & Community

Assess Satisfaction
1. Distribute and collect parent satisfaction forms.
2. Distribute and Collect teacher satisfaction forms.

Parent Preparation
1. Awareness Activities
2. Informational Materials
3. Opinionnaires/Surveys

General Teacher Preparation
1. Distribute & Collect GTNAs*
2. Distribute & Collect TEAMs

Specific Teacher Preparation
1. Distribute & Collect Regular Education MESAs
2. Arrange CEOs

* Each of these items is discussed in detail in later chapters.

3. Involve staff and parents in the planning process. The more involvement individuals have in the development of a program, the more "ownership" they take for it, and the more committed they are to seeing the program succeed. Anticipate resistance, since change almost always results in fear of the unknown. The more involved people are and the more receptive planners are to listening to positive and negative suggestions, the more likely it is that participants will become involved and committed. Be sure that input is obtained from the principals in schools where integrated programs will be housed.

4. Analyze the current special education program in terms of student identification, referral, assessment, programming, and evaluation. Clearly describe the existing system.

5. Develop an ideal integration plan that addresses all aspects related to preschool integration including organizational structure, staff and space needs, curriculum adaptations, personnel preparation, technology needed, socialization, assessment, programming, and evaluation. Assess needs for implementing this plan.

6. Develop a specific integration plan that takes into account the existing special education program and the ideal integration plan. The integration plan should include easily communicable goals; time lines; implementation steps; responsibilities; specific sites to be used; staff, parent, and student preparation activities; awareness activities; financial and other resources needed; and evaluation procedures. Figure 2.3 provides an overview of some planning strategies useful in establishing an integrated program (Taylor, 1982). Some integration options to consider include tutors, buddies, small and large groups, teacher trades (e.g., self-contained teacher teaches a regular class), and the use of aides (see Chapters 8 and 9 for more information on options).

Activity 3—Implementation

Implementation of activities 1 and 2 is the focus of the remaining chapters of this book. In essence, the administrator needs to take responsibility for determining the future direction and goals of the integrated preschool program, involving others as much as possible and presenting the program to staff and parents. To do so, the administrator needs the necessary information, needs a plan, needs to implement the plan, and needs to monitor progress.

Figure 2.3. Planning Strategies

---

1. Create a task force to develop an integration plan.

2. Designate a faculty member or consultant to plan for integration.

3. Conduct inservice session for regular and special education staff.

4. Arrange visits for special educators to regular classes (schools) and vice versa.

5. Meet with administrators and teachers at the integration site.

6. Arrange for students with handicaps to use as many school facilities as possible (Preferably at the same time as students without handicaps are using the facilities).

7. Teach students with handicaps age-appropriate behavior in regular schools.

8. Involve parents in integration planning.

9. Arrange a faculty "Drop-in" to answer questions about integration.

10. Give regular students a day off to visit programs for students with handicaps (or regular time daily or weekly to serve as tutors and buddies).

11. Develop a handbook on special education for regular teachers and one on regular education for special education teachers.

(Adapted from Taylor, 1982)

Steps for Involving Administrators

The FMS steps for involving administrators include (see Figure 2.4):

1. Initiating contact with or responding to contact by administrators.
2. Introducing administrators to the specific program.
3. Obtaining and maintaining administrative commitment.
4. Providing support to administrators.

A description for each follows.

Initiating Contact with Administrators

Several purposes for initiating contact with administrators exist. The purpose(s) of a specific contact depends on who is initiating the contact and the variables related to the administrator being contacted. It is also probable that an administrator is the one initiating contact with someone knowledgeable about integration. The purpose of the contact can be:

1. To determine the administrator's knowledge of integration;
2. To determine the administrator's knowledge of the laws and state guidelines pertaining to integration;
3. To determine the administrator's philosophical and fiscal commitment to integration;
4. To get an administrator's assistance in
   a. involving others,
   b. planning,
   c. responding to a request, or;
5. If initiated by the administrator, to provide information, materials, and/or assistance.

Several approaches can be used to initiate contact with school administrators. One option is to begin by having a discussion with the appropriate administrator(s). The typical administrator contacted is the school principal in a small school, the director of special education in a large school or in a school district. Other administrators contacted could include the director of regular education, the superintendent, the pupil personnel director, or a member of the school

Figure 2.4. Flowchart of Administrator Involvement in Integration

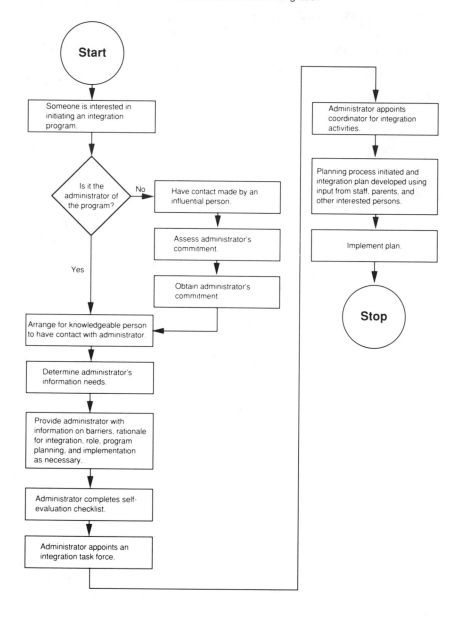

board. This discussion can be initiated by anyone who is knowledge-able about integration and mainstreaming including a PTA member, a state education agency staff member, a parent, or a staff member from the target school. The discussion can be scheduled in the adminis-trator's office; at a staff inservice; at a state, regional, or national confer-ence; or anywhere else deemed appropriate by the relevant parties. The focus of this discussion should be on establishing or strengthen-ing a working relationship with the administrator and on assessing the administrator's level of (a) knowledge about what integration is and how to make it a practical reality, (b) philosophical and fiscal com-mitment to integration, and (c) knowledge of the laws and state guide-lines pertaining to integration. These points can be assessed with the administrator's permission by rating each administrator on the Edu-cator Rating Form (see Appendix 2.D). The Educator Rating Form was designed to determine how committed an educator is to establishing and maintaining an integration program.

A second useful option is to have administrators attend a pre-sentation on integration at which they can gain information, hear questions and comments by others, and have the opportunity to ask questions. This presentation can focus on any aspects of what inte-gration is and how to make it a practical reality. It could be on imple-mentation, on laws, or on other aspects of integration.

A third option is to send or provide this information to each administrator so she or he may review it within the daily schedule. Some materials that may be given to the administrators during this initial contact stage include the FMS brochure (Appendix 2.E), written definitions of terms such as *integration* and *mainstreaming* (see Chapter 1), the Integration Self-Evaluation Checklist for Administrators (see Appendix 2.A), and the List of Goals and Activities That Demonstrate Commitment to Integration (Appendix 2.B).

Introducing Administrators to the Specific Program

Within 1 week of the initial contact, the administrators should be con-tacted again to determine if they are interested in learning about and/or implementing the FMS integration model. If the administrator is inter-ested, the person who introduced or initiated the contact should make arrangements for additional meetings in which the administrator can learn more about the FMS model. To avoid overwhelming adminis-trators with new information and responsibilities, these meetings should be arranged to fit the needs and schedule of the administrator. During these meetings the components of the FMS model should be presented and the administrator(s) should be provided with samples of appropriate materials. The components include (a) an introduction to the integration model, (b) administrative preparation and commitment, (c) staff preparation, (d) parent preparation, (e) peer preparation, (f) the placement decision process, (g) integration, and (h) evaluation. Each of these tasks is dealt with in detail in later chapters of this book.

If the administrator is initially not committed to establish an integrated preschool in his or her school, two obvious choices are available. First, efforts can be directed at obtaining commitment for integration from this administrator. Second, efforts can be directed to obtaining commitment from other key administrators. Both options can be pursued by educating the administrator on the benefits of integrated preschools and by reminding the administrator of her or his legal responsibilities toward children with handicaps. These procedures are described in the next section of this chapter.

Obtaining and Maintaining Administrative Commitment

While administrators are being introduced to the integration process, efforts should also be directed toward enhancing the administrators' commitment to having a successful, functional, and integrated preschool program in their school. Administrative commitment to integration can be achieved in several ways. One way to strengthen administrative commitment to integration is to have influential parents or community figures who support integration visit with the administrator, with her or his supervisor, or with the superintendent of schools. Preparing parents or other community members to support and/or provide leadership for an integration effort can be accomplished through individual meetings with the parents and community leaders or through social activities where all parties involved can meet and help each other learn about and learn how to support an integration effort and how to impact administrators. If personal visits cannot be arranged, petitions and phone calls by influential parents and other interested parties can also be very effective in securing limited commitment. If the barrier to commitment is financial, parent petitions may be of assistance in securing the necessary financial resources from the school district and the state. Care must be taken when going to a higher level administrator to overcome resistance by a lower level administrator to assure that all other options have been exhausted.

It should be recognized at the outset that change will generally be resisted, often due to a lack of knowledge. Producing change can be a very slow process or can be achieved relatively quickly depending on the approach used, the skills of those involved, and the power of those involved. It is always preferable to implement system change using a consensual, congenial, and cooperative approach. Sometimes this is not possible. In those cases, one may need to be very assertive. Assertiveness is often seen as aggression on the part of an administrator; thus, it is useful to have the support of a group, particularly if the group includes an influential person who is respected by the administrator (often the contact person is the most critical element in producing change). Consistent progress over time is preferable to no change.

Another way to gain administrative commitment to integration is to introduce administrators to materials and support networks offered by experts in the field. This includes the FMS project's materials and procedures, which are discussed in this and other chapters of this book. These materials provide the administrator with procedures that have been proven effective in integrating children with handicaps into regular education environments. It may also be helpful to introduce the administrator to effective integration programs that are already functioning in the immediate vicinity.

Finally, it may be necessary to remind administrators of their legal obligations to children with handicaps by providing the handbook, *Public Law 94-142, Section 504, and Public Law 99-457: Understanding What They Are and Are Not* (Ballard et al., 1987), or an equivalent publication. Unfortunately, parents of children who have handicaps may have to request a due process hearing if they are not satisfied with the school's integration efforts.

During efforts to obtain administrator commitment, it is important to keep in mind that administrators should not be publicly embarrassed in the presence of their staff or parents of children who attend the school. One cannot make friends by embarrassing an administrator. Other approaches are more useful for obtaining commitment. Substantial signs of commitment include, but are not limited to, written and/or verbal assurances of commitment, the forming of a task force to develop an integration plan, and efforts to secure the resources needed to implement the integration plan (e.g., monies, space, materials, and staff). The List of Goals and Activities That Demonstrate Commitment to Integration in Appendix 2.B is an expanded list of items that are indicative of commitment to integration.

Providing Support to Administrators

Support should be provided to administrators throughout the process of introducing, obtaining, and maintaining a commitment to preschool integration. This support comes in several forms and should be designed to help administrators develop a functional and effective integration program. One form of support consists of providing materials from experts in the field. Which integration materials to give to administrators for support and when to give them is dependent on the specific situation. If scheduling allows, it may be better to break the initial presentation into two sessions or to plan for several follow-up meetings rather than risk overburdening an already busy administrator. Aside from the materials previously discussed, the following materials were designed for use mainly by administrators and are described below: the List of Goals and Activities That Demonstrate Commitment to Integration (Appendix 2.B), Methods for Integration (Figure 2.5), and the Administrator Planning Form (Figure 2.6).

The List of Goals and Activities That Demonstrate Commitment to Integration (Appendix 2.B) provides a listing of activities to be initiated by an administrator to prepare staff, parents, peers, and others for mainstreaming; common obstacles that are encountered; and possible sources of support in carrying out integration activities and overcoming obstacles.

The Methods for Integration (Figure 2.5) is also a useful handout for introducing integration to educators. This is a one-page handout that lists techniques and facts that should be taken into consideration when developing a plan for integration.

Once the agency decides to develop an integration plan, the Administrative Planning Form (Figure 2.6) can be used as an outline. Similar to the List of Goals and Activities That Demonstrate Commitment to Integration, this form has seven sections used to:

1. Establish integration goals.
2. List activities to accomplish the goals.
3. Identify obstacles that may need to be overcome in achieving a goal.
4. Identify available support to overcome obstacles.
5. Establish time lines.
6. Establish staff responsibilities.
7. Identify methods for determining progress toward goal achievement.

Steps After Commitment Is Obtained

Once a commitment to integration is made, the education agency is faced with many administrative questions that must be answered. A

Table 2.5. Methods for Integration

Here are some ideas and techniques that will help assure that integration will be a positive experience in your classroom. (These thoughts can guide decision-making at the IEP meeting.)

---

1. INTEGRATION is more than just physical placement. Remember the equation: INTEGRATION = SOCIAL AND INSTRUCTIONAL INTERVENTION = CHILD PROGRESS

Remember that for children with greater impairments, social interactions can occur both within and outside of the self-contained class!

2. INTEGRATION is carried out for a reason and must be stated as an objective which indicates what the child is expected to gain from the experience. An objective which states, "The child will participate in lunch with other preschoolers." is inappropriate, since it states what will happen to the child, not what the child is expected to learn. An alternative objective could state. "The child will initiate conversation with nonhandicapped peers at least twice during lunchtime."

3. INTEGRATION should offer some benefit for children without handicaps, such as better understanding of individual differences; increased responsibility and leadership; or opportunities to develop fluency on an academic task, while tutoring another student. These benefits will not occur unless someone assumes responsibility for preparing the regular peers for the presence of the new student, discussing and practicing ways to interact, and following up with solutions to questions or difficult situations as problems arise.

Table 2.5. (continued)

4. INTEGRATION needs to be successful. Select an activity where the children with handicaps can demonstrate adequate skills.

5. INTEGRATION requires communication: Collect the child's test and program data, and personal information which the receiving teacher may need, then send it and follow up with a personal visit. The Child Profile and the MESA can be used for this purpose.

6. INTEGRATION involves parents. Solicit their ideas, identify their integration concerns, and answer their questions. Follow-up written communications help reinforce decisions or information communicated verbally.

first step may be one or more "brainstorming" sessions by staff members or a task force to examine possible problems related to implementation of the integrated preschool program, along with possible solutions. On the basis of these sessions, an individual may suggest that a task force be formed to develop an integration plan. A tentative plan for implementing either the FMS model or another integration plan can also be developed.

Influential parents are not only a resource helpful in obtaining commitment from administrators to integrate programs, they can also be helpful as a source of support for the administrators by forming support groups to assist administrators or the task force in obtaining monetary support from the local or state government through visits, phone calls, and formal requests to appropriate agencies. It may be necessary to involve the parents in social activities where they can be educated about integration and the benefits it has for all involved as discussed in Chapter 4 of this manual.

Proper use of the media can also be a very forceful source of support for administrators. Media coverage, if properly used, can mobilize public and private support for those committed to implementing integration programs. Media can disseminate progress reports, individual and group successes with integration, and news updates about ways in which the community can become involved.

Figure 2.6. Administrator Planning Form

Goal	Data/Method for determining progress toward goal (End Product)	Activities for achieving goal (Resources to Use)	Obstacles to overcome	Support to overcome obstacles	Start Date	Completion Date	Persons(s) Responsible	Rating Very Useful=VU Useful=U Irrelevant=I Non applicable=NA

Decisions must also be made in areas concerning the type and intensity of preparation activities that will be conducted for staff, parents, students with handicaps, and their regular class peers; any necessary curriculum modification; placement procedures; and program evaluation. These areas are examined in the following sections of the manual.

In summary, several follow-up sessions will need to be scheduled to determine the administrator's knowledge about and commitment to integration. A measure of the administrator's knowledge about integration can be determined by filling out items such as the Educator Rating Form (Appendix 2.D) and The Integration Self-Evaluation Checklist for Administrators (Appendix 2.A). Each item included in this chapter was designed to help administrators develop a preschool integration program. In developing a program, it is important to determine the administrator's knowledge and commitment to integration so that the strengths and deficits of the administrator can be determined and so an action plan to address deficit can be formulated.

Appendix 2.A.
The Integration Self-Evaluation Checklist for Administrators
Sebastian Striefel, Joel Allred,
Maria Quintero, & LeAnn Hyer

Rationale

Many reasons exist on why Public Law 94-142 and Public Law 99-457 (Education for all Handicapped Children Acts) have not been fully implemented, including; 1) the expectation of state education departments for only minimal compliance with the requirements of PL 94-142 and PL 99-457; 2) the disincentive provided to local school districts because special education students, particularly those in self-contained programs, generate additional dollars above and beyond those generated by regular students; 3) the failure to perceive the dignity of children with disabilities and the extent of their rights; 4) the attitudes and ideologies of those who do not believe children with moderate and severe disabilities are best served in integrated classrooms; 5) the lack of data to demonstrate the cost effectiveness of integrated programs in the short or long term; and 6) the fact that most programs are managed by administrators who were not trained in special education and are thus often not familiar with what is needed (Berres & Knoblock, 1987). The Self-Evaluation Checklist is concerned directly with the evaluation and re-education of administrators, but indirectly with providing guidance for planning for functional integration of children who have handicaps into settings with those who don't. The information for this checklist was based on work by Crisci (1981), Pasanella and Volkmor (1981), and Sharp (1982).

Purposes

The Self-Evaluation Checklist has several purposes for use with administrators such as principals, directors of special education, and supervisors. First, it can provide them with a method for evaluating their familiarity with integration needs and requirements. Second, the checklist items provide a listing of tasks administrators can engage in to facilitate and demonstrate support for the functional integration of children who have handicaps into settings and activities with their non-handicapped peers. Third, the checklist items can provide guidance to an administrator in developing a simple plan for initiating or improving the services provided to those who have

Appendix 2.A. (continued)

handicaps. Fourth, the checklist items can assist self-evaluators in formulating an appropriate philosophy for educating everyone in the least restrictive environment (LRE). Fifth, the Self-Evaluation Checklist when completed by several or all administrators in a school or school district can be used by a task force comprised of teachers (both regular and special educators), administrators, parents, and appropriate others to develop and implement a comprehensive integration program, including, but not limited to, teacher training and support, parent preparation, and preparation of children both with and without handicaps. The major use for the checklist is by administrators who are motivated to change their own behavior and that of their staff.

Description

The Integration Self-Evaluation Checklist for Administrators includes two major sections: 1) The Self-Evaluation Checklist and 2) The Corrective Action Needed Summary. The Self-Evaluation Checklist consists of 34 items. All of the items are directed specifically toward administrators such as the school principal; however, others such as teachers may also find completion of the checklist beneficial in assessing their own behavior.

Since integration is not a discrete, one-time action, but rather is an ongoing process, a self-evaluator may wish to repeat the self-evaluation periodically. Additional items specific to the setting can easily be added as desired.

The Corrective Action Needed Summary sheet has two sections. In the first, labeled "Corrective Action," a listing is made of all items from the Self-Evaluation Checklist that were marked "no" or "don't know." Second, in the section entitled "Implementation Steps," space is provided so that a set of steps for implementing changes can be written for each item listed on the Corrective Action section.

Disadvantages

The biggest disadvantage is that an administrator can complete the form in such a way that s/he "looks good." Failure to complete the Self-Evaluation Checklist honestly may abort its usefulness unless an administrator's supervisor also completes the checklist and does so honestly. In such cases discrepancies between different administrators' self-evaluations will be obvious immediately. The checklist was not designed for the purpose of having one administrator evaluate another administrator's performance, but rather was designed as a planning tool.

Appendix 2.A. (continued)

Instructions for Use

Read each item and place a check mark in either the yes, no, not applicable, or don't know column. Your first impression is probably the best response. Be honest; trying to impress others will not help you in correcting deficits in your program.

After completing the checklist turn to the section entitled "Corrective Action Needed" and make a list of the items for which corrective action is needed and list the steps you will take to make the needed changes. Since the expected response for each item is a "yes" response, all items marked "no" or "don't know" should be included on the "Corrective Action Needed" sheet. For example, if item 28, "Have you made integration a part of each teacher and other staff member's job description?" was marked "no" you would complete the "Corrective Action Needed" section as appropriate to your setting. See the example that follows.

Example

- -

Corrective Action

1. Incorporate integration into each teacher and staff member's job description.

Implementation Steps

1. Do I need approval from some other administrator or a union to make such a change? If so, get it.

2. Decide how to word the new responsibility on each person's job description and the time lines for implementation.

3. Discuss the change with all affected staff either in a staff meeting or one by one. Modify plan as appropriate.

4. Follow up by providing each staff member with a corrected copy of his or her job description.

5. Monitor to assure that staff comprehend and implement their new responsibility.

Appendix 2.A. (continued)

Check the most appropriate answer for each item.

YES NO NA DK

1. Do you have a functional understanding about what mainstreaming is and is not?

2. Do you have an operational definition of mainstreaming?

3. Do you currently educate all children in the least restrictive environment that will meet their needs?

4. Do you designate and implement educational programs for children who have handicaps in the school, in accordance with approved policies, procedures, and guidelines of LEA, State Dept. of Education, PL 94-142 and PL 99-457?

5. Do children with and without handicaps ride on the same buses?

6. Do all children (those with and without handicaps) in your school or district (a) enter the same door(s) at school, (b) follow the same schedule, (c) have access to all facilities, and (d) eat lunch at the same time and in the same location?

7. Is the school district and/or local Board of Education committed to implementing the legal requirements of PL 94-142 and PL 99-457?

8. Have costs been worked out with (a) local school districts, (b) intermediate units, and (c) the state so that no district will be disadvantaged by moving into an integrated program?

9. Do you (a) participate in planning for specific education programs in the school and (b) make budget recommendations to the superintendent/school board?

10. Has a district or school-wide planning committee been organized to determine questions which will probably be raised (a) in the community, (b) by the school board, (c) by parents, and (d) by regular educators and (e) have factual answers been prepared to respond to these questions?

11. Was mainstreaming first initiated with (a) principals, (b) teachers, and (c) staff who are supportive of mainstreaming children who have handicaps?

12. Did you initiate mainsteaming in schools with low annual teacher and pupil turnover rate?

13. Do you participate in LEA planning for special education services?

Appendix 2.A. (continued)

	YES	NO	NA	DK

14. Do you (a) coordinate and administer special education services in the school? If you do not coordinate and administer special education services in the school, have you (b) assigned someone who does and (c) is this person qualified and trained in the implementation of special education services?

14.(a)
  (b)
  (c)

15. Do you supervise or arrange for a qualified administrator to supervise educational personnel providing integrated services to the children in the school?

15.

16. Do you supervise or arrange for a qualified administrator to supervise appropriate assessment as a result of a screening procedure?

16.

17. When a referral is received from teachers, parents, and others, do you assist in reviewing the progress of students suspected of having handicapping conditions?

17.

18. Do you attend IEP meetings? If not, is a qualified person attending in your place?

18.

19. Do you promote and model positive attitudes for school personnel and parents to encourage acceptance and inclusion of children with handicaps in regular classes and in interaction with regular students?

19.

20. Do you interact with, observe, and work with children who have handicaps in the regular and special education teaching areas whenever possible?

20.

21. Do you (a) supervise the maintenance of child records at the school level and (b) protect the confidentiality of these records?

21.(a)
  (b)

22. Are visual warnings about fire and other alarm systems provided where the welfare and safety of hearing impaired students are involved?

22.

23. Are you encouraging inservice training and continuing education for teachers?

23.

24. Are you making periodic needs assessments among regular and special educators to determine appropriate topics for workshops?

24.

25. If teachers request assistance, do you provide or arrange for specialized assistance?

25.

26. Do the teachers and staff members have a clear understanding about how mainstreaming will be implemented?

26.

27. Does your district or local school (a) have collective bargaining and negotiations with teachers and others? If so, have you (b) made certain that the school integration policy is discussed with them?

27.(a)
  (b)

28. Have you made mainstreaming a part of each teacher and/or other staff member's job description?

28.

Appendix 2.A. (continued)

	YES	NO	NA	DK
29. Is there a working plan in your school and/or district for implementing PL 99-457 by the school year 1990-91?				
30. Are you (a) avoiding overloading administrators or teachers who are willing to assist in implementing mainstreaming? If not, have you (b) considered distributing the load equally?				
31. Is there a written rationale of integration provided for substitute teachers and families moving into the school district?				
32. Have you established policies and procedures for the selection, training, and implementation of buddy systems and peer tutoring programs?				
33. Are you educating teachers, both regular and special, that their work is not the same but each should understand the other's work and recognize the balancing factors which make them relatively equivalent?				
34. Do you need outside consultation to improve the degree of integration occurring in your program?				

Corrective Action Needed Summary

Corrective Action	Implementation Steps
(list all items for which the "no" or "don't know" column was checked)	(list the corrective action steps needed for each item listed on the "Corrective Action" section)

Appendix 2.A. (continued)

Corrective Action Needed Summary continued	
Corrective Action	Implementation Steps

Appendix 2.B.

List of Goals and Activities That Demonstrate

Commitment to Integration

Sebastian Striefel, Joel Allred,
& Maria Quintero

Rationale and Purpose

This listing was developed for teachers and administrators to use as a blueprint of goals and activities that can assist educators in the development and implementation of integration activities in their district/school. Many administrators and teachers who wish to integrate in their schools may not have a systematic plan designed for integration. Moreover, they may not have obtained commitment to integration from those who are involved in education in the district/school. This product outlines integration goals and activities which demonstrate commitment to goals and provides methods for obtaining commitment from administrators, teachers, school staff, the community, and parents of and children with and without handicaps. Also included are goals and activities for conducting an IEP meeting.

As a guide to administrators and teachers, goals and objective methods for determining progress toward goal achievement or end products for each goal are listed. Also included for each goal and objective method are resources to use for achieving the goals, obstacles to overcome when working on each goal, and support systems to overcome obstacles. Included with the product is a column for implementation time lines and dates of completion, a column for placing the name of person(s) who are responsible for each goal and objective, and a rating scale for evaluation of use with this product (i.e., very useful, useful, irrelevant, not applicable).

This product was developed with the intent of providing teachers and administrators with a comprehensive plan for integration in a district/school and to assess their individual integration programs. The list of goals, end products, resources to use, potential obstacles to overcome, and support to overcome obstacles is by no means complete. Based upon the particular needs, there exist other goals, end products, resources to use, obstacles, and support to overcome obstacles which we may not have addressed. Every educator has concerns and problems which are unique and individual to their situation. The VSSM Project developed this product in order to assist educators in formulating their own integration plan and determine whether there is commitment to integration from existing personnel in their school/district. If the methods developed in this product can assist or help you develop this product further, then we have succeeded. If there are any areas that we have overlooked, the VSSM Project would appreciate your input.

Instructions

Use this product as a blueprint to follow in terms of integration activity in your school/district. Goals are provided which may be applicable to your school/district. If

Appendix 2.B. (continued)

commitment to a specific goal has not been met, use objectives stated in the end products section as a guide to follow. Use the listing of resources to achieve the end product objectives. Pay particular attention to the obstacles that you may encounter while obtaining commitment from the respective persons in each goal area. Support to overcome obtacles has been provided and may assist you with concerns you may have in your area. Again, this is not a complete listing of goals, end products, resources, obstacles, or support to overcome obstacles. You may want to add or delete as your needs occur.

Place starting and completion dates for goals and name(s) of person(s) who are responsible for each goal and objective. In the final column, rate whether the goals and objectives were very useful, useful, irrelevant, or not applicable. Any additional comments can be noted on the back of each sheet.

Additional blank forms are provided on which you can place additional information, goals, end products, resources to use, obstacles, support to overcome obstacles, time lines and completion dates, and rating scale of usefulness.

It is suggested that the integration task force composed of administrator(s), special education teacher(s), regular education teacher(s), a school psychologist, and parents be organized to carry out the implementation of this product. In cases where no task force exists, it may be time consuming and difficult for one or two people to carry out the tasks required for implementing integration in a school/district. The use of this listing coupled with FMS Products (i.e., MESA, TEAM, CEO, etc.) is recommended to assist educators with integration activities.

Appendix 2.B. (continued)

Goal	Data/Method for determining progress toward goal (End Product)	Activities for achieving goal (Resources to Use)	Obstacles to overcome	Support to overcome obstacles
1.0 To obtain and maintain administrative commitment to implementing a successful integration program.	1.10 Administrator has scheduled inservice for staff on integration. 1.11 Administrator has requested additional resources to make integration work via memo, letter, etc. 1.12 Written documents (PL 94-142) explaining requirements for educating persons with handicaps are presented to administrators (i.e., principals, supervisors, superintendents, etc). 1.13 Integration plan with implementation guidelines has been designed, written, and made available for implementation in school/district (definition, rationale, etc.). 1.14 Training needs have been identified via formal written needs assessment for integration in school/district. 1.15 Inservice training has been implemented via workshops, classes, inservices, etc., for needs identified via formal written needs assessment.	1.20 General presentation to obtain Administrator Awareness and Commitment to integration. 1.21 Assess administrator knowledge and commitment to integration via discussion, questionnaires, etc. 1.22 Brochures, questionnaires, abstracts, articles, and other relevant integration materials provided to administrator to discuss the points of integration s/he may have questions or concerns about. 1.23 Awareness activities via film, puppet show, panel discussions, etc., are presented. Specific presentation regarding tools and methods of integration. 1.24 Visits made to administrators by informed, influential parents, state officials, etc. Social activity(ies) for administrators, parents, children, staff, teachers, school board members, etc.	1.40 Lack of motivation (lack of commitment to spearhead activity, resistant to change, does not want to issue change that will elicit negative feedback, traditional attitudes and practices, fears due to lack of understanding, apathy, no desire to participate, etc.). 1.41 Lack of knowledge and understanding (i.e., of education associations, PTA, advocacy groups, philosophies of education, etc.). 1.42 Time conflicts (i.e., work schedule conflicts, time required to prepare and implement integration, etc.). 1.43 Money concerns (incentives, reinforcement to teachers, career ladder costs, credit costs, hiring substitutes,	1.50 Teachers, parents, and influential persons in community who have had success in integration to present their positive experiences and share testimonial of the need for effective integration to administrators. 1.51 Administrator commitment to breaks, credit, salary increases, lane changes, support, substitutes (aides), positive reinforcement, anonymity of surveys and/or questionnaires of staff and teachers, etc. 1.52 Demonstration of tools (i.e., MESA, TEAM, CEO, checklists, etc.) and use of professionals (i.e., FMS, etc.) from university and other professional levels. 1.53 Groups and parent organizations to provide positive pressure for integration at school.

Appendix 2.B. (continued)

Goal	Data/Method for determining progress toward goal (End Product)	Activities for achieving goal (Resources to Use)	Obstacles to overcome	Support to overcome obstacles
1.0 To obtain and maintain administrative commitment to implementing a successful integration program.	1.16 Administrator has made a written and/or verbal commitment of "Ownership" toward children with handicaps.	1.25 Locate and obtain written/verbal commitment from people in areas located in district/ school for integration activities.	(cont.) 1.43 ...costs of materials and/or equipment for integration, etc.).	(cont.) 1.53 ...district, and/or state levels.
	1.17 Administrator has assigned person(s) to coordinate integration activities via written confirmation and acceptance.	1.26 Secure and obtain support materials from experts to assist in integration effort.		1.54 Support from school board officials, state education officials, directors of education, etc.
	1.18 Administrator, in writing, has requested/ formed an integration task force.	1.27 Provide written handbook of guidelines and policies (regarding integration and education of children with handicaps in the least restrictive environment-LRE) to administrators, teachers, staff, parents, etc.		1.55 Provision of systematic plan for integration (i.e., activities, assessment, needs acquisition schedules, etc.) which is presented in a thorough and organized manner at staff meetings, orientations, etc.
	1.19 Administrator has committed time and/or money (dollar amount, and percent/number of full-time equivalents available in written form).	Maintaining Administrator Commitment via Ongoing Support.		
		1.28 Surveys, checklists, MESA, TEAM, etc., provided to administrator to demonstrate and explain integration tools available.		1.56 Workable integration model (materials and procedures) available.
		1.29 Administrators participate in brainstorming session to discuss points in effective integration, answers questions, addresses concerns, etc.		1.57 Meet administrators on "Neutral Turf" (i.e., hotel conference room, restaurant, etc.) to discuss plans and present integration ideas.

Appendix 2.B. (continued)

Goal	Data/Method for determining progress toward goal (End Product)	Activities for achieving goal (Resources to Use)	Obstacles to overcome	Support to overcome obstacles
1.0 To obtain and maintain administrative commitment to implementing a successful integration program.		1.30 Provide written definition and rationale as part of integration plan. 1.31 Design tentative model or classroom plan via written blueprint of plans and procedures. 1.32 Parent support and parent advocacy groups organized by parents of children with and without handicaps to provide support and put pressure upon the administrator and teachers, if needed. 1.33 Administrative/Superintendent support of administrator and teachers in school/district via money, credits, lane changes, etc. 1.34 Staff in school support of administrator via memos, letters, verbal reports to keep administrator informed and aware of integration progress. Staff can also put pressure upon administrator to make changes (i.e., inservice needs, credits, money, etc.). 1.35 Task force arranges with media (TV, radio, newpaper releases, etc.) to disseminate progress of school/district and news of MS successes.		1.59 Allowance of time or arrangements for follow-up visits with administrators to discuss questions, concerns, etc. 1.60 Conferencing with another administrator who is using an integration model successfully.

Appendix 2.B. (continued)

Goal	Data/Method for determining progress toward goal (End Product)	Activities for achieving goal (Resources to Use)	Obstacles to overcome	Support to overcome obstacles
2.0 To obtain and maintain teacher and staff commitment to implement a successful integration program.	2.10 Staff have requested inservice/help/etc. to implement a successful integration program.	2.20 Staff are presented with a written list of needs and goals of children with handicaps in order to educate them to the needs of integration.	2.30 Lack of teacher understanding of the long-range goals of the program, time, dedication, and understanding of integration.	2.50 Informal discussions with teachers. Playing "Devil's Advocate" to elicit honest responses.
	2.11 Staff have volunteered to talk to parents or other staff about integration.	2.21 Barriers of fear and misunderstanding are removed via presentations, discussions, and inservices.	2.31 Withholding true feelings with regard to integration.	2.51 Rewards for participation (i.e., carrier ladders, credit, salary increases, leave days, teacher trade-off, etc.).
	2.12 Staff have volunteered to integrate children in their classroom.	2.22 Staff are presented with a written form of PL 94-142 and PL 99-457 to acquaint them with federal laws governing the education of children with handicaps.	2.32 Forms (MESA/TEAM etc.) which are invalid, incomplete, not turned in on time, etc.	2.52 Write and obtain monies from the state and federal governments via grants, etc.
	2.13 Administrator has obtained written and/or verbal commitment from staff to become involved in integration.	2.23 Staff are assessed using TEAM/ 23 Competencies/etc. to determine skills and possible technical assistance needs. (Names of participants with their respective responses to skill levels and technical assistance needs must be safeguarded to maintain confidence and limit the linking of names to specific skill deficits and needs).	2.33 Lack of time (due to commitments, outside activities, other items which have higher priority, etc).	2.53 Provision of specific ideas for teachers to study and think about in planning meetings.
	2.14 Staff have volunteered to train other teachers on how to integrate.	2.24 Committee is organized to analyze teachers' skills and technical assistance needs.	2.34 Lack of money (due to costs for aides, materials, incentive, credits, etc.).	2.54 Provision of specific inservice days with arrangements to have substitute coverage for classes.
	2.15 Staff have volunteered to provide technical assistance to other teachers who are integrating.		2.35 Inability to solve concerns between teachers/ acministrators, professional consultants, parents, etc.	2.55 Look for ideas and specialists within own school to provide experts at inservices and workshops for teachers.
	2.16 Staff have requested the formation of an integration task force and/or to be on the task force.			

Appendix 2.B. (continued)

Goal	Data/Method for determining progress toward goal (End Product)	Activities for achieving goal (Resources to Use)	Obstacles to overcome	Support to overcome obstacles
2.0 To obtain and maintain teacher and staff commitment to implement a successful integration program.	2.17 Staff have organized/requested regular meetings for purposes of planning, communication, resolving problems, etc., with staff who are involved in integration. 2.19 Staff/task force have requested a systematic plan for the purposes of organizing the means for meeting teacher needs identified by needs assessment (i.e., university courses, workshop schedules, regular staff inservices, etc.).	2.25 Technical assistance needs are prioritized in order of most critical to least critical to integration effectiveness for each teacher by integration committee. 2.26 Based upon assessment results, workshops, seminars, inservices, etc., are organized by committee to meet teacher's needs. Speakers, locations, and materials are prepared. Organization of training is designed to meet teacher needs and provide follow-up services where needed in areas noted by teachers on the TEAM/MESA/PK/23 Competencies. 2.27 School administrator schedules substitutes and makes necessary arrangements for class coverage during training time of teachers. 2.28 A long-range plan is designed by principal and/or mainstreaming committee to assist teachers in skills acquisition over time. This plan may include inservices, college courses, workshops, listing of names of experts (in house and surrounding areas) who may help in training, monies earmarked for teacher materials, monies to pay for guest experts, teacher salaries, career ladders, etc.	2.36 Lack of anonymity with results of surveys (MESA/TEAM/PK/23 Competencies, etc). 2.37 New teachers may not know needs and/or have concerns about skills, needs, etc. 2.38 Fears (i.e., reprisal from administrator, admitting weaknesses in terms of skill levels, threatened by outside professionals, etc.). 2.39 Teachers who refuse to participate, attend meetings, complete paperwork, etc. 2.40 Teachers who dislike being observed and evaluated. 2.41 Lack of teacher validity on the team. 2.42 Too many goals to be a realistic plan to accomplish.	2.56 Use university and outside professional resources (i.e., FMS projects, etc.) to assist teachers in gaining needed skills to integration. 2.57 At meetings, provide refreshments (i.e., juice, sweet rolls, coffee, etc.). 2.58 Obtain and use teacher input, suggestions for possible goals, and methods for meeting goals. 2.59 Locate individuals who are willing to serve, who are leaders, and let them set the example for others to follow. 2.60 Hold regular and consistent meetings to assist and update teachers. 2.61 Assure that all surveys will be kept confidential (i.e., coded; Smith = 1, Jones = 2).

Appendix 2.B. (continued)

Goal	Data/Method for determining progress toward goal (End Product)	Activities for achieving goal (Resources to Use)	Obstacles to overcome	Support to overcome obstacles
2.0 To obtain and maintain teacher and staff commitment to implement a successful integration program.			2.43 Teacher apathy.	2.62 Goals for specific completion dates.
			2.44 Writing and copy costs of paper, etc., to be given to teachers as prep material.	2.63 Development of advisory committee to oversee teacher preparation and relieve burden placed upon administrator to supervise.
			2.45 Lack of commitment from administration.	2.64 Consistent and regular training inservices and workshops which are well planned and organized to meet teacher needs.
			2.46 Teachers with traditional and/or poor attitudes. An unwillingness to participate.	
			2.47 What inservice takes priority over other inservices and scheduling times.	2.65 Someone assigned to relay messages to teachers regarding dates, times, and locations of meetings.
			2.48 Teachers who do not feel they need to attend inservices or feel that said inservices are not for them.	2.66 Use of parent groups to put pressures upon teachers and administrators to improve education for children with handicaps.

Appendix 2.B. (continued)

Goal	Data/Method for determining progress toward goal (End Product)	Activities for achieving goal (Resources to Use)	Obstacles to overcome	Support to overcome obstacles
3.0 To make parents and community aware of integration program.	3.10 A school-wide awareness plan is available in written form. 3.11 A record of awareness activities completed is available in written form including number of brochures/pamphlets distributed, talks given, letters mailed, etc.	3.20 Administrator assigns person(s)/committee to coordinate parent awareness activities for integration. (Committee may consist of teachers, parents, community leaders, PTA supervisors, etc.) 3.21 Committee writes goals and expectations for parent and community awareness. 3.22 Committee gains verbal/written monetary support from the community for awareness campaign via media, events, socials, PTA meetings, etc. 3.23 Committee conducts needs assessment of parents and general community to determine questions, concerns, etc. 3.24 Committee organizes inservices, socials, etc. to dispel misconceptions and concerns via films, discussions, guest lecturers, etc. 3.25 Posters and fliers are distributed by committee explaining integration activities. 3.26 Letters and memos are sent to parents and community leaders announcing meetings,	3.40 General public apathy toward mainstreaming. 3.41 Accountability of group for assignment, monthly reports, etc. 3.42 Misconceptions, fears, etc. 3.43 Lack of time (too many other commitments, etc.). 3.44 Parents' (of children without handicaps) negative attitudes. 3.45 Lack of time lines for completion of newletters, meetings, etc. 3.46 Lack of administrator and teacher support. 3.47 Parents refuse participation by their children in integration activities.	3.60 Knowledgeable people on task force/committee to do informal educating of committee members, volunteers, etc. 3.61 Use of PTA meetings to disseminate information. 3.62 Support from district and state superintendents. 3.63 School administrator who is committed to parent groups (via monetary support, paper, photocopy costs, etc). 3.64 Use of professional projects (i.e., university research, FMS Project, etc.) to assist parent groups in community awareness activities, etc. 3.65 Well-publicized meetings via posters, radio, newspaper ads, etc.

Appendix 2.B. (continued)

Goal	Data/Method for determining progress toward goal (End Product)	Activities for achieving goal (Resources to Use)	Obstacles to overcome	Support to overcome obstacles
3.0 To make parents and community aware of integration program.		(cont) 3.26 ...inservices, newsletters, etc.	3.48 Newsletters not read by community.	3.66 Use of volunteers from the community.
		3.27 A handbook of people's names (professionals, parents, community leaders, etc.) is designed to help organizers and committees select advocates for MS for inservices, panel discussions, etc., to answer questions and concerns.	3.49 Community backlash. 3.50 Lack of money (for news-letters, fliers, posters, etc.).	3.67 Specific assignments to specific people with specific dates of completion. 3.68 Provide an open door for future questions or problems that may arise.
		3.28 Committee contacts media (newspaper, television, radio, etc.) to make community aware of integration plans, goals, expectations, PL 99-457, feature stories,etc.		3.69 Person with specific responsibility to make contact with people via telephone, memos, letters, notes, etc.
		3.29 Committee organizes handicap awareness day/week/etc. in the community.		
		3.291 Activities may include: afterschool night, puppet shows, slide shows, assuming a handicapping condition (i.e., being confined to a wheelchair, cotton taped over eyes and/or ears, etc.).		
		3.30 Committee gradually turns responsibility over to parent group for that school/district. Parent group answers to committee and continues to work with them as needs arise.		

Appendix 2.B. (continued)

Goal	Data/Method for determining progress toward goal (End Product)	Activities for achieving goal (Resources to Use)	Obstacles to overcome	Support to overcome obstacles
4.0 To prepare peers and environment for integration activities.	4.10 Student has participated in general preparation activities for his/her class. 4.11 Students have participated in organized activities for class preparation based upon class needs. 4.12 Students have participated in regular integration follow-up sessions with class. 4.13 Environment is prepared to receive students which are being integrated. 4.14 Activities for ongoing preparation are designed by the teacher (i.e., tutoring buddies, grouping, etc.). 4.15 Peers are knowledgeable about handicapping conditions and comfortable in environment.	4.20 Teacher assesses class knowledge about integration and children with handicaps via questionnaires, interview, discussion, survey, etc. 4.21 Teacher provides a question-and-answer period for students to eliminate their concerns and answer their questions. 4.22 Teacher arranges for professional projects (i.e., FMS, etc.) to present preparation activities (i.e., puppet shows, skits, role-play situations, video programs, movies, etc.). 4.23 Teacher designs handicap awareness activities via simulation of handicapping conditions (i.e., wheelchair obstacle course, crutch races, patches over eyes, cotton in ears, etc.). 4.24 Teacher allows for children to interact with integrated student(s) via buddy/tutor activities on a scheduled basis. 4.25 Teacher provides regular and consistent sessions for follow up and review of handicapping awareness (monthly, etc.).	4.30 Under- or overestimating peer prep needs. 4.31 Noncooperative regular education teachers. 4.32 Student prejudices fostered by parents. 4.33 Children who are absent when preparation activities take place. 4.34 Uncorrectable obstacles (i.e., concrete support barriers, etc.). 4.35 Lack of time (i.e., time to prepare peers, adapt environment, etc.). 4.36 Lack of money (i.e., money to purchase prep materials, make environmental adaptations, etc.).	4.40 Use of video equipment to show educational films, slides, etc. 4.41 Peer prep activities (i.e., puppet shows, films, slide-sound presentations, discussions, role play, etc.). 4.42 Administrators who support peer and environmental preparation via monies, materials, equipment, etc. 4.43 Support groups (i.e., parent groups, teacher groups, etc.) to put positive pressures upon district/school personnel to make changes as needed in environment. 4.44 Use of influential people to discuss positive integration experiences to commit-tees and administrators in order to garner support for changes, etc.

Appendix 2.B. (continued)

Goal	Data/Method for determining progress toward goal (End Product)	Activities for achieving goal (Resources to Use)	Obstacles to overcome	Support to overcome obstacles
4.0 To prepare peers and environment for integration activities.		4.26 CEO review. 4.27 Task force (administrator, teachers, parents, etc.) to put pressure upon district for environmental changes (i.e., ramps, railings, larger lavatory facilities, etc.).	4.37 Lack of administrative support (principal, district/ state superintendents, etc.) to make necessary changes in environment, allocate monies for changes.	4.45 See goals 1.55, 1.56, 1.57, 1.59.
5.0 To prepare a child, who is identified as a candidate to be integrated, to function appropriately when placed in a integration environment.	5.10 Teacher expectations (i.e., academic, social, etc.) for any child entering teacher's class have been identified via assessment measure (not child specific). 5.11 Teacher expectations (i.e., academic, social, etc.) for a specific child entering teacher's class have been identified via assessment measure. 5.12 Child's skill levels (i.e., academic, social, etc.) have been identified to determine successes and deficits. 5.13 Child has been trained to meet integration teacher's expectations in deficit areas.	5.20 General inventory given to all possible mainstreaming teachers in a school/district at beginning of year or when applicable. 5.20 Integration committee and/or principal assesses potential integration teacher's expectations and technical assistance needs via Teacher Expectations and Assistance for Mainstreaming (TEAM). 5.21 Integration committee reviews all TEAM evaluations to determine teacher expectations and technical assistance needs.	5.40 Lack of time (to make observations, fill out MESA,TEAM, scheduling conflicts, etc.). 5.41 Lack of support from teachers, administrators, parents, etc. 5.42 Lack of motivation (teacher reluctance to participate, etc.). 5.43 Lack of money (i.e., funding for substitute to take class while teacher observes pupil, fills out forms, provision of incentive pay, career ladder, credit, etc.).	5.50 Administrator support via $$ for aides, substitutes, to take class for teacher while forms are filled out, observations are made, etc. 5.51 Use of aides to manage classes while teachers fill out forms, make observations, etc. 5.52 Support of special educator via training time, equipment, and modification programs.

Appendix 2.B. (continued)

Goal	Data/Method for determining progress toward goal (End Product)	Activities for achieving goal (Resources to Use)	Obstacles to overcome	Support to overcome obstacles
5.0 To prepare a child, who is identified as a candidate to be integrated, to function appropriately when placed in a integration environment.	5.14 Child has been acquainted with his/her potential receiving environment (i.e., physical structure, pupils, aides, class rules, grading procedures, etc.).	Specific inventory given to possible integration teachers in school/district once a specific child has been identified as a candidate for integration. 5.22 Special educator-completed child portion of the Mainstreaming Expectations and Skills Assessment (MESA) for a specific child identified for possible mainstreaming activities. 5.23 Potential receiving teacher(s) have completed teacher portion (expectations and technical assistance needs) of the IESA based upon a specific child's skill previously completed by special educator. 5.24 Special educator obtains completed MESA from potential integration teacher(s). 5.25 Special educator notes skills needed for the child entering the potential receiving teacher's classroom. 5.26 Special educator designs a systematic plan for training identified child in areas needed for meeting potential receiving teacher's expectations prior to integration.	5.44 Student who is not ready for total integration. 5.45 Reluctance of special ed teacher to "let go" of child. 5.46 Over- or underestimating student competencies. 5.47 Lack of validity of teacher's responses on TEAM, MESA. 5.48 Forms and papers which travel between teacher's and/or administrators (paper shuffle).	

Appendix 2.B. (continued)

Goal	Data/Method for determining progress toward goal (End Product)	Activities for achieving goal (Resources to Use)	Obstacles to overcome	Support to overcome obstacles
5.0 To prepare a child, who is identified as a candidate to be integrated, to function appropriately when placed in a integration environment.		5.27 Prior to integration, the target child is introduced to the potential receiving teacher. 5.28 Prior to integration, the target child is introduced to the potential receiving environment (i.e., physical structure; classroom, desks, storage facilities, lockers, etc.) via informal and casual walk-through of classroom. 5.29 Prior to integration, the target child has been introduced to the potential receiving class (i.e., pupils, aides, tutors, buddies, etc.) via formal introduction and orientation. 5.2901 Prior to integration, the potential receiving teacher has discussed the program, policies, goals, grading, seating, recess, rules, homework, attendance, etc., with the child's parents. 5.30 Prior to integration, the target child will have observed the class for the specific time in which s/he may be participating. This observation should occur on a "regular" school day which would allow the child to see and feel the flow of the potential receiving environment in which s/he may be participating.		

Appendix 2.B. (continued)

Goal	Data/Method for determining progress toward goal (End Product)	Activities for achieving goal (Resources to Use)	Obstacles to overcome	Support to overcome obstacles
6.0 To conduct Individualized Education Plan (IEP) meeting.	6.10 People involved in the decision-making process for the IEP (i.e., administrator, teachers of special and regular education, psychologists, specialists, parents, child when appropriate, etc.) have been notified of date, time, and location of meeting.	Pre-IEP 6.20 See goals 5.10 - 5.27.	6.30 Lack of time (to attend meeting, to fill out forms, to discuss integration objectives, to observe child, too busy to attend, other obligations, etc.).	6.40 Teacher/administrator support.
	6.11 People involved in the IEP decision-making process have met at the appointed time and location.	6.21 A written memo, letter, etc., was sent to the IEP committee to notify them of the date, time, and location of the IEP meeting.	6.31 Motivation (incomplete paperwork from committee members, unwillingness to participate, lack of teacher/administrator commitment, too much paper work to complete, apathy, etc.).	6.41 Use of prior reminders (i.e., phone calls, memos, etc., with advance planning).
	6.12 Child's skill levels (i.e., academic, social, etc.) for a specific child have been identified via testing measures to determine successes and deficits.	6.22 Follow-up and confirmation of IEP meeting date, time, and location were made via telephone, personal visit, etc., to all persons involved in the IEP process.	6.32 Insufficient data to make decisions.	6.42 Planning ahead of time to distribute and collect surveys, questionnaires, testing results, etc.
	6.13 Environmental adaptations have been planned for via written objectives and dates for completion.	6.23 Placement options were finalized via written goals and objectives from the IEP committee members based upon goals 5.10 - 5.27 and 6.12.	6.33 Incorrect data, observations, recommendations, etc.	6.43 Maintain positive discussions during meetings. Keep all committee members involved via assignments, answering questions, etc.
	6.14 Time lines have been set for peer prep, child prep, teacher training, parent involvement, re-evaluation times, etc.	6.24 Time lines were set for peer prep, child prep, teacher training, parent involvement, re-evaluation times, etc., via written goals and objectives with dates for completion. (See goals 5.28 - 5.32.)		6.44 Allow flexibility in scheduling with parents and other committee members.
	6.15 Alternative strategies (i.e., the use of tutors, buddies, groupings, etc.) have been planned for via possible integrated child.	6.25 Alternative strategies (i.e., tutoring, buddies, groupings, etc.) were planned with dates for implementation.		6.45 Arrange for substitutes, aides, etc., to cover class while in meetings.

Appendix 2.B. (continued)

Goal	Data/Method for determining progress toward goal (End Product)	Activities for achieving goal (Resources to Use)	Obstacles to overcome	Support to overcome obstacles
6.0 To conduct Individualized Education Plan (IEP) meeting.	6.16 Placement(s)/options and programs have been finalized for child via written plan. 6.17 IEP forms have been dated and signed by persons involved in the IEP process.	6.26 Goals and objectives for assisting child to become proficient in deficit areas were written and dates for re-evaluation were scheduled (see goal 5.27). 6.27 IEP forms were signed and dated by IEP committee members involved with the child's placement decisions.		6.46 Complete that paperwork which does not require committee members' participation (i.e., names, dates, DOB, address, etc.). 6.47 Select one teacher to be a representative for a group of teachers in order to communicate effectively at the IEP.

Appendix 2.C.

Integration Task Force Overview

What is an integration task force?

A group of individuals (regular and special educators, principal, school psychologist, counselor, parents of children with and without handicaps, PTA representative, etc.) who work together to establish an integration program.

What does a task force do in terms of integration activities?

Activities vary based upon school needs and organization of the task force. Typically, a task force assists the principal in planning and maintaining an organized system of integration activities within a school. Activities may include but are not limited to:

1. General peer, parent, and community preparation for integration.

2. Systems for designing and implementing peer tutors and buddy systems within schools.

3. Support system for special and regular educators (i.e., classroom support, organization of teacher, child, and parent training, inservices).

4. Support to principal (i.e., IEP support, fund-raising, organization of training programs for teachers).

5. Long-term support to integration via awareness activities, training of new team members, organization of parent groups, etc.

How should the integration task force be organized?

See Figure 2.2 for a sample of Task Force organization.

Integration Task Force Evaluation Questionnaire

School/District _____ Date_____
Position on Task Force _____

Directions: This questionnaire was designed to assess the organizational structure and function of a task force. We are interested in discovering effective practices and techniques, assisting school administrators and others with the organization of integration task force guidelines, and improving the educational system within a school/district in terms of integration practices. Please take a few minutes to repond to questions about your task force. In responding to the questions on this form, make your reponses descriptive and honest. One member of the task force will collect the questionnaires and return them to the task force. All identifying comments will be kept confidential from all task force members. Data from this survey will be summarized into one form for the task force records.

Appendix 2.C. (continued)

1. Were goals and objectives for the task force discussed? **Yes No**
   a. If **yes**, were the goals and objectives clear to you? If not, why were they not clear to you?_____
   _____

   b. If **no**, what structure was provided and what directions were discussed?
   _____
   _____
   _____

2. If your response to question #1 was <u>yes</u>, were methods for evaluating those goals and objectives designated? **Yes No**

3. If your response to question #1 was <u>no</u>, what methods for evaluation of task force effectiveness were discussed?
   _____
   _____
   _____

4. Functioning as a task force, do decisions come from a general consensus of team members or come from the top down? Please describe. _____
   _____
   _____
   _____
   _____

5. Describe the pros and cons of your task force.
   Pros:_____
   _____
   _____
   Cons:_____
   _____
   _____

6. What suggestions do you have to improve the structure and effectiveness of the task force with which you are involved? _____
   _____
   _____
   _____
   _____
   _____

7. How often does the task force meet (i.e., weekly, monthly)? _____

8. Is the meeting formal or informal? _____

9. Is the entire task force committee invited to each meeting? **Yes No**

10. Is every member of the task force treated equally? **Yes No**

Appendix 2.C. (continued)

11. Is notification of meetings given early enough to fit it into your schedule? **Yes No**

12. Presently, how effective is the task force? In other words, what benefit does the task force make to the integration effort in your school/district at the present time?

_____
_____
_____
_____
_____
_____
_____

If you have additional comments, questions, or concerns, please respond below:

_____
_____
_____
_____
_____
_____
_____
_____
_____
_____
_____
_____
_____
_____
_____
_____
_____
_____
_____
_____
_____
_____
_____
_____
_____
_____
_____
_____

Thank you for your time and efforts in responding to this questionnaire. If you have further comments, questions, or concerns, please contact:

Appendix 2.D.

Educator Rating Form

Gary Percival, Sebastian Striefel,
& Joel Allred

Purpose and Instructions for Educator Rating Form

Purpose

The purpose of the Educator Rating Form is to determine those educators who seem most willing or motivated to establish and maintain functional integration in their schools. The reason for locating those most willing to implement integration in their schools is to be able to work with these individuals first. This will ensure the best possible results from the integration process so that other schools and educators will have a positive example in the further implementation of integrated preschools.

Instructions

The Educator Rating Form is to be filled out by a person interviewing the educator to see how amenable the educator is to the integration process. Each item is scored as yes or no, or on a five-point continuum with the higher scores indicating more of a willingness, on the part of the educator, to help the integration process. Several questions ask for a description or a list. These should be filled out by the interviewer to help assess the strong points and the needs of the educator.

Appendix 2.D. (continued)

EDUCATOR RATING FORM

Educator's Name_____ School_____

Interviewer_____ Date_____

1. Did Educator initiate a request for information?

   NO   YES

       If yes describe motivation (i.e. District Supervisor request or directive, self-motivation, etc.):

     If no who did?

2. How did Educator rate self on knowledge about integration?

1	2	3	4	5
knows little				knows a lot

3. Is integration already implemented in the school district?

   NO   YES

       If so, describe (i.e. physical, social, instructional):

4. Does Educator have a goal to initiate integration in the school?

1	2	3	4	5
weak				solid

       If so, describe:

5. Are there barriers that interfere with or preclude integration in the school?

1	2	3	4	5
many				none

       Describe barriers:

6. Will Educator be supported by staff, parents, administrators?

1	2	3	4	5
limited				full

Appendix 2.D. (continued)

7. Did Educator ask questions about integration?

| 1 | 2 | 3 | 4 | 5 |
| none | | | | many |

| 1 | 2 | 3 | 4 | 5 |
| naive | | | | sophisticated |

(i.e., Do the questions show a lack of knowledge or a abundance
of knowledge about integration?)

| 1 | 2 | 3 | 4 | 5 |
| superficial | | | | in-depth |

(i.e. Are the questions surface questions with no desire
to understand, or do they show understanding or a desire
to understand integration?)

8. Did Educator verbalize reservations about integration?

| 1 | 2 | 3 | 4 | 5 |
| many | | | | few |

Describe reservations:

9. Did Educator commit resources?

| 1 | 2 | 3 | 4 | 5 |
| none | | | | many |

List resources committed (i.e. photocopying, paper, personal time,
teachers' time, etc.):

10. Did Educator make specific comments about facilitating the integration process?

| 1 | 2 | 3 | 4 | 5 |
| none | | | | many |

11. Did Educator ask what is the next step in implementing integration in the school?

NO   YES

If yes, describe motivation:

12. Did Educator invite us back for a follow-up?

NO   YES

Describe motivation:

Appendix 2.E.

Functional Mainstreaming for Success Brochure

A successful mainstreaming program is one in which both children with and without handicaps receive quality services at the same time.

The FMS model promotes mainstreaming by:

1. Providing procedures and materials for two systems of mainstreaming:

   a. **Reverse Preschool Mainstreaming** - Desegregation of programs that previously served only children with handicaps while maintaining quality service for children with handicaps.

   b. **Transition**- Integration of children with handicaps into regular programs.

2. Identifying the needs that will arise with the mainstreaming of a particular student with handicaps, and addressing those needs through:

   a. Environmental modifications

   b. Staff training and technical assistance

   c. Training of target child

   d. Parent preparation and training

   e. Peer preparation

   f. Effective grouping, use of peers, curriculum modification and teaching techniques

Functional Mainstreaming for Success

FMS Project
Developmental Center for Handicapped Persons
Utah State University
Logan, Utah 84322-6840

A 3-year demonstration project funded by the
Handicapped Children's Early Education Programs
U.S. Office of Education

Appendix 2.E. (continued)

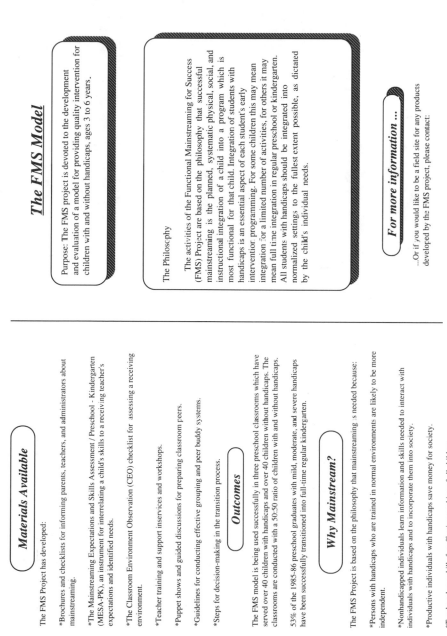

The FMS Model

Purpose: The FMS project is devoted to the development and evaluation of a model for providing quality intervention for children with and without handicaps, ages 3 to 6 years.

The Philosophy

The activities of the Functional Mainstreaming for Success (FMS) Project are based on the philosophy that successful mainstreaming is the planned, systematic physical, social, and instructional integration of a child into a program which is most functional for that child. Integration of students with handicaps is an essential aspect of each student's early intervention programming. For some children this may mean integration for a limited number of activities, for others it may mean full time integration in regular preschool or kindergarten. All students with handicaps should be integrated into normalized settings to the fullest extent possible, as dictated by the child's individual needs.

For more information ...

...Or if you would like to be a field site for any products developed by the FMS project, please contact:

Materials Available

The FMS Project has developed:

*Brochures and checklists for informing parents, teachers, and administrators about mainstreaming.

*The Mainstreaming Expectations and Skills Assessment / Preschool - Kindergarten (MESA-PK), an instrument for interrelating a child's skills to a receiving teacher's expectations and identified needs.

*The Classroom Environment Observation (CEO) checklist for assessing a receiving environment.

*Teacher training and support inservices and workshops.

*Puppet shows and guided discussions for preparing classroom peers.

*Guidelines for conducting effective grouping and peer buddy systems.

*Steps for decision-making in the transition process.

Outcomes

The FMS model is being used successfully in three preschool classrooms which have served over 40 children with handicaps and over 40 children without handicaps. The classrooms are conducted with a 50:50 ratio of children with and without handicaps.

53% of the 1985-86 preschool graduates with mild, moderate, and severe handicaps have been successfully transitioned into full-time regular kindergarten.

Why Mainstream?

The FMS Project is based on the philosophy that mainstreaming is needed because:

*Persons with handicaps who are trained in normal environments are likely to be more independent.

*Nonhandicapped individuals learn information and skills needed to interact with individuals with handicaps and to incorporate them into society.

*Productive individuals with handicaps save money for society.

*Teachers learn skills for effective teaching of all children.

Chapter 3

. . .

Staff Preparation: Procedures and Materials

Efforts to develop an integrated program will often be resisted by a school's staff. Resistance usually arises from apprehension of change and legitimate concerns about the difficulties of meeting the needs of children with handicaps in less restrictive settings. This chapter presents a model of staff preparation for dealing with these concerns, and procedures and materials to assist the reader in staff preparation. Staff preparation includes (a) orienting staff to integration and integrated service delivery, (b) assessing staff training needs and locating training resources, (c) conducting training to meet those needs, and (d) providing ongoing staff training services (see Figure 3.1).

Orientation

Many teachers' concerns about integration will diminish once the teachers have been provided with information about what to expect. Resistance to change is often based on the reluctance of individuals to admit that they may need new skills, rather than resistance to the philosophy of integration itself. Orientation may include introducing new administrative policies, discussing the integration time lines, making staff aware of administrative commitment to the integration

Figure 3.1. Flowchart of Staff Preparation Activities

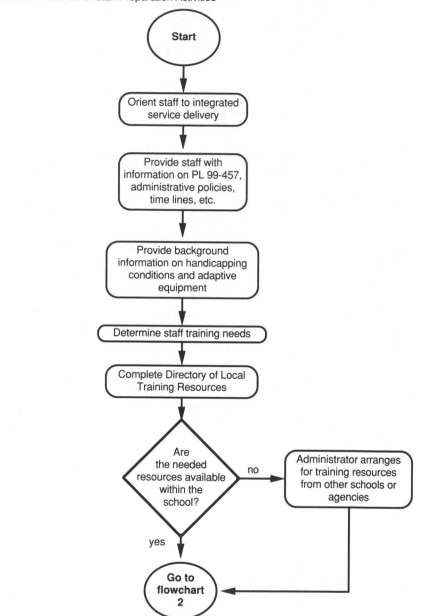

Figure 3.1. (continued)

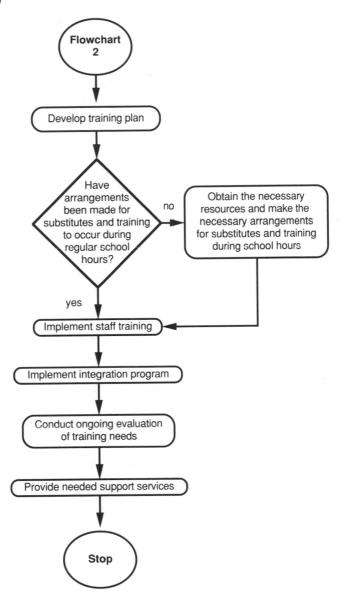

process, defining integration and mainstreaming, and making staff aware of the legal requirements of P.L. 94-142 and P.L. 99-457. Several methods including memos, handouts, inservices, informal discussions, and presentations may be used to present general information about policy changes regarding mainstreaming.

Questions Teachers Often Raise About Mainstreaming (Appendix 3.A) was developed to provide information about the rationale and procedures involved in integration, promoting integration among students with and without handicaps, and concerns often held by teachers.

Another valuable resource, *Public Law 94-142, Section 504, and Public Law 99-457: Understanding What They Are and Are Not* (Ballard et al., 1987), discusses the federal laws concerning mainstreaming and integration. One challenge for both educators and parents is to meet the adaptive equipment needs of children with handicaps at home and school. At home, children sometimes require special equipment to assist them in performing everyday activities (e.g., communication and mobility). In the classroom, schools are obligated to provide adaptive equipment that is deemed necessary for a child's academic success under Public Law 94-142, Public Law 99-457, and Section 504 of the Rehabilitation Act.

Parents, teachers, and administrators who are suddenly faced with a need for special equipment and are not familiar with handicapping conditions, available adaptive equipment, and possible sources of funding may feel as if they are lost in a maze of government programs, advocacy groups, and overwhelming information. The lack of guidance in seeking information may lead parents, teachers, or administrators to believe they are incapable of acquiring the needed equipment. In many cases, however, resources are available and can be found with a little effort.

Adaptive Equipment and Materials for the Mainstreamed Classroom: A Resource Guide (Appendix 3.B) contains information on meeting the adaptive equipment needs of children with handicaps. The adaptive equipment resource guide is designed to provide general information on the topics of assessing adaptive equipment needs, determining how to best fulfill a given need for adaptive equipment, the types of adaptive equipment available, building adaptive equipment, and sources of information and funding for adaptive equipment and materials. Although this guide can be used by anyone interested in meeting the needs of children with handicaps, the main emphasis is on obtaining and using adaptive equipment to facilitate the integration of students with handicaps into regular education settings.

Determining Training Needs and Locating Resources

After orientation, the training and preparation needed by school staff to insure success must be determined. The integration task force's coordinator for teacher preparation (Chapter 2) should form a committee to conduct an assessment of (a) staff training needs and (b) available resources for meeting these identified needs.

The FMS project has developed several instruments that can be used to assist a task force in determining a preschool's staff readiness to implement integrated services. Each of the FMS instruments is described below, and a copy of each is provided in the appendices of this chapter.

Assessing Teacher Skills

Based on a review of the literature on teacher training, integration, and mainstreaming, the FMS project has identified 23 major skill areas that are important for successful integration. The General Teacher Needs Assessment (Appendix 3.C) consists of (a) a listing and definition of each of the skill areas and (b) a needs assessment form for all areas and their subskills. The General Teacher Needs Assessment is used to identify skills in which a teacher feels he or she may need training, as well as the skills in which the teacher is able to train others.

The Teacher Expectations and Assistance for Mainstreaming in Preschool and Kindergarten (TEAM-PK) (Appendix 3.D) identifies the communication, social, work, and self-help expectations of teachers and the maladaptive behaviors of children who might be placed in their classrooms. It also identifies areas in which teachers may request technical assistance and support when children with handicaps are placed in their classrooms.

Needs Assessment

The information gathered by the TEAM-PK and the General Teacher Needs Assessment is used by the staff training committee to determine and prioritize staff training needs. By identifying teachers' expectations, technical assistance, and training needs, the task force is better able to plan inservices and locate the resources necessary to better prepare teachers both before and during the process of integration.

Forms or surveys used to conduct a needs assessment should be completed anonymously and the results kept confidential. If staff members feel threatened by the assessment, they should be assured that it is only being conducted to determine the preschool's overall training needs (i.e., handicapping conditions, adapting curricula, knowledge of different types of evaluation, teaching social skills, etc.). To assure confidentiality, the principal might ask the task force to prepare a written summary of the results of the needs assessment, and then destroy the original forms to protect staff anonymity and increase the likelihood of obtaining accurate responses.

Locating Resources

The results of a needs assessment can often be overwhelming. At first, it may seem to the committee that they have a long list of training needs, but no trainers. What many administrators and teachers do not realize is that trainers and other resources can often be found locally. The Directory of Local Training Resources (Appendix 3.E) is intended to provide teachers, trainers, principals, and district administrative staff with a method for developing an organized and readily usable listing of resources for training. Although focused on increasing successful integration, the resources identified are useful for all teachers and all students.

If the directory is limited to resources within a single school, the staff training committee should complete the directory. If the directory is used to identify resources within a district, a larger group effort is appropriate. Such a group may include principals, teachers, and district administrative and training staff. The final completed copy is then sent to all interested parties.

Conducting Training to Meet Needs

Based on the results of the needs assessment and the completed directory, the staff training committee can now organize training activities (i.e., inservices, workshops, and discussion groups). It may be possible to find needed trainers from within the school's staff. In this case, the administrator will need to arrange for class coverage during the time teachers are trained and develop a system to compensate teachers who conduct inservices on their own time. If outside trainers are needed, the committee may be able to find educators from local universities who would be willing to conduct inservices free of charge. If trainers cannot be found locally, special funding may need to be requested from the school district to pay for speakers' time, travel costs, and materials. It is also recommended that reciprocal training with other schools and agencies, such as Head Start, be considered.

Many of the staff's concerns about integration diminish once they have knowledge of what to expect. Information is also a large part of obtaining staff commitment to integration. Most administrators generally find that if they are constructive and open about giving, asking for, and receiving feedback about how the program is being conducted, the staff will begin to show their commitment to integration. Additional activities that will help obtain commitment include (a) hiring substitutes when staff training is scheduled, (b) assuring that the integration program is not an overload activity, and (c) scheduling training during regular work hours.

Signs of staff commitment include teachers volunteering to integrate children into their classrooms, teachers offering to provide technical assistance to other teachers, suggestions by staff members on how to make an integration program more effective, and staff members requesting the formation of a committee or task force and/or offering to serve on the committee.

Ongoing Evaluation and Availability of Support Services

The need for staff training and support is an ongoing part of implementing an integrated preschool program. It is essential that a process be established to assure that training and support not be a one-time event, but rather that they be available when and as needed. Regular contact with staff and observation of implementation activities will provide the opportunity to determine the need for training and support services.

Staff who are implementing an integrated preschool program for the first time will have many questions and concerns on a weekly, if not daily, basis. These issues and concerns must be addressed if the program is to succeed. Having weekly discussions with all staff involved in the implementation activities in a group setting is very useful in identifying problems, sharing ideas, arranging for needed resources, providing additional training, and assuring that staff feel that their efforts are important and are being supported. Failure to provide ongoing training and support will result in staff dissatisfaction, turnover, and resistance.

Appendix 3.A.

Questions Teachers Often Raise About

Mainstreaming

What is mainstreaming?

Mainstreaming refers to the placement of children with handicaps into settings and activities with their nonhandicapped peers. This placement can be as comprehensive as full-time placement in a regular program or as limited as eating lunch or having recess together. Mainstreaming can be physical -- children attending the same school but in separate classrooms or in the same activities but with no interaction. Mainstreaming can be social -- children with handicaps interacting during recess with their nonhandicapped peers. Mainstreaming can be instructional -- children with handicaps spending part or much of the day in the regular classroom. Ideally, maintreaming becomes integration through the planned physical, social, and instructional inclusion of children with handicaps in all normal activities with peers without handicaps so their growth and development is enhanced to their fullest potential.

Why mainstream?

When well planned and well managed, mainstreaming is beneficial to all involved. Children with handicaps benefit because they learn to function in the "mainstream of society." Their independence, social skills, and overall learning increase. Mainstreaming may also decrease the amount of time children with handicaps spend on nonproductive tasks such as being transported to special schools.

Children without handicaps can learn to respect differences in other people and can learn to respect that everyone has varying strengths and weaknesses. They can also learn patience and better communication skills under the guidance of the teacher.

Teachers can benefit by having their skills broadened and, consequently, fine-tuned. Mainstreaming, when well implemented, demands communication among teachers and specialists. Many programs have benefited from mainstreaming by having more and better communication among staff, parents, and administrators.

Who decides which children are mainstreamed?

Programs for children with handicaps are determined by the child study team which includes the parents, teachers, specialists, administrators, others as needed, and the student, if appropriate. In setting early intervention objectives, the team considers the child's current abilities and the long-term goals for the child, as well as the child's learning styles and needs. When the objectives planned for a child can be met in a more integrated setting, then it is this team's responsibility to arrange for the child to be mainstreamed and to provide the support that is needed.

Appendix 3.A. (continued)

What should I do when I see children with handicaps in the hallway, playground, etc.?

The best general answer to this question is that adults should behave as they would with any child. If the child with handicaps is misbehaving, he or she should be disciplined. If not, then a normal greeting and conversation would be appropriate and useful for helping the child practice social skills.

What should I tell children without handicaps about the children with handicaps?

Children are usually very interested in how people vary and how they are alike. Teasing often results from lack of knowledge and fear. Teachers can help children by having an open discussion with their class, by answering the children's questions simply and frankly, by pointing out that children with handicaps have more similarities to nonhandicapped peers than differences, and by helping the children in their class consider ways in which they can play with, help, be friends with, or work with children with handicaps.

How can I facilitate interaction between the children with and without handicaps?

One important step to helping children communicate with each other is for teachers to model the language and social skills they want children to exhibit - by initiating conversations with children with handicaps, by inviting them to join activities, and by making them feel that they are an important part of the group. In these activities the teacher must often arrange for the children to interact; for example, initiating art activities that are team-oriented but non-competitive, such as making a mural or papier-mâché sculpture.

Peer buddy systems are also useful by providing parameters and guidelines for interactions. In a peer buddy system children with handicaps and children without handicaps are assigned to each other as buddies for non-academic activities.

How do I meet the needs of children with handicaps, and am I qualified to fulfill them?

Providing services to children with handicaps can appear to be an overwhelming task, because these children have skill levels that are seemingly widely divergent from the rest of the group. However, an early intervention program is uniquely suited for addressing the needs of a very broad range of students. The variety of skills demonstrated by "normal" students allows for integrated groupings throughout the day, which combine children with similar strengths and deficits. This system is particularly effective in programs where children are grouped by skills and interests, not solely by age levels. A teacher who already approaches children as individuals should have little difficulty planning for the individual needs of the child with handicaps.

In specialty areas, (e.g., language, and physical therapy) teachers must always have access to professionals in these fields. It is the responsibility of a program administrator to facilitate this access, so that quality services can be maintained for all children. Finally, it is naive to assume that staffing patterns will not change; additional

Appendix 3.A. (continued)

people are very likely to be needed. However, paid aides are only one option; many programs have succeeded with sibling, community group, and elderly volunteers; parent volunteers; and cooperative credit-earning practicum assignments for college or high school students.

Wouldn't this take time away from the other children in my program?

In order to ensure that the mainstreaming experience is successful for the child with handicaps, the other children, and the teacher, extra time may be needed initially from the teacher. However, this extra time should not be at the expense of the child's peers. Continuity of programs for the mainstreamed child can be facilitated when the previous specialists, service providers, and parents have meetings to discuss the child's functioning before, during, and after integration. When the planning which takes place in these meetings is detailed and flexible, the extra time will have been used before placement. The child should function appropriately in the new setting, and only occasional check-up meetings should be necessary.

Which of my class activities would interest the children with handicaps?

Just as nonhandicapped children have different needs and interests, so do children with handicaps. An important consideration in deciding which activities might be appropriate is whether the activity is beneficial to all involved. For example, an art activity can require cutting out and counting animal figures (for higher-skilled children), labeling animal names and body parts (for intermediate-skilled children) and color recognition (for low-skilled children). All of these objectives can be addressed at the same learning center.

My classroom is overcrowded, my materials are out of date, and there are a number of children in my classroom who need special attention. Why do children with handicaps get so much funding and extra assistance?

There are two basic answers to this question. One reflects a particular moral stance, the other a more practical one. In part, the moral argument is that children with handicaps are already burdened. They are children with the odds against them. Ethically, everything that can be done for them should be. On the practical side, the cost to society over the long run will be diminished if intensive, high-quality intervention is made early, and children with handicaps become productive members of the workforce. One study found that for every dollar spent on a high-quality preschool program for children with intellectual handicaps, there was a $7 return to society over the lifetime of the child.

If I run into a problem, how do I get help?

This varies from agency to agency. The principal, parent, teacher, or specialist may be the appropriate person to approach in many settings. Local universities and civic groups can offer technical assistance and personnel resources.

Appendix 3.B.

Adaptive Equipment and Materials for the Mainstreamed Classroom:

A Resource Guide

Brian Sevy, Maria Quintero, LeAnn Hyer,
Steve Campbell, & Sebastian Striefel

Introduction

One challenge for both educators and parents is to meet the adaptive equipment needs of children with handicaps at home and school. At home, children sometimes require special equipment to assist them in performing everyday activities (e.g., communicating and manipulating electrical switches). In the classroom, schools are obligated to provide adaptive equipment which is deemed necessary for a child's academic success under P.L. 94-142, P.L. 99-457, and Section 504 of the Rehabilitation Act.

Parents, teachers, and administrators who are suddenly faced with a need for special equipment and are not familiar with handicapping conditions, available adaptive equipment, and possible sources of funding may feel as if they are lost in a maze of government programs, advocacy groups, and overwhelming information. The lack of guidance in seeking information may lead a parent, teacher, or administrator to believe that they are incapable of acquiring the needed equipment. In many cases resources are available and can be found with little effort.

This guide is designed to provide general information on the topics of assessing adaptive equipment needs, determining how to best fulfill a given need for adaptive equipment, and sources of information and funding for adaptive equipment and materials. Although this guide can be used by anyone interested in meeting the needs of children with handicaps, the main emphasis is on obtaining and using adaptive equipment to facilitate the integration of students with handicaps into regular education settings.

Definition

Adaptive equipment and materials are defined in this guide as any device or aid that will help a person with handicaps function in the regular classroom or another "normal" environment. These include items that would facilitate or augment communication, reading, writing, mobility, self-care, seating, and other demands of the environment.

Assessing Individual Needs

Careful evaluation of the child's needs and products available is essential in fitting the proper equipment and materials to the demands of the environment. The individual functioning of students must be considered in many areas including communication, reading, writing, self-care, movement, accessibility, etc. This is especially true in assessing the needs of severely and/or profoundly handicapped children. If careful

Appendix 3.B. (continued)

evaluation is not taken into account, it may endanger the safety or limit the potential growth of the individual. Since a child's functioning needs are apt to change over time, any evaluation has to be ongoing.

Matching Equipment to the Child's Need

Once a child's needs for adaptive equipment have been assessed, the task becomes one of choosing a particular piece of equipment from the variety of products commercially available. Some factors that may be considered in making the choice include: present and future functioning needs; physical abilities; cognitive abilities; motivation; language skills; environmental constraints; vocational, educational, leisure, and residential goals; cost; durability; and functionality (Cadez et al., 1986).

Types of Equipment Available by Need

The information cited in this section is simply designed to make the reader aware of some equipment and materials that exist, and to give some suggestions on facilities and special provisions. Each situation will be different, and will require discretion on the part of the student's evaluation team in terms of what is necessary to meet the needs of the mainstreamed child. We do not intend to imply that all of these items are necessary for each handicapping condition, or that this section lists everything which is currently available.

As a function of the Technology-Related Assistance for Individuals with Disabilities Act of 1988 (P.L. 100-407), there will be statewide assistive technology service systems in all states within 3 to 5 years. Such systems will be a great source of technical assistance in finding appropriate adaptive equipment and materials. (Additional information concerning P.L. 100-407 may be found under State Government in the section "Sources of Materials and Funding.")

Materials for the Visually Impaired

    Classroom Equipment:*
      Tape recorder
      Typewriter
      Braille writer
      Braille slate and stylus
      Large type, tape recorded, or braille books
      Magnifying lenses
      Lamps
      Abacus
      Tactile-braille maps and globes
      Bold-line paper, raised-line paper, black felt-tip pens, large pencils
      Yellow acetate to bring out contrast in purple dittos
      Raised line drawing kit
      Closed circuit T.V. system to increase print size
      Walking cane
      Talking (speech output) calculators

Appendix 3.B. (continued)

Computerized/High-Tech Equipment:**
    Braille compatible microcomputers, and computers with braille keyboards and
        printers: equipment that can translate normal text to braille transcription.
    Text readers: devices that interface with computers that scan printed text and
        convert it to braille, voice, or discernible vibrations felt by the index finger.
    Voice response/voice output computers.

Facilities and Provisions:
    Audible or tactile substitutes for visual signs.
    Textured footing on stairs and walkways
    Railings for stairs and doorways
    Audible danger signs (i.e., high voltage and emergency exits, etc.)
    Evacuation safety procedures and personnel
    Braille names on doors, braille numbers and instructions on telephones and
        switches.

Specialists:
    Ophthalmologist
    Optometrist

    *   Many of these items are provided with federal funding from the
       American Printing House for the Blind (see "Other Sources" section
       herein).
    ** Many of these computerized devices are peripherals that can be
       added to existing microcomputers.

Materials for the Hearing Impaired:

Classroom Equipment:
    Visual aids such as models and slides, etc.
    Captioned films (see "Other Sources" section herein)
    Communication Board
    Speech Synthesizer
    Frequent use of written materials and handouts
    Carbon paper or duplicating notebooks
    Telecaption attachment to T.V. set to access close-captioned television
        programs or videotapes
    Hearing aids and batteries for each of the specified hearing aids
    Telephone hearing aid connectors
    Volume control implanted in the phone

Computerized/High-Tech Equipment:
    Communication Technology device (Com-Tek), a device that amplifies the
        speaker's voice
    Teletype (TTY) and Telecommunication (TDD) devices and/or computer
        modem links for telephone communication
    FM systems to decrease backgroud noise amplification
    Voice input/visual display computer: a device that converts a teacher's voice
        into printed text on a screen

Appendix 3.B. (continued)

Specialists:
Audiologist
Speech and Language Pathologist
Speech Therapist
Sign language interpreters
Vocational Rehabilitation Counselors for the deaf for those who have financial
burdens and are unable to provide their own equipment and materials

Materials for the Physically Impaired

Classroom Equipment:
Communication board
Speech synthesizer
Typewriter

Computerized/High-Tech Equipment:
Eye movement keyboard: a device that substitutes eye movement for finger
touch and enables typing
Computerized switches and remote controls: devices that require very little
motor ability (e.g., tongue, breath, etc.) yet they provide accessibility to a
number of devices

Facilities and Provisions:
Accessible doorways, ramps, drinking fountains, lavatories, etc.
Evacuation safety procedures and personnel
Space adjustment to allow mobility
Medication responsibilities, storage, and procedures are clear

Specialists:
Physical Therapist
Recreation Therapist
Occupational Therapist

Building Adaptive Equipment

Courses on building adaptive equipment are sometimes offered by colleges and universities through special education or physical rehabilitation departments. Another possible resource for educators is the book <u>Designing and Constructing Adaptive Equipment on Your Desktop</u> which is available from the Department of Special Education, Utah State University, Logan, UT 84322-6500.

If there isn't any adaptive equipment available or costs are prohibitive, working with a creative rehabilitation engineer, physical therapist, or other technically skilled persons can be successful (Reynolds & Birch,1982). Sometimes the only solution to a certain classroom adaptation problem is a little creativity and ingenuity. Boy Scouts, for example, are usually open to suggestions for completion of service hours and Eagle Scout Projects. By working with someone knowledgeable about adaptive equipment, a scout may be able to design and build a piece of adaptive equipment. Since many companies will contribute the supplies for Eagle Projects, the equipment can be developed at no cost to the parents or the school.

Appendix 3.B. (continued)

Sources of Information

Information Centers
With the rapidly increasing technological advances in adaptive devices, it would be difficult for any one person to be familiar with them all. There are a number of centers in the country which organize such information and provide to those in need. The Center for Special Education Technology Information Exchange is a federally funded center that gives free information on request, and provides a toll free hotline enabling interested parties to talk with staff, listen to recorded messages on various topics in special education technology, and request specific information (see "Other Sources" section herein).
There are also several private organizations providing similar services. The Easter Seals organization has information centers and facilities which lend out adaptive equipment in cities around the country. Other possible sources of information are hospital rehabilitation units and local colleges or universities.

Parents
Educators often find that parents are more familiar with their child's handicap than anyone else, and parents of children with handicaps are often familiar with special equipment, materials, information centers, or special programs that may assist in their child's education. Parent support groups may also be a source of information.

School Special Education Staff
Individual schools or school districts often have special education resource personnel that can aid parents in the selection and procurement of adaptive equipment and materials, as well as provide knowledge of funding. Such specialists can also be an invaluable source of information on a child's needs and how to meet them.

Sources of Materials and Funding

Federal Government
There are federal programs that directly aid in the education of children with handicaps by providing special materials and equipment such as media materials and captioned films for the hearing impaired and books in braille, cassette, or other media for the visually impaired. See the Catalogue of Federal Domestic Assistance (CFDA) published by the federal government for further information.
One program, the American Printing House for the Blind, has a budget appropriated by Congress to provide textbooks on cassette or other educational aids for visually impaired students (Singleton, & Madge, 1980). Many states have material centers that administer American Printing House for the Blind items as well as other materials and equipment (Rossi, 1979). Other federal programs are given in the "Other Sources" section herein.

State Government
Most states have ongoing programs for providing educational materials and equipment for individuals who are handicapped. These programs may be either broadly defined, or specific to a single disability such as those devoted to the visually or hearing impaired. Contact your state Office of Special Education or local special education groups for information on existing state and school district programs.

Appendix 3.B. (continued)

An act recently passed by the federal government can be expected to bring about rapid changes in the existence of state programs concerning adaptive equipment. Under the Technology-Related Assistance for Individuals with Disabilities Act of 1988 (P.L. 100-407), Congress has made competitive grants available to state governments for the development of programs to serve the following purposes: identification and assessment of needs for technology-related (i.e., adaptive equipment) assistance; identification and coordination of resources; provision of assistive technology devices and services; dissemination of information; training and technical assistance; public awareness programs; and assistance to statewide and community-based organizations which provide assistive technology services. As funding from this act becomes available, statewide adaptive equipment services should increase dramatically.

<u>Insurance</u>

A family's health insurance can sometimes help pay for adaptive equipment. Careful documentation and written recommendations from education specialists or staff members of evaluation centers is essential to this process. In making the request, it is sometimes useful to also include a doctor's prescription, a statement of current skills, the prognosis for future health and functioning without the device, and a description of the equipment (Cadez et al., 1986). Careful wording of the request may be crucial. For example, while insurance policies will not provide for educational equipment per se, a policy may provide for a prothesis to facilitate normal functioning.

<u>Private Corporations, Foundations, and Service Clubs</u>

Another good source of funding can be corporations. Charitable donations and gifts are an important part of maintaining a "socially responsible" image for many corporations--not to mention the tax advantages (Belnap, 1987). Private foundations can also be an effective source of funding as many have commitments especially to education and special education (H. Sokoloff, 1985). Service clubs (e.g., Kiwanis, Lions Club, Shriners, etc.) are yet another potential source.

Relevant References

Interview with Mr. Kerry Belnap. (1987, March). Utah State University Office of Development, Logan, Utah 84322.

Cadez, M.J., Clark, K., Cocklin, M., Harris, P., & Killoran, P.M. (1986). <u>Designing and Constructing Adaptive Equipment on Your Desk Top.</u> Logan, UT: Utah State University, Department of Special Education.

Kentucky Department of Education. (1980). <u>The Specialists Who Help Our Child</u>. Frankfort, KY: Bureau of Education for Exceptional Children.

Reynolds, M., & Birch, J. (1982). <u>Teaching Exceptional Children in All America's Schools</u>. Reston, VA: Council for Exceptional Children.

Robinson, G. (1986, May). Insurance can help pay for adaptive equipment. <u>The Exceptional Parent</u>, <u>16</u>(3), 11-15.

Appendix 3.B. (continued)

Rossi, P. (1979, Fall). Management of a statewide textbook and materials center for the visually impaired. Education of the Visually Handicapped, 11(3), 85-88.

Singleton, L., & Madge, L. (1980). Resources for teaching social studies in the mainstreamed classroom (MAVIS Sourcebook 6). Boulder, CO: Social Science Education Consortium.

Sokoloff, H. (1985, March/April). Funding special needs. Media & Methods, 21(7), 38-39.

Sokoloff, M. (1985, March/April). Linking the new technologies with special education. Media & Methods, 21(7), 12-16.

Weinberg, S. (1985, September). Over the hurdles. American School and University, 58(1), 21-23.

Weisenstein, G., & Pelz, R. (1986). Administrators Desk Reference on Special Education. Rockville, MA: Aspen.

Other Sources

Corporate and Private Foundation Directories

The following directories can be found in public or college libraries or from funding specialists:

Corporate 500: The Directory of Corporate Philanthropy. Public Management Institute, San Francisco, 1986.

Handicapped Funding Directory by Burton J. Eckstead. Oceanside, NY: Research Grant Guides.

Taft Corporate Giving Directory. Comprehensive profiles of America's major corporate foundations and charitable giving programs. Washington DC: Taft Corporate Information System.

Taft Foundation Reporter. Comprehensive profiles and analysis of America's private foundations. Washington DC: Taft Foundation Information System.

Sources of More Specific Information

The American Printing House for the Blind (APH) is a private agency funded and designated by the federal government as the official supplier of materials and equipment for visually impaired students under college age. APH provides a variety of educational materials and equipment such as cassette players, speech compressors, braille writing equipment, abacus, and textbooks in various media (e.g., large type, tape recorded, braille). Procurement of items can be arranged through the agency with which the child is registered--usually the state Department of Education. Catalogues are available for materials and equipment, 1839 Frankfort Ave., Louisville, KY 40206.

Appendix 3.B. (continued)

Books for the Blind and Physically Handicapped (CFDA number 42.001) provides cassette players and books on cassette, record, and in braille for those either visually impaired or physically unable to read regular books. Contact the National Library Service for the Blind and Physically Handicapped, 1291 Taylor Street NW, Washington DC 29524, (202) 287-5100. (The National Library Service for the Blind and Physically Handicapped reference circular 78-4 can be found in libraries or government document depositories.)

The Center for Special Education Technology Information Exchange is a federally funded organization dedicated to providing information on special education technology to parents, teachers, administrators, and other concerned parties. Staff members answer a toll free hotline at 1-800-345-TECH on weekdays from 1 p.m. to 4 p.m. Eastern time. Before and after this period, there is a taped message service with over 200 recordings on different topics on special education technology. A directory of the messages can be obtained by contacting the center at 1920 Association Drive, Reston, VA 22091, (703) 620-3660. Hotline and taped messages, 1-800-345-TECH.

This organization also provides an electronic bulletin board (TECH.LINE) on SpecialNET toll free. The caller is able to request follow-up information free of charge.

Handicapped Media Services and Captioned Films (CFDA number 84.026). One of the functions of this program is to provide a free loan service for films, media materials, and equipment for the educational, cultural, and vocational education of the hearing impaired. For more information contact your state Office of Education or the Division of Educational Services, Special Education Programs, Office of Assistant Secretary for Special Education and Rehabilitative Services, Department of Education, Washington DC 20202.

IBM Corporation, Directory of Services and Specialized Equipment for the Physically Impaired, IBM Corporation, 18100 Fredrick Pike, Gaithersburg, MA 20879 (301) 640-5444. **Note: This office only provides information on services and equipment, they do not take requests for money.**

Minnesota Educational Computing Consortium, 3490 Lexington Ave., St. Paul, MN 55112, (612) 418-3500.

Phonic Ear, Inc., 250 Camino Alto, Mill Valley, CA 94941, (415) 383-4000. This company provides information on communication devices and how to obtain funding for them. They also publish a newsletter titled "The Many Faces of Funding."

Recording for the Blind is a source of taped materials and recording services for the visually or physically handicapped. A catalogue can be ordered from 215 East 58th Street, New York, NY 10022. If a particular book cannot be found in the catalogue or from other sources, applications can be made for recordings to be produced.

Appendix 3.C.

General Teacher Needs Assessment

23 Critical Skills for Mainstreaming

Paul R. Adams, MS
Sebastian Striefel, Ph.D.
Maria Quintero, Ph.D.
John Killoran, M.Ed.

Purpose: Teachers and/or supervisors can assess teacher skills in 23 major areas. This assessment will identify skill areas in which a teacher has the expertise to train other teachers, and will identify the areas in which a teacher desires to upgrade personal skills. The completed forms can also be used by the supervisor to develop a training plan for the school or district.

Instructions:

1. Read the listing under each area (e.g., "Prepare class for mainstreaming").

2. Rate skill level by thinking through the following questions:

    -What has been my training, both formal and informal?

    -How does my expertise compare with most of my professional peers?

    -What are my strengths?

    -What additional knowledge do I want to acquire?

    -What skills would I like to acquire or upgrade?

    -How might additional training increase my overall effectiveness as a teacher?

3. For each item, use the following code and circle the number that best describes skill level.

    1 = Teacher has no skill in executing this activity. Would need training and also in-class assistance to complete the activity.

    2 = Teacher has partial skills to execute the activity, and could do so with training and no in-class assistance (except perhaps a demonstration).

    3 = Teacher has skill to execute the activity and could do so without training or in-class assistance.

    4 = Teacher is highly skilled in executing the activity and could train others in that area.

Appendix 3.C. (continued)

CODE: 1 = No skills; training and in-class help would be required

2 = Partial skills; training required, but in-class help is not needed

3 = Good skills; no training or in-class help required

4 = Excellent skills; can train colleagues in this activity

1. Prepare Class for Mainstreaming

	1	2	3	4
a. Conduct puppet shows, discussions, and other class preparation activities.	1	2	3	4
b. Discuss difficulties specific to the student to be mainstreamed.	1	2	3	4
c. Conduct discussions on recognizing and accepting similarities and differences between people.	1	2	3	4

2. Assess Needs and Set Goals

	1	2	3	4
a. Understand the tests commonly used in your school.	1	2	3	4
b. Know how they are administered.	1	2	3	4
c. Interpret the results obtained.	1	2	3	4
d. Use the results to set goals for the student.	1	2	3	4

3. Evaluate Learning

	1	2	3	4
a. Understand differences between criterion and norm-referenced tests.	1	2	3	4
b. Collect data on student progress to use for: measuring progress toward goals, feedback for the student, feedback for the parents.	1	2	3	4
c. Use data as a basis to change goals, as needed.	1	2	3	4

4. Curriculum

	1	2	3	4
a. Have general knowledge of curricula used in your school.	1	2	3	4
b. Keep current on new curricula and materials appropriate for grade level(s) you teach.	1	2	3	4
c. Adapt existing curricula to meet the IEP goals of individual students.	1	2	3	4

5. Parent - Teacher Relationships

	1	2	3	4
a. Understand the parent involvement mandated by PL 94-142.	1	2	3	4
b. Establish and maintain regular, positive communications with parents.	1	2	3	4
c. Involve parents in the classroom or program when appropriate.	1	2	3	4
d. Know referral procedures for other services family may need (e.g., therapy, welfare).	1	2	3	4

Appendix 3.C. (continued)

CODE:	1 = No skills; training and in-class help would be required
	2 = Partial skills; training required, but in-class help is not needed
	3 = Good skills; no training or in-class help required
	4 = Excellent skills; can train colleagues in this activity

6. Teaching Fundamental Skills

a. Know methods for training academic basics.	1	2	3	4
b. Know methods for teaching non-academic survival skills (e.g., health, safety, leisure time, problem-solving) appropriate to your grade level.	1	2	3	4
c. Understand the specific skills needed by a particular mainstreamed student, and how to teach those skills.	1	2	3	4

7. Exceptional Conditions

a. Develop basic understanding of handicapping conditions.	1	2	3	4
b. Understand the adaptations needed to work with students who are handicapped.	1	2	3	4
c. Acquire a thorough understanding of the handicapping conditions of any student in your class.	1	2	3	4

8. Professional Consultation

a. Know how to access specialists for consultation about students with handicaps.	1	2	3	4
b. Collect information to document concerns in special areas.	1	2	3	4
c. Accept and use constructive feedback from consultants.	1	2	3	4

9. Nature of Mainstreaming

a. Understand the district/school definition and rationale for mainstreaming.	1	2	3	4
b. Understand the educational guidelines mandated by PL 94-142.	1	2	3	4

10. Student - Student Relationships

a. Develop skill in structuring and teaching positive student - student interactions.	1	2	3	4
b. Use peer buddies and peer tutors.	1	2	3	4
c. Demonstrate equity when dealing with all students.	1	2	3	4
d. Group students in ways which promote social interactions.	1	2	3	4

11. Attitudes

a. Self: Recognize and overcome personal biases and stereotypic, preconceived ideas of students with handicaps and of mainstreaming. Demonstrate knowledge of how personal attitudes can affect teacher behavior and student learning.	1	2	3	4
b. Other Adults: Provide accurate information to help modify misconceptions held by other (parents, colleagues, etc.)	1	2	3	4
c. Students: Promote acceptance of the student with handicaps by: noting difficulties and modeling appropriate behaviors.	1	2	3	4

Appendix 3.C. (continued)

CODE: 1 = No skills; training and in-class help would be required

2 = Partial skills; training required, but in-class help is not needed

3 = Good skills; no training or in-class help required

4 = Excellent skills; can train colleagues in this activity

12. Resource and Support Systems

a. Know how to access and use agencies, programs, and individuals in the school or district who can serve as resources.   1   2   3   4

13. Learning Environments

a. Arrange a classroom or other setting so that students with handicaps can have both complete and safe access.   1   2   3   4

b. Establish a positive climate for learning by modeling acceptance of individual differences, and encouraging each student's best effort.   1   2   3   4

14. Interpersonal Communication

a. Demonstrate competence in oral and written communication skills.   1   2   3   4

b. Know one's personal style of communication (e.g., personal responses to stress, feedback, compliments).   1   2   3   4

c. Know how to adapt information for different audiences (e.g., parents, teachers, general community).   1   2   3   4

15. Teaching Communication Skills

a. Have sufficient knowledge of language skills at the age level which you teach to be able to note strengths and deficits in individual student's expressive and receptive communication.   1   2   3   4

b. Teach language skills in task-analyzed, generalizable steps.   1   2   3   4

16. Administration

a. Function as a supervisior of aides and volunteers, as well as students.   1   2   3   4

b. Manage and coordinate schedules and programs of specialists and consultants.   1   2   3   4

c. Involve administrator by seeking feedback early, as well as by asking for resources when needed.   1   2   3   4

17. Individualized Teaching

a. Show skill in assessing individual needs and in adapting instruction to the individual.   1   2   3   4

b. Show skill in collection of progress data.   1   2   3   4

c. Know methods for individualizing instruction within groups.   1   2   3   4

Appendix 3.C. (continued)

CODE: 1 = No skills; training and in-class help would be required

2 = Partial skills; training required, but in-class help is not needed

3 = Good skills; no training or in-class help required

4 = Excellent skills; can train colleagues in this activity

18. Class Management

a. Organize and control classrooms to facilitate learning.	1	2	3	4
b. Demonstrate skill in group alerting, guiding transitions, arranging/organizing materials, crisis intervention, positive reinforcement of individuals and groups.	1	2	3	4

19. Teaching Techniques

a. Understand and use appropriate teaching techniques for group and individual instruction.	1	2	3	4
b. Show ability and willingness to be flexible and to change procedures to accommodate individual students.	1	2	3	4

20. Legal Issues

a. Understand the legal implications of PL 94-142 for educational services in public schools.	1	2	3	4
b. Know rights of persons with handicaps.	1	2	3	4
c. Understand school/district policies for mainstreaming.	1	2	3	4
d. Understand "due process."	1	2	3	4

21. Behavior Modification

a. Identify problem behaviors precisely.	1	2	3	4
b. Identify desirable behaviors.	1	2	3	4
c. Know how to identify and use effective reinforcers.	1	2	3	4
d. Monitor changes in behavior.	1	2	3	4

22. Task Analyze Skills

a. Understand the rationale for task analysis.	1	2	3	4
b. Demonstrate ability to task analyze a variety of necessary student skills.	1	2	3	4
c. Consolidate discrete tasks into total desired behavior.	1	2	3	4
d. Demonstrate ability to collect progress data.	1	2	3	4

23. Teaching Social Skills

a. Know the social skills expected of students at the grade level you teach.	1	2	3	4
b. Know how to identify strengths and deficits in social skills for students that you teach.	1	2	3	4
c. Know how to systematically train social skills using curricula and/or incidental opportunities.	1	2	3	4

Appendix 3.D.

Instruction Manual

TEAM-PK Profile
**Teacher Expectations and Assistance for Mainstreaming in
Preschool and Kindergarten**

John Killoran M.Ed., Sebastian Striefel Ph.D.,
& Maria Quintero Ph.D.

Introduction
Since the passage of Public Laws 94-142 and 99-457, increasing numbers of students who are handicapped are being integrated for all or part of their school day. As such, all educators are becoming increasingly responsible for educating children who are handicapped. The Teacher Expectations and Assistance for Mainstreaming (TEAM-PK) Profile identifies the expectations classroom teachers have of children who are enrolled in their classrooms and also identifies areas in which classroom teachers will require assistance if integration is to be successful.

Rationale
Integrating a child who is handicapped into a classroom where a teacher is willing and prepared to teach that child may increase the chances for successful integration (Striefel & Killoran, 1984a). By identifying a teacher's expectations and technical assistance needs, the teacher may be provided with the necessary training to be better prepared before and during the integration process.

Materials Needed
The TEAM-PK Profile instruction manual and protocol and recent school assessment information.

Time for Administration
Expectations Profile - 10 to 15 minutes.

General Description
Section I contains five categories of items which describe child behaviors typically demonstrated in the school setting. The categories are:

1. Classroom Rules - e.g., replacing materials and cleaning work places.

2. Work Skills - e.g., recognizing materials which are needed for tasks.

3. Self Help - e.g., eating lunch with minimal assistance.

4. Communication - e.g., following group directions, and

5. Social - e.g., social amenities.

Appendix 3.D. (continued)

Within the five categories there are 27 items that describe behavioral skills and competencies which facilitate successful classroom adjustments and positive social relationships with peers in normal settings.

Specific Instructions

Section I
In Section I, you are being asked to code your expectations of children in your classroom. Simply code each behavior as (C) Critical, (D) Desirable, or (U) Unimportant by circling C, D, or U as appropriate in the boxes to the right of each item.

(C) **Critical** indicates that you expect each child in your classroom to be acceptably skilled in this behavior (the child must demonstrate the behavior on 90% of opportunities to do so).

(D) **Desirable** means that you would like the student to demonstrate the behavior.

(U) **Unimportant** indicates that the behavior is unimportant for the student to demonstrate at entry into your classroom.

Technical assistance (TA) refers to having assistance for helping you with specific needs that arise in teaching children who are handicapped. TA can include a) demonstration via modeling, b) discussion, c) feedback, d) reading materials, and e) provision of curricula.

After coding each item in Section I, indicate with a check mark those skills which you would be willing to train in your classroom if technical assistance were available to you in the column labeled "Technical Assistance."

The priorities column is for use of the child study team in setting priorities.

The TEAM-PK Profile has been adapted, with permission from: The SBS Inventory of Teacher Social Behavior Standards and Expectations; The Walker-Rankin Rating Scale of Adaptive and Maladaptive Child Behavior in School by Hill M. Walker, PhD, and Richard Rankin, PhD, University of Oregon; and the Mainstreaming Expectations and Skills Assessment by John Killoran, MEd, Sebastian Striefel, PhD, Maria Quintero, and Trenly Yanito, MS.

Appendix 3.D. (continued)

TEAM-PK
Teacher Expectations and Assistance for Mainstreaming In Preschool and Kindergarten

John Killoran, M.Ed.
Sebastian Striefel, Ph.D.
Maria Quintero, Ph.D.

Name of Person Completing Form _____

Class Taught _____

Date of Rating _____

Have you previously worked with students who are handicapped?

Yes _____   No   _____

If yes, what handicapping conditions? _____

Appendix 3.D. (continued)

Teacher Expectations Codes C = Critical D = Desirable U = Unimportant	Expectations by Teacher	Technical Assistance	Priorities by Child Study Team
Classroom Rules			
1. Follows established class rules.	C D U		
2. Moves through routine transitions smoothly.	C D U		
3. Uses appropriate voice volume in classroom	C D U		
4. Uses appropriate signal to get teacher's attention when necessary (i.e., raises hand).	C D U		
5. Waits appropriately for teacher response to signal.	C D U		
6. Replaces materials and cleans up own work space.	C D U		
7. Recognizes and stays within area boundaries in classroom.	C D U		
Work Skills			
1. Does not disturb or disrupt the activities of others.	C D U		
2. Produces work of acceptable quality given his/her skill level.	C D U		
3. Asks for clarification on assigned tasks when initial instructions are not understood.	C D U		
4. Follows one direction related to task.	C D U		
5. Occupies self with age-appropriate activity assigned by an adult.	C D U		
6. Recognizes materials needed for specific task.	C D U		
7. Selects and works on an activity independently.	C D U		
8. Recognizes completion of task/activity, indicates to adult that s/he is finished and stops activity.	C D U		
9. Works on assigned task for 5 minutes.	C D U		
10. Self corrects errors.	C D U		
11. Recalls and completes task demonstrated previously.	C D U		
12. Uses crayons and scissors appropriately without being destructive.	C D U		

Appendix 3.D. (continued)

Teacher Expectations Codes C = Critical D = Desirable U = Unimportant	Expectations by Teacher	Technical Assistance	Priorities by Child Study Team
Self-Help			
1. Monitors appearance, e.g., keeps nose clean, adjusts clothing, uses napkin.	C D U		
2. Locates and uses a public restroom with minimal assistance in the school.	C D U		
3. Puts on/takes off outer clothing within a reasonable amount of time.	C D U		
4. Eats lunch or snack with minimal assistance.	C D U		
5. Independently comes into the classroom or house from bus or car.	C D U		
6. Goes from classroom to bus or car independently.	C D U		
7. Knows way and can travel around school and playground.	C D U		
8. Responds to fire drills as trained or directed.	C D U		
9. Seeks out adult for aid if hurt on the playground or cannot handle a social situation, e.g., fighting.	C D U		
10. Follows school rules (outside classroom).	C D U		
11. Stays with a group according to established school rules, i.e., outdoors.	C D U		
12. Recognizes obvious dangers and avoids them.	C D U		
Communication (Includes gesture, sign, communication board, eye pointing, speech, and other augmented systems).			
1. Attends to adult when called.	C D U		
2. Listens to and follows group directions.	C D U		
3. Communicates own needs and preferences, e.g., food, drink, bathroom.	C D U		
4. Does not ask irrelevant questions which serve no functional purpose or are not task related.	C D U		
5. Stops an activity when given a direction by an adult to "stop."	C D U		
6. Attends to peers in large group.	C D U		
7. Responds to questions about self and family, i.e., personal information.	C D U		
8. Responds appropriately when comments/compliments are directed to him/her.	C D U		
9. Responds to questions about stories.	C D U		

Appendix 3.D. (continued)

Teacher Expectations Codes C = Critical D = Desirable U = Unimportant	Expectations by Teacher	Technical Assistance	Priorities by Child Study Team
Communication (Cont.)			
10. Protests appropriately.	C D U		
11. Requesting assistance from adult or peer, i.e., help in cafeteria, bathroom, mobility.	C D U		
12. Responds without excessive delay.	C D U		
13. Uses intentional communication (speech, sign, or gesture)	C D U		
Social Behaviors			
1. Uses social conventions, e.g., help in cafeteria, bathroom mobility.	C D U		
2. Complies with teacher commands.	C D U		
3. Takes direction from a variety of adults.	C D U		
4. Separates from parents and accepts school personnel.	C D U		
5. Follows specified rules of games and/or class activities.	C D U		
6. Makes choice between preferred items or activities.	C D U		
7. Initiates interaction with peers and adults.	C D U		
8. Plays cooperatively.	C D U		
9. Respects others and their property.	C D U		
10. Defends self.	C D U		
11. Shows emotions and feelings appropriately.	C D U		
12. Responds positively to social recognition and reinforcement.	C D U		
13. Interacts appropriately at a snack or lunch table.	C D U		
14. Expresses affection toward other children and adults in an appropriate manner, i.e., is not overly affectionate by hugging, kissing, and touching.	C D U		
15. Refrains from self-abusive behavior, i.e., biting, cutting, or bruising self, head banging.	C D U		
16. Refrains from physically aggressive behavior toward others, i.e., hitting, biting, shoving.	C D U		
17. Does not use obscene language.	C D U		
18. Discriminates between edible and non-edible toys and objects.	C D U		
19. Uses play equipment in an age-appropriate manner during unstructured activities with limited adult supervision.	C D U		

Appendix 3.E.

Directory of Local Training Resources

Purpose: This directory is intended to provide teachers, teacher trainers, principals, and direct administrative staff with a method for developing an organized, readily usable listing of local resources which may be helpful in training teachers in the skills necessary for successfully integrating students who have handicaps. Although the focus is on increasing successful mainstreaming, a casual glance will show that the resources identified are useful for all teachers and all students. It is expected that a completed directory will help increase the cost-effective use of training time and money when responding to teacher training needs.

Description

Components: The Directory of Local Training Resources has four components, including: 1) Teacher Competencies, 2) the Competency Training Grid, 3) the Directory of Trainers, and 4) the Directory of Resource Organizations.

Component I - Teacher Competencies
This component contains a listing and definition of 23 competencies synthesized from a literature review on the competencies essential for successful mainstreaming.

Component II - Competency Trainer Grid
This component consists of a grid which lists, on a single page, all 23 teacher competencies and the name of one or more trainers who could effectively train teachers in those competencies.

Component III - Directory of Trainers
This component lists all of the trainers identified in component II, and includes the address, phone number, and name of school or agency for each trainer.

Component IV - Directory of Resource Organizations
This component identifies resource organizations that could provide training, technical assistance, and/or materials. It includes land-grant universities which offer extension courses, local college education departments and special education departments, the Comprehensive System of Personnel Development (CSPD) serving your state, Regional Resource Centers, and model programs that may exist in the local area (i.e., any existing project, program, or classroom that will allow teachers to observe or be trained to use competencies which are being modeled in real-life contexts). Component V also includes an "Other" category for miscellaneous resources available locally.

Appendix 3.E. (continued)

Component I - <u>Teacher Competencies</u>

Instructions: Read each competency thoroughly and thoughtfully.

1.   <u>Prepare Class for Mainstreaming</u>: prepare members of regular class for entrance of students with handicaps: conduct pre-placement preparation and awareness activities on handicapping conditions in general (i.e., discussion of specific student behaviors, training on how to respond to inappropriate behaviors, training on how to respond to inappropriate behaviors); identify commonalities as well as differencies between students.

2.   <u>Assess Needs and Set Goals:</u> master the basic diagnostic, measurement, and assessment skills necessary to determine each student's present level of functioning and educational needs; use that information to set realistic, measurable goals for each student both for the class as a whole and for subsets within the class.

3.   <u>Evaluate Learning</u>: understand difference in purpose and use of norm-referenced and criterion-referenced evaluation; collect and record student progress toward goal attainment; provide feedback to students and parents on goal attainment; and use evaluation data to assess goal attainment in order to measure terminal outcomes and set new goals.

4.   <u>Curriculum</u>: general knowledge of K-12 curricula; understanding of curriculum principles and structures; understanding of the relationship to child development and of schools as social institutions.

5.   <u>Teacher-Parent Relationships</u>: fulfill all parent participation responsibilities as mandated by P.L. 94-142; develop and maintain advocacy, rather than an adversarial role, with parents; utilize parents in training roles where possible; refer parents to appropriate agencies as requested (i.e., parent training sessions, counseling, advocacy, etc.).

6.   <u>Teaching Fundamental Skills</u>: functional skills: reading, writing, spelling, arithmetic, study, speaking; life maintenance skills: health, safety, law, consumerism; personal development skills: goal setting, decision making, problem solving, career development, recreation.

7.   <u>Exceptional Conditions</u>: rudimentary understanding of exceptional children, their special needs, and how to accommodate those needs; knowledge of specialists and resources available to assist with particular educational needs of specific children.

Appendix 3.E. (continued)

8. Professional Consultation: knowledge and practical skills required for effective consultation (i.e., know who has expertise in particular areas and how that person can be contacted; identify and collect essential information which the consultant will require; ability to solicit and effectively use constructive feedback on your own performance).

9. The Nature of Mainstreaming: understanding of definition, rationale, philosophy, legal issues involved, and delivery system models.

10. Student-Student Relationships: demonstrate equity when dealing with students; group children to increase social interactions; use systematic teaching strategies to increase social interactions; use peer buddies and peer or cross-age tutor systems to increase social interactions as well as academic learning.

11. Attitudes: evaluate attitudes of handicapped and nonhandicapped students, parents, and school administrators through formal and informal evaluations; where necessary, re-educate handicapped and nonhandicapped students, parents, and school administrators (e.g., provide factual information regarding handicapped persons; avoid referring to students by labels, classifications of handicaps, or stereotypes); demonstrate knowledge of how personal attitudes can affect teacher performance and student learning; strive for honest awareness of personal predjudices, stereotypes, and attitudes toward all students.

12. Resources and Support Systems: demonstrate knowledge of local agencies, programs, individuals, and audiovisual or curricular materials which can serve as resources in teaching; use available personnel, material, and program resources effectively in teaching activities.

13. Learning Environment: arrange physical characteristics of a learning environment to facilitate ease of access by students with handicaps; establish a positive emotional/psychological climate conducive to learning (e.g., model the acceptance of all students in the class; encourage creativity, productivity, achievement of all the highest quality of work each individual can accomplish; promote peer buddies, tutors, and group activities for learning tasks where appropriate).

14. Interpersonal Communication: demonstrate competence in oral and written communication skills; demonstrate skill in identifying one's own personal styles of communication (e.g., identify: how one responds to feedback; mannerisms and phrases common in one's own style and how others may interpret them); use active communication skills appropriate to audience in dealing with parents, students, administrators, and professional colleagues.

Appendix 3.E. (continued)

15. Teaching Communication Skills: assess strengths and deficits in student's oral and written communication skills; including both receptive and expressive skills; task analyze appropriate skills and teach in ways that maximize generalization; acquire student-specific skills in nonverbal communication (gestures, sign language, augmentative communications systems).

16. Administration: function as a supervisor (i.e., supervise aides and volunteers; coordinate services provided by other professionals such as speech and physical therapists); work effectively with administrators, especially school principals (i.e., advise administrator of needed equipment and materials; keep administrator informed of ongoing activities, including potential or actual problems, be able to solicit and accept constructive feedback from administrator regarding your own performance).

17. Individualized Teaching: competence in assessing individual educational needs and in adapting instruction to the individual; skill in keeping records of individual progress toward objectives; knowledge about diverse models for individualized instruction.

18. Class Management: ability to organize classrooms for instructional purposes and manage them effectively to meet the needs of students (skills include: group alerting, guiding transitions, arranging/organizing materials, crisis interventions, creating a positive affective climate, and reinforcing individuals within a group).

19. Teaching Techniques: demonstrate proper teaching techniques for group and individual instruction (e.g., correction procedures, prompts, modeling, commands, rates of reinforcement); demonstrate flexibility for modifying teaching strategies.

20. Legal Issues: understand legislative background of P.L. 94-142; knowledge of state law and Department of Education guidelines on mainstreaming; knowledge of due process; knowledge of school reponsibilities to students with handicaps; knowledge of teacher, parent, and student rights.

21. Behavior Modification: demonstrate skill in identifying problem behaviors, identifying desirable behaviors, identifying effective reinforcers, differential reinforcement of desirable behaviors, decreasing incidence of problem behaviors, and measuring changes in behaviors.

22. Task Analysis Skills: identify skill areas necessary for specific students; analyze material into concepts or subskills; break down skills into measurable subskills; scope and sequence skills to be taught; measure progress of skill achievement; consolidate components into total desired behaviors.

Appendix 3.E. (continued)

23. Teaching Social Skills: use formal and informal assessments to identify student's social strengths and deficits; task analyze social skills to be trained; use systematic social skills training curricula and programs to increase student's social behaviors; use informal teaching strategies to increase student's social behaviors; incorporate generalization strategies in social skills programing; monitor child's progress in social skills acquisition.

Component II - Competency Trainer Grid

Instructions:

Step 1 - For each of the 23 competencies, one at a time, consider the following questions:

a. Which people in our school or district have the most knowledge and practical experience in this competency area?
b. Of those people, who would be best to train fellow teachers? ("Best" means in terms of revelant experience.)
c. Does the person (or persons) identified have the time to do training, or could time be made available by changing that person's responsibilities, or could compensatory pay or time off be arranged?
d. Is the person (or persons) identified willing to do the training? (This step will require personal contact with the individual.)

Step 2 - Write the name of the trainer in the upper portion of the grid. Then mark an **X** under the trainer's name in the space opposite the relevant competency.

Note 1: More than one trainer might be available to train the same competency area. If so, mark all such trainer names opposite that competency.

Note 2: A single, very experienced trainer may have the expertise in multiple areas. If so, mark each area in which this person is able and willing to train.

Note 3: If no suitable teacher or other staff member can be identified within the school or district, refer to the resource organizations listed in Component V for assistance.

Step 3 - Repeat Steps 1-2 for each of the remaining competency areas.

Step 4 - If teacher needs assessments have identified other competency areas of high training interest, select the most urgent competencies and list them in the blank spaces provided (i.e., #s 24-26). Then repeat Steps 1-2 for each of these competency areas.

Appendix 3.E. (continued)

Name	Notes:
School	
Date	

Competency/Trainer Grid
FMS Project
Utah State University

Names of Resources

Teacher Competencies

1. Prepare Class for Mainstreaming												
2. Assess Needs and Set Goals												
3. Evaluate Learning												
4. Curriculum												
5. Teacher - Parent Relationships												
6. Teaching Fundamental Skills												
7. Exceptional Conditions												
8. Professional Consultation												
9. The Nature of Mainstreaming												
10. Student - Student Relationships												
11. Attitudes												
12. Resources and Support Systems												
13. Learning Environment												
14. Interpersonal Communication												
15. Teaching Communication Skills												
16. Administration												
17. Individualized Teaching												
18. Class Management												
19. Teaching Techniques												
20. Legal Issues												
21. Behavior Modification												
22. Task Analysis Skills												
23. Teaching Social Skills												

Appendix 3.E. (continued)

Component III - <u>Directory of Trainers</u>

Instructions: List the names of all trainers identified in Component II. The address, phone number, and name of the school or agency represented should be listed for each trainer. This section will not be necessary if all the trainers are "in-house" at a single school. Use additional sheets of paper as necessary.

Name	Agency Represented	Address	Phone Number

Component IV - <u>Directory of Resource Organizations</u>

Instructions: Write the names of resource organizations that could provide training, technical assistance, or materials that will assist teachers in mainstreaming. Be sure to include the name of at least one specific contact person within each resource organization.

<u>Resource Organizations</u> (include contact person, address, and phone number)

1. Colleges/Universities

    a. <u>Land Grant University</u> providing <u>Extension Courses</u> in your area

    b. <u>Education Department</u> (local college/university)

    c. <u>Special Education Department</u> (local college/university)

    d. <u>Other</u>

Appendix 3.E. (continued)

2. Comprehensive System of Personnel Development (<u>CSPD</u>) serving your area

3. <u>Regional Resource Center</u> serving your area

4. <u>Model Programs</u> (name of program, contact person, address, phone number)

5. <u>Other</u> (name of resource agency, contact person, address, phone number)

Chapter 4

. . .

Modifying Service Delivery to Integrate Preschool Classrooms

The importance of providing preschool special education in least restrictive environments is emphasized in the implementation regulations of P.L. 99-457, which mandate that services be provided to the maximum extent appropriate to meet the needs of each individual child in settings that serve nonhandicapped children. As a result, many early childhood and special education practitioners must significantly modify and adapt the manner in which they deliver services since, in an integrated setting, services must meet the needs of children both with and without handicaps. This modification entails the merger of traditional early childhood and behavioral special education teaching techniques into a system that allows children to learn using the most normal and least restrictive interventions possible while maintaining the availability of intensive special education and behavioral intervention for children with special needs. Chapter 4 serves as an overview of this modification, details of which are discussed in subsequent chapters.

The FMS Service Delivery Model

The FMS service delivery model is committed to providing preschool special education services in totally integrated settings. However, this integration goes beyond mere physical placement, and incorporates systematic instruction and social interventions as primary program components. In the FMS model classrooms, preschool-age children with handicaps are instructionally and socially grouped with nonhandicapped peers throughout the day. Classrooms are noncategorical; that is, children with mild to severe and profound handicaps, across categorical labels, are placed in classes with nonhandicapped students. Classes are also cross-aged, serving children 3 through 5 years of age.

A typical integrated classroom can efficiently serve 16 children. The mix of children includes 50% (8) who have handicaps (e.g., two mild, four moderate, and two severe). The remaining eight children are nondelayed (i.e., normal). Classrooms are staffed by a certified teacher and two full-time teaching assistants or child development associates. It is critical that the mix of staff include individuals trained and/or experienced in both early childhood and special education, since teaching in integrated settings demands competence in both. One teacher can have both sets of skills or, in settings where more than one integrated classroom is housed adjacently, the skills could be available across two or more teachers who do joint planning and sharing of ideas and activities. Many states, including Utah, where the FMS model was developed, have adopted preschool special education certification standards that require competencies in both special and early childhood education (see Appendix 4.A). Related services (e.g., physical therapy) are provided through a systematic consultative model (Striefel & Cadez, 1983a) or directly by therapists.

Most children attend school for 2.5 to 3.5 hours per day, 5 days per week, although children could attend school for longer periods of time dependent upon their IEP. Instruction is initially delivered in large and small groups or coincidentally. IEP goals and objectives are generally addressed in these groups. In cases where a child is so severely delayed that no progress is occurring or a child has a need no other child has, the child's IEP team may decide to provide services using intensive one-to-one microsessions. Microsessions are used only as needed, so that the child may participate in other activities where language, social, and group attending activities can be developed and practiced. During one-to-one sessions, peers should be used as tutors and as models wherever possible. The length and types of services a child receives are dependent on that child's individually determined IEP.

Skills needed for success in future integrated settings are identified and taught with an emphasis equal to that of deficit skills. Through this combined use of traditional group curricula, individualized special education, and future-referenced instruction, all children can be provided an appropriate, IEP-driven education in integrated settings through the use of least intensive instruction.

Least Intensive Service Delivery

The term *least restrictive instruction* is often confused with least restrictive placement. Therefore, the FMS model has replaced the concept of least restrictive instruction in the delivery of services to children in integrated preschool classrooms with the term *least intensive instruction*. Least intensive service delivery refers to the teaching of a skill using the least intensive teaching technique and/or instructional grouping needed for a child to learn a targeted skill. The components of least intensive service delivery include:

1. Instruction that combines developmental and behavioral teaching techniques to teach children using only the intensity that they require to learn effectively.

2. Transdisciplinary, consultant-based staff to provide most related services such as motor, speech, and language training.

3. The use of nonobtrusive data collection procedures for measuring student progress.

4. The use of least restrictive and nonaversive behavioral treatment techniques that can be implemented within natural environments and that rely on naturally occurring reinforcement as much as possible.

Traditional Group Curricula Versus Individualized Special Education Curricula

The FMS model was designed to incorporate the strengths of developmental groups and behavioral special education teaching methods to meet the individual needs of all children in integrated settings, including providing intensive and systematic intervention for children with handicaps.

Developmental Curricula. Simply stated, curricula refers to the systematic arrangement of time, procedures, materials, and tasks (Findlay et al., 1976). In developmental curricula, this arrangement is based on addressing the common characteristics and needs of more than one student at a time (Findlay et al., 1976) and usually incorporates skills that are age-appropriate, developmentally sequenced and taught through exploration of the child's naturally occurring environments. Although instruction is individualized, this individualization is often not specific enough to meet the needs of some children with handicaps. Children with handicaps often require (a) greater numbers of trials to learn a skill than their nonhandicapped peers; (b) smaller groups with more task-analyzed instruction and individual attention than occur in regular preschool programs; (c) more specific behavioral interventions, rates of reinforcement, and direct instruction; and (d) specific procedures for generalizing learned skills across new settings, adults, and peers (Brown et al., 1983; Stokes & Baer, 1977). Unfortunately, children with handicaps often have difficulties learning incidentally and find it more difficult to generalize new and previously learned skills to other situations and settings than their peers (Stokes & Baer, 1977). This is especially true when students with handicaps are in segregated settings.

Thus, the curricula often require specific procedures for facilitating generalization of skills across stimuli, staff, settings, and time for each individual child in ways not required for nonhandicapped learners (Striefel & Cadez, 1983a; Whitney & Striefel, 1981). In traditional preschool programs, individualized instructional objectives are usually not identified (O'Connell, 1986), and behavioral teaching techniques are not employed to the same degree or intensity needed for children with handicaps. In the FMS model, individualized task-analyzed instructional objectives are identified and behavioral teaching techniques that result in more rapid learning for children with handicaps are used.

Developmental curricula usually follow a unit or theme approach to planning in which lesson plans are developed around a specific theme and all weekly activities address this theme. Themes are usually nonoperationalized concepts such as animals, holidays, or helpers. Progress monitoring, or determining if the child has mastered the unit's objectives, is usually confined to pre- and posttesting, if it occurs at all.

Advantages of group curricula include the efficiency of teaching the entire class simultaneously and the presence of opportunities for children to learn through repetitive and naturally occurring interactions with peers and their environment (Widerstrom, 1982). Unfortunately, in nonintegrated classrooms specific child deficits may not be quickly identified (the exception being children who exhibit behavioral deficits), and if developmental delays or significant skill deficits are suspected or identified, the child is typically referred elsewhere for services rather than receiving services in the normal preschool setting.

Individualized Special Education. In traditional individualized special education commonly used in early intervention programs, the focus is on meeting the needs of an individual child rather than on the needs of a group. Instruction is developed for a particular child and implemented in small groups with frequent one-to-one instruction, traditionally in separate therapy settings and self-contained classrooms.

The advantage of traditional special education lies in its reliance on behavioral teaching techniques and systematic components of instruction that have been demonstrated to be effective for teaching children with handicaps (Greer, Anderson, & Odle, 1982), including:

1. Criterion-referenced assessment to identify a child's strengths and deficits.

2. Program development that prioritizes a child's needs and develops goals and objectives to systematically teach a child.

3. One-to-one instruction, using discrete trial training in self-contained settings.

4. Frequent progress monitoring of the child's skill acquisition.

5. Revision of the teaching program based on the child's progress in mastery of the skill being taught.

Unfortunately, traditional special education as it is commonly applied may be self-defeating to the process of integration. The emphasis on one-to-one and small group instruction in therapy rooms and self-contained classrooms often hinders the student's generalization and transfer of skills to settings other than those in which they are taught. In addition, the specificity of instruction and reliance on mass trial training often teach the child to respond to a limited number of stimuli with a limited number of responses that often do not occur in the natural environment. Teaching activities are not naturally occurring nor consistent with developmentally age-appropriate activities and often lack a valid function. Frequently used behavioral interventions may be difficult to implement in integrated and normalized settings; thus, they may often be implemented incorrectly.

Traditional special education allows the student to be successful in the special education setting; however, when the school setting is restricted to the separate school or to a self-contained classroom, such instruction actually increases the child's dependency on special education, limits interaction in the community, prohibits ongoing social interaction in the community, and prohibits ongoing social interaction between students with handicaps and their peers (Widerstrom, 1982).

A Comprehensive Model of Integrated Service Delivery

To optimize the acquisition of skills by students in integrated settings, the strengths of developmental and traditional special education approaches must be merged (Figure 4.1). At first appearance, it may seem that the use of developmental approaches with traditional special education are mutually exclusive within a single setting; however, with careful planning and individualization within group activities, this merger is readily accomplished. Effective grouping in integrated preschools is an ongoing process which changes across activities and skills being taught, and as children master skills. The groups that are established today may not be useful in a month's time, since the rate of skill acquisition in preschoolers is extremely variable. Likewise, effective grouping for teaching cognitive skills in all probability will differ from groups for language, self-help, and social skills development; that is, most children will actually be in several different groups throughout the school day. Combining developmental groups and behavioral special education into systematic least intensive service delivery includes a range of instructional techniques from intensive discrete trial training to incidental teaching conducted by teachers, tutors, and buddies.

Consultant-Based Service Delivery

The FMS project uses a transdisciplinary, consultant-based model to provide most related services including motor, speech and language to children with identified deficits. In addition, therapists also provided intensive direct services as identified in a child's IEP, or if the child is not making sufficient progress in group settings. Consultants may be program employees or individuals serving in a contracted fee-for-service capacity. In settings where related services are provided through contracted employees who are serving in a fee-for-service capacity, it is imperative that the consultants be skilled in transdisciplinary programming and that they are willing to use the following consultant-based model. In the FMS consultant-based model, the consultant or therapist is responsible for:

1. Criterion-referenced assessment in areas of identified or suspected delay.
2. IEP development (goals, objectives, criteria, and schedules for evaluation).

Figure 4.1. Flowchart of Modified Service Delivery for Integrated Preschool Programs

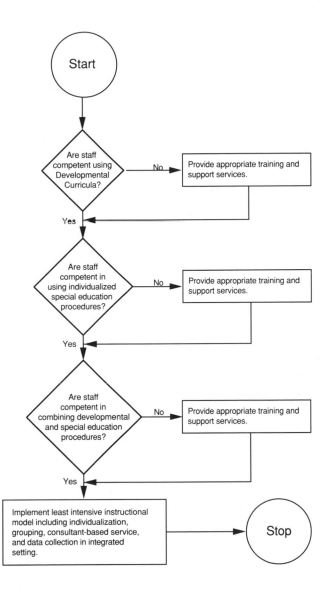

3. Instructional program development.

4. Staff training for implementing child-specific instructional programs.

5. Child progress monitoring and instructional program changes.

Criterion-Referenced Assessment.   Criterion-referenced testing, utilizing age-appropriate best practices and instruments, is conducted by the appropriate consultant to identify all areas of suspected delay that are in need of remediation, as well as skills needed in future environments. Instruments used by the FMS model are discussed in Chapter 8. (For further information related to the selection of appropriate early childhood assessments and practices, the reader is referred to *Assessment: Best Practices for Assessing Young Children*; Danielson, Lynch, Monyano, Johnson, & Bettenburg; 1988.)

IEP Development.   The results of these assessments are then used to develop specific IEP goals and objectives, as well as to determine the intensity and/or groups in which instructional programs will be conducted. IEP development is discussed in detail in Chapter 7.

Instructional Programs.   Instructional programs are developed to implement identified IEP goals and objectives. Programs may be as simple as written suggestions to be implemented incidentally during group activities (e.g., using graduated prompting and praising to teach a child reciprocal stair-walking on the slide during free play) or coincidental teaching programs that structure instruction at the time of day in which using the skill would naturally occur (e.g., prompting a student to socially greet and initiate a conversation with a peer upon arrival at school). More intensive group intervention may be programmed through the use of commercially prepared curricula (e.g., DISTAR or Peak Language kits) or systematic discrete trial training programs which use behavioral special education techniques to remediate severe deficits. These intensive special education programs are referred to as microsessions in the FMS model. Instructional programming is detailed in Chapter 8.

Staff Training.   Staff training for the implementation of microsessions is conducted through a systematic hand-shaping procedure in which the trainer systematically trains and transfers program implementation to the classroom teacher, paraprofessional staff, peer, or parent. This training, known as the *Microsession Training and Transfer Procedure* (Killoran et al., 1987), includes training in (a) gaining the child's attention; (b) presenting commands (teacher says/does); (c) obtaining child responses; (d) reinforcing, correcting, ignoring, and prompting; and (e) recording child progress. The process was developed based on research by Sanok and Striefel (1979). Weekly supervision by the classroom teacher or consultant is required to make needed program changes and to insure the continued appropriate implementation of the program.

Child Progress Monitoring and Nonobtrusive Data Collection.   Child progress data are collected through a variety of means, dependent upon the intensity at which the program is developed, and vary from simple anecdotal recording and checklists, weekly or daily probes, to recording of distributed and massed discrete trials. Data are collected nonobtrusively and only in numbers sufficient to be useful to individual instructional decision-making. Monitoring child progress allows the teacher to record goals as completed on the IEP, as well as make systematic changes to children's programs. Several types of data assist the teacher in revising the IEP. The extent and type of data collected is dependent upon the teaching intensity and grouping used and the skill being trained. In all cases, student progress is monitored through yearly re-evaluations with criterion-referenced assessment instruments. Instructional programs in group settings are monitored through checklists, pre/posttesting, and daily and weekly progress.

Coincidental teaching programs should have data systems that allow for the collection of data on a daily or weekly basis depending on the needs of the child. Data should be collected on a daily basis during skill acquisition and on a weekly basis once the skill is mastered to insure maintenance of the skill.

Microsessions incorporate the most sophisticated data collection system, usually incorporating discrete trials. Whereas daily data are preferable in microsessions, the size and time allotment for small groups may necessitate taking less frequent data.

When considering the design of a nonobtrusive data collection system, McLean and Snyder-McLean (1987) suggest the following as options:

1. Daily, continuous training response data collected for every student, every program, every day.

2. Training response data collected on all programs every third day, for any one student (assuming three students in a group).

3. Training response data collected for all students, but on only one or two programs per day.

4. Training response data collected for all students and all programs, but only the *last* 3 to 5 trials are recorded.

5. Training response data collected for all students and all programs, but recording only the *first* 3 to 5 trials.

6. Data not collected in daily training activities; but "test" sessions scheduled at regular intervals and at any indication that the student's level of performance has changed.

7. Some combination of the above.

More information on data-based decision-making can be found in *Serving Children and Adolescents with Developmental Disabilities in the Special Education Classroom: Proven Methods* (Striefel & Cadez, 1983a).

In summary, the development of integrated classrooms requires the incorporation of the best practices found within both regular and special preschool education to meet the needs of all students in integrated settings.

Appendix 4.A.

Utah Preschool Special Education Teacher

Certification Standards

Professional Education Standards

STANDARD I. The program shall require experiences to develop knowledge, skills, and attitudes in the prospective teacher which will enhance pupil self-esteem and confidence and promote constructive interaction among people of differing economic, social, racial, ethnic, and religious backgrounds.

STANDARD II. The program shall require study of general principles of life-long human growth and development and the relationship of teaching and learning theories to physical, social, intellectual, and emotional development.

STANDARD III. The program shall require study of research about teacher characteristics and behaviors as they affect the learner.

STANDARD IV. The program shall require study of the communication processes and skills for use between the teacher and pupil and between the teacher and others.

STANDARD V. The program shall require study of techniques for diagnosing the capabilities of the learner and for designing instructional programs for all pupils in the least restrictive environment.

STANDARD VI. The program shall require study of the application of methods and techniques in a clinical setting in the particular field of specialization.

STANDARD VII. The program shall require study of methods of teaching reading in the prospective teacher's area(s) of specialization.

STANDARD VIII. The program shall require study of skills and strategies to be used in classroom management of individual, small, and large groups under varying conditions.

STANDARD IX. The program shall require prospective teachers to observe and analyze a variety of teaching models and to assess their own teaching effectiveness and professional growth needs.

STANDARD X. The program shall require study of the leaders, ideas, and movements underlying the development and organization of education in the United States.

Appendix 4.A. (continued)

STANDARD XI. The program shall require study of the state laws and State Board of Education policies which specify content, values, and other expectations of teachers and other professionals in the school system.

STANDARD XII. The program shall require study of techniques for evaluating student progress, including the use and interpretation of both standardized and teacher-made tests.

STANDARD XIII. The program shall require study of the knowledge and skills designed to meet the needs of students with handicapping conditions in the regular classrooom. These shall include, but not be limited to, the following content domains: (1) Knowledge of handicapping conditions, (2) knowledge of the role of regular education teachers in the education of students with handicapping conditions, (3) skills in assessing the educational needs and progress of students with handicapping conditions in the regular education classroom, (4) skills in the implementation of an educational program for the student with handicaps educated in the regular classroom, and (5) skills in monitoring student progress.

Preschool Specific Education Certification Standards

STANDARD I. The program shall require the study of normal and atypical child development from birth to five years of age with emphasis upon the implications of the learning process at these ages.

STANDARD II. The program shall require the study of psychological and sociological concepts and generalizations dealing with social and emotional development.

STANDARD III. The program shall require study and experiences designed to develop skills in observing , recording, and assessing children's behavior in order to plan an appropriate instructional program and learning environment.

STANDARD IV. The program shall require study and experiences in the disciplines which provide content knowledge needed to teach expressive and receptive language development.

STANDARD V. The program shall require study and experiences in the disciplines which provide content knowledge needed to teach fundamental cognitive and preacademic skills.

STANDARD VI. The program shall require experiences in organizing, planning, and implementing programs to promote gross and fine motor development.

STANDARD VII. The program shall require experiences in organizing, planning, and implementing programs to develop self-care skills.

Appendix 4.A. (continued)

STANDARD VIII. The program shall require study and experiences in health care, nutrition, and safety for young children in home, group care, and school settings.

STANDARD IX. The program shall require study and experiences designed to develop competence in enabling children to express themselves creatively in a variety of ways, including experience through the arts.

STANDARD X. The program shall require study designed to develop competence in facilitating independent learning and decision-making skills in young children.

STANDARD XI. The program shall require study and experiences designed to examine characteristics of different learning environments appropriate for children from infancy through kindergarten.

STANDARD XII. The program shall require study and experiences designed to develop skills in the use of state and local resources and appropriate referral strategies.

STANDARD XIII. The program shall require experiences designed to develop the skills and abilities to work with parents and other adults in the home, school, and community.

STANDARD XIV. The program shall require study in undertaking the organization and administration of the pre-kindergarten program.

STANDARD XV. The program shall require study and experiences designed to develop skills to work as a member of an interdisciplinary team and to develop an understanding of disciplines related to special education.

STANDARD XVI. Assessment: Eligibility determination; strength and weakness determination.

The program shall require demonstrated competence in selection, design, administration, and interpretation of a representative sample of age-appropriate, norm-referenced, criterion-referenced and ecological assessments to determine the discrepancies between academic, behavioral, and life skill demands (requirements) and actual student performance.

STANDARD XVII. Planning: Establishing goals and objectives for students based upon individual assessment, coordination of services, identification of resources, and implementation of activities.

The program shall require demonstrated competence in:
    (1) projecting long-term outcomes and establishing appropriate annual goals and short-term objectives utilizing assessment data;

Appendix 4.A. (continued)

    (2) designing, planning, and coordinating age-appropriate academic and social integration and transition programs within regular school and community environments;

    (3) designing a plan for assessing and coordinating resources available in the student's natural environment to implement long-term outcomes, annual goals, and short-term objectives and identify a representative sample of such resources, both human and technological;

    (4) designing appropriate, systematic, data-based, daily individual student activities based on student performance and relevant long-term outcomes, annual goals, and short-term objectives which provide for new skill development, practice, and application across environments;

    (5) coordinating all services (required related services and a representative sample of support services including peer tutors, parents, volunteers) necessary to implement daily individual student activities which provide for new skill development, practice, and applications across environments;

    (6) developing an Individual Education Plan (IEP) which is an integrated management tool and which meets federal and state requirements;

    (7) coordinating case management activities including service delivery and transition.

STANDARD XVIII. Implementation: Actualization of planning and utilization of effective pedagogy across levels including: Development, remedial, functional, and compensatory.

The program shall require demonstrated competence in:
    (1) Knowledge of scope and sequence across functional life skills, preacademic skills, and behavior skills;

    (2) conducting concept and task analysis to identify performance demands for skill use and application;

    (3) teaching discrete skills, including selection and sequencing instructional examples to facilitate aquisition, strategies of trial distribution, systematic strategies of response prompting and fading, and systematic strategies for rewarding correct student responses and correcting student errors in individual, small group, and large group instruction;

    (4) conducting general case analysis of performance demands;

    (5) designing, implementing, and evaluating applied behavior analysis including related ethical issues;

Appendix 4.A. (continued)

(6) implementing effective techniques of consultation, collaboration, and teaming;

(7) utilizing the transdisciplinary approach to instruction.

STANDARD XIX. Evaluation: Monitoring student progress; formative and summative program evaluation.

The program shall require demonstrated competence in:
(1) Designing and implementing data collection systems that measure the accuracy, rate, duration, fluency, and independence of student performance;

(2) designing and implementing data collection systems that measure performance across novel stimuli (generalization) and time (maintenance) and in natural (noninstructional) settings;

(3) selecting data collection systems which match the target behavior and intended outcome of Instruction;

(4) adjusting instructional procedures based on student performance data;

(5) measuring consumer (e.g., parent, cooperating agency, etc.) and team (e.g., therapist, regular educator, paraprofessional, etc.) satisfaction with student educational programs and in adjusting classroom procedures, methods of communication with significant others, and/or educational programming based on consumer or team feedback.

Chapter 5

•   •   •

Parent Preparation for Integration

P.L. 94-457 emphasizes that services for young children who have handicaps should involve parents as active participants in their child's program. However, when parents are faced with a proposal for integration of their child into more normalized environments, concerns about integration often become obstacles to implementation (Bloom & Garfunkel, 1981; Kroth & Krehbiel, 1982; Noel, 1984; Pasanella & Volkmor, 1981; Stetson, 1984; Striefel, Killoran, & Quintero, 1985a, 1985b, 1986). Likewise, parents of children without handicaps express concerns about the impact of integration on their child. Carefully planned parent preparation activities can allay concerns and develop parental support for, and participation in, integration.

The purposes of parent preparation are to (a) inform parents of children with and without handicaps about the purposes and philosophy of integration and changes that integration would produce in the present program, (b) answer parents' questions and concerns, and (c) promote positive relations between the program and the local community. These purposes can be achieved through the following activities:

1. Establishing a system of communication.

2. Using the communication system to address concerns.

3. Establishing goals and expectations.

4. Maintaining parent involvement.

129

Issues, procedures, and materials for each component of successful parent involvement are addressed in this chapter.

Establishing a System of Communication

The key to promoting parent participation and fostering parent support is good communication between parents and program personnel. The establishment of good communication requires consideration of (a) mode of communication, (b) timing of the information related to integration, and (c) content.

Mode of Communication

An ongoing exchange of information between parents and schools may best be established through regular contacts such as written notes concerning the child's progress; occasional telephone calls to parents; brief photocopied materials such as happy faces or symbols indicating good or bad days; verbal or written requests for specific information (e.g., potential IEP goals); and by providing more extensive materials such as handbooks, programs, or articles on current issues in special education that seem appropriate for reading by specific parents (Krehbiel & Sheldon, 1985; Kroth & Krehbiel, 1982; Pasanella & Volkmor, 1981; Price and Weinberg, 1982; Weisenstein & Pelz, 1986). Whenever written material is used, special attention must be given to the use of technical vocabulary or jargon that may be confusing and uninformative to parents. Staff may choose to rewrite technical materials using vocabulary that is more common in the community, or materials may be presented verbally instead of in written form.

Parent involvement groups are another method for communication between the teacher and parents. Group work has the advantage of providing services to a number of people at the same time. A disadvantage of group activities is that opportunities for individualized, personal attention may be reduced. Additionally, integrated parent groups can emphasize a child's handicap for the child's parents, as they listen to parents of children without handicaps discussing what may appear to be relatively minor problems (e.g., parents discussing their child's occasional use of profanity while other parents are concerned that their child may never speak at all). Integrated parent groups require that staff who serve as facilitators be alert to possible emotional reactions of parents, and that staff be prepared to intervene as needed or refer parents to other sources (e.g., psycho-logical counseling).

Timing

The timing of communication with parents of children with handicaps must also consider how prepared a parent may be to accept the infor-mation (Krehbiel & Sheldon, 1985). The stages of acceptance and emo-tional adjustment that have been documented in the adjustment of parents to the presence of an offspring with a handicap suggest that, although information may be given to parents, the parents may not be at a point of acceptance or understanding to assure the effective-ness of the communication (Marion, 1981). It may be necessary to repeat and/or reformat information as parents progress in the accep-tance of their role as parents of a child with handicaps and as they adjust to their child's participation in an integrated setting. Staff may become impatient with parents who appear not to have "listened" when information was first provided. This staff frustration is understandable, and points out the need for staff to be acquainted with the process of parents' adjustment to the handicapping condition of their child and the impact of the disability on the family. By understanding the process that a family is experiencing, staff can serve as sources of sup-port, and can avoid feeling frustrated when information has to be repeated or worded in different ways.

Content

The most common information about integration given to parents is usually embedded within written material that encompasses the process of special education, and includes an explanation of parents' rights under P.L. 94-142 and/or P.L. 99-457, descriptions of the process of special education (referral, evaluation, IEPs, etc.), and procedural safeguards. Within such documents, references to integration are brief, and generally lack specificity of how parents can be active par-ticipants in the process. Parents are often left more confused because of the large amount of information and the complexity of the language used.

The FMS project developed specific brochures (see Appendix 10.A and Appendix 6.A in Chapters 10 and 6, respectively) about inte-gration to answer questions of parents of children with and without handicaps. Additionally, individual programs may develop pamphlets or fliers that define integration within their specific setting, and that provide vital program information such as classroom hours and costs. After parents have received general information to address commonly asked questions, they may still have concerns related to specific needs that may need to be addressed. A parent needs assessment can be conducted, and from the results, parent training programs can be designed to address these needs. This process not only pinpoints concerns, but it also provides a self-report method for assessing the utility and impact of parent information, materials, and procedures. Appendix 5.A includes a copy of the Parent Integration Opinionnaire, an instrument for identifying parent concerns about integration, which can be used to develop a training program to address specific concerns. The Parent Integration Opinionnaire lists 14 common concerns about integration. Parents are instructed to indicate their agreement/disagreement with each statement (Column 1) and to indicate if they feel that the concern is a good reason for not integrating a student (Column 2). The assumption in an integrated model is that there are no good reasons for not integrating preschool students. Any items marked "Yes" in Column 2 or any items with responses of "Strongly Agree/Agree" suggest possible areas of concern that may be addressed in parent sessions. The opinionnaire can also serve as a pre-/postmeasure of changes in parents' opinions about integration.

Parent training programs in an integrated model should also include generic topics of interest to all parents. These topics may include child development, accessing community resources, behavior management, and general child health and care issues. One instrument for assessing these needs and interests is the Assessment of Parent Needs and Interests (Appendix 5.B). This instrument allows parents to indicate areas in which they would like their child to have more training (e.g., in self-help skills such as dressing or toileting). Additionally, parent involvement in a child's program is encouraged by asking parents to rate their child's needs in areas of self-help, motor, language, and communication skills. All of these parent questionnaires can be sent home for completion at the parents' leisure, or can be completed at a general parent meeting, such as a parents' night or a PTA meeting.

Using the Communication System: Addressing Parent Concerns

Parents of children in integrated programs may have numerous questions about integration. Program personnel must anticipate these questions and be prepared to address parents' concerns in an honest, informative manner. Most concerns parents commonly have about integration are centered around (a) knowledge about integration, (b) quality of education, (c) support services, (d) social isolation, (e) inappropriate models, and (f) safety.

Knowledge of Integration

Many concerns about integration stem from a lack of knowledge of what is actually meant by integration or the related concept, mainstreaming. Each program must define integration clearly and be able to state the benefits of integration for participating children. The FMS project developed a parent brochure to answer specific questions about integration (see Appendix 10.A). However, during the initial meeting at which integration is discussed, parents may need an opportunity to be verbally reassured by having staff available to personally answer their questions. During this sensitive period when parents are seeking direction for their child's future, written materials may appear cold and impersonal and may be insufficient to address concerns.

Quality of Education

Parents of children with handicaps often express concern that the teacher may be too busy to provide sufficient time and attention to their children (Bloom & Garfunkel, 1981; Demerest & Vuoulo, 1983; Mlynek, Hannah, & Hamlin, 1982). Similarly, parents of children without handicaps express concerns over the quality of education their children might receive because a teacher may devote more time to meet the more demanding needs of the child with handicaps (Bloom & Garfunkel, 1981; Demerest & Vuoulo, 1983; Karnes, 1980; Mlynek, Hannah, & Hamlin, 1982). Additionally, parents of children without handicaps report that an integrated program may lack creativity, stimulating learning experiences, and playmates for their child (Winton, Turnbull, & Blacher, 1983).

In response to these concerns, aides, volunteers, and peers serving as buddies, models, confederates, and tutors have been used to provide additional attention. These measures, however, cannot substitute for good classroom organization that allows the teacher time to contact each child personally on a daily basis. Without careful planning, the possibility exists that the quality of education may be reduced. Teachers must remain alert to this possibility. One indicator for parents that their child is being attended to appropriately is a teacher's ability to comment on the child's day or on some specific aspect of the child's progress. Such comments can be very reassuring for parents, as well as being indicative of staff that remain sensitive to the needs of individuals in their classroom.

Support Services

Parents of children with handicaps also report being concerned that related services (motor, language) for their child will be reduced or eliminated by integration, and that their child's integration may be limited by inadequate transportation, furniture, and/or building structure (e.g., ramps, wide halls, bathroom stalls). Yet, physical barriers cannot be used as a legal reason for denying a child access to a free, appropriate public education in least restrictive environments (Elbaum, 1981; Pasanella & Volkmor, 1981; Quintero & Striefel, 1986).

Although reduction of services can be a realistic trade-off when a child moves into a regular program, parent education agencies, advocacy groups, and advocates of integration have attempted to educate parents concerning the fact that services dictated by the child's needs and documented on an IEP cannot be refused. Likewise, inaccessibility is not permissible for denying integrated services. Parent training about rights and due process appears to have impacted educators, as indicated by increased information and training for educators to assure that they safeguard the rights of parents and students, thereby reducing the chances of parent-initiated litigation.

Parent concerns about the environment and available services can be addressed and reduced by specifically delineating for a parent the services and/or environmental modifications or features that will be available. Specific information may detail the name and credentials of the person responsible for delivering the needed special service, the time(s) of day, day(s) of the week when the service will be provided, the setting of the service delivery, and the plan for evaluating progress and generalizing the learned skill to the integrated setting if the child receives the service in a setting apart from his or her peers. A program must assure access to staff or consultants who can address the special therapeutic and training needs of children with handicaps. Without these resources and a firm commitment to meet each child's individual needs, a program cannot adequately address the needs of children with handicaps and parents are unlikely to support an integration effort.

Social Isolation

Prior to mainstreaming, parents of children with handicaps commonly express concerns that their children will be teased by others in the class, or will be ostracized during informal class activities (Bloom & Garfunkel, 1981; Demerest & Vuoulo, 1983; Mlynek, Hannah, & Hamlin, 1982; Schanzer, 1981). This situation can arise when a child is excluded from a group activity because of the limitations of the handicapping condition, or when others provide too much assistance, thereby limiting the child's opportunity to develop more independence.

Parents of children with handicaps also report concern over the potentially negative reactions they anticipate from other parents as a result of the integration of the student who has a handicapping condition (Cansler & Winton, 1983; Demerest & Vuoulo, 1983).

One method for addressing this concern is to clearly communicate and demonstrate to parents the procedures that will be used to promote and support positive child interactions (e.g., prompting and praising, buddy systems, functional grouping). When program staff openly discuss the possibilities that social isolation can occur if program staff are not attentive and activities well planned, parents are reassured that their concern is genuinely acknowledged and that a system is in place to address the problem.

The social isolation that parents themselves fear may be more difficult to address. Some programs have attempted to structure meetings of both parents of children who have handicaps and parents of children who are not handicapped (integrated meetings) to promote positive relations among parents of children with and without handicaps. However, integrated meetings may actually be difficult for some parents of children with handicaps, because the handicapping condition is more obvious when contrasted with the abilities of children who do not have handicaps (Turnbull & Blacher-Dixon, 1980). It may be speculated that since parents have experienced a history of societal pressure and negative responses to their child, the process of feeling accepted may require a long period of time to evolve. Program staff should continue to encourage equal parent participation, facilitate parent communication for common needs such as carpooling, and involve parents in joint program activities (e.g., working on the Christmas pageant committee).

Inappropriate Models

Parents of children without handicaps express concern that their children may learn inappropriate behaviors from children who have handicaps (Cansler & Winton, 1983; Gresham, 1982; Price & Weinberg, 1982). Conversely, parents of children with handicaps may express concerns about their child learning "normal" behaviors, such as cursing or fighting. While these concerns are commonly cited, they are also addressed more easily than other worries about integration. Parents can be reassured that most children imitate desirable and undesirable behaviors; that this imitation is normal; and that if the behaviors are corrected as needed or given minimal attention, the behaviors will extinguish. These statements have been supported through observations of children in integrated settings where children without handicaps either did not imitate less mature behaviors or, if they did, they quickly extinguished these imitations when no rewards were given for behaving inappropriately (Cansler & Winton, 1983; Price & Weinberg, 1982).

Safety

Parents of children without handicaps occasionally are concerned about their children's safety when in proximity to children with handicaps. The inadequate social skills of some children can result in potentially unsafe encounters such as physical aggression. This problem can be aggravated by the poor communication skill of the child with handicaps, resulting in nonreinforcing experiences for children without handicaps who attempt to initiate social interactions (Gresham, 1982). Conversely, parents of children with handicaps express concern that other children may encourage their child to engage in inappropriate, harmful, or dangerous acts that could humiliate or even endanger a child.

In response to this concern, peer buddies have been successfully used to help protect the target child, as well as to model appropriate behaviors (Odom et al., 1985). More importantly, however, staff must foster a sense of competence in their ability to discipline and manage a classroom to insure safety. At times, behavior consultants or school psychologists may be required to develop and/or implement programs for individual students who require more than the standard classroom procedures. This is a resource that administrators should prepare to access, so that problem behaviors exhibited by a selected individual can be successfully eliminated without completely removing the child from the program.

Establishing Goals and Expectations

It is often assumed by staff that all parents of children with handicaps are equally interested in, or available to become involved in, their child's education. In reality, although the law mandates that parents be allowed to become actively involved in the development and approval of the Individualized Education Program (IEP), the level of participation remains a personal matter. Many factors may affect parents' motivation to be involved in their child's program, and it is important for staff to consider these factors as they interact with their students' parents.

In examining the reasons for parent reticence to participate in programs, Cansler and Winton (1983) determined from parent reports that their child's integration was frequently the first time that parents of young children actually compared their child directly with nonhandicapped children of the same age, and this created emotional difficulty for parents. For example, one parent indicated that it was difficult for her to attend a parent meeting for learning to handle the behavior difficulties of 3-year-olds. She reported that she wished her child could be capable of such misbehavior. It is easy to appreciate how parents may seek to avoid such pain, and thus limit participation in their child's program.

Parents can also resist involvement because they have become too involved in the past (Winton & Turnbull, 1981). Since integration is a relatively new activity for many schools and teachers, parents have been called on to fill an informational gap ranging from providing information about the child's history and medical services to demonstrating management techniques and training personnel. The extensive involvement of some parents in their child's education (often stemming from a realistic fear that appropriate services will not be available otherwise) is overwhelming to many parents and results in less involvement over time (Winton & Turnbull, 1981).

In light of these and numerous other pressures on parents (e.g., marital conflicts, siblings' needs, finances, etc.), conflicts can develop when school personnel expect parents to become involved in other ways, such as through classroom assistance, when the parents do not desire this level of involvement. Conversely, if a school assumes that all parents desire only to be involved in an informational capacity, problems can arise when the parent who wishes to be more active cannot be accommodated.

Lack of flexibility in defining the roles of parents invariably results in frustration for parents and staff. Expectations for parent involvement need to consider the different family structures in modern society (e.g., single parents, working parents), as well as the individual interests of parents. Professionals who attempt to involve a parent who opts for less involvement may need to accept that parent's decision, without assuming that they have failed in not involving the parent further.

One option for individualizing parent involvement is through the use of an individualized parent/family plan to delineate the level of involvement mutually agreed upon by staff and parents (Bauer & Shea, 1985). Compliance with the goals in the plan can also be used as a measure of involvement, without comparing types of involvement across different family systems.

In accordance with the issues discussed previously, parent involvement is defined in this book as a continuum of options that allow choices for parents to assume varying levels of responsibility in the process of their child's education. Inherent in this definition is the acceptance of any parent involvement as "good," without attaching relative value to commitments of more or less time. The Options for Parent Involvement questionnaire is presented in Appendix 5.C to assist parents in identifying the type(s) of activities in which they can or would like to participate. The information obtained through this questionnaire can assist staff in planning activities that suit each family, rather than assuming that one type of activity will suffice, only to find that few parents participate on a regular basis.

Maintaining Parent Involvement

Although parent involvement implies that the process is ongoing, very few sources have offered suggestions for continuing involvement after the child's placement. Sources that offer suggestions agree that a specific listing of assignments and activities is more successful than open-ended invitations to participate (Cansler & Winton, 1983; Kroth, 1980; Reynolds & Birch, 1982).

A significant amount of responsibility for continued parent involvement will rest on school personnel. Consequently, personnel training activities should include information about parent adjustment to integration and the difficulties that parents may face when their child is placed in an integrated setting. This information may help professionals to better understand the reluctance of some parents to attend activities that may be painful from a parent perspective. Furthermore, since professionals and parents now both have access to community resources (Reynolds & Birch, 1982), there is an increasing likelihood that they will share information about parent support groups and resources.

Appendix 5.A.

PARENT INTEGRATION OPINIONNAIRE

Sebastian Striefel & Joel Allred

Purpose:

This instrument is designed (a) to determine parents' views about integration and (b) to determine what issues are seen by parents as possible reasons for not integrating students with handicaps.

Description:

The Opinionnaire has two sections. The first section has three columns. In the column on the left, labeled **Item**, are fourteen statements reflecting issues that are sometimes associated with integration. The middle column, labeled **Column 1**, asks "How much do you agree or disagree with this statement?" followed by a four-point scale ("Strongly Agree", "Agree", "Disagree", "Strongly Disagree"). The column on the right, labeled **Column 2**, asks "Do you feel this is a good reason for not integrating students with handicaps?" followed by a series of "Yes" and "No" choices.

The second section of the Opinionnaire is made up of six questions which ask for information that can be used in the interpretation of the results (e.g., age, gender, education and opinion of integration).

Instructions:

After reading each statement in the **Item** column, the parent indicates the extent to which s/he agrees by circling one of the responses under **Column 1** . The parent then answers the question under **Column 2** by checking either "Yes" or "No." After completing the first section, the parent answers the six questions at the end of the form.

Using the Results:

To analyze the results, compile the total number of responses and then compute the percentages of occurrence for each type of response. The information given in **Column 1** is used as a general assessment of the respondents' views toward integration. **Column 2** provides information which may be used by administrators and educators to prioritize any issues which should be addressed. The responses in Section 2 can be used to divide the respondents into groups (e.g., groups of parents of children with and without handicaps) for comparison.

Appendix 5.A. (continued)

Parent Integration Opinionnaire

The following statements reflect issues that sometimes arise with integration. For each item please circle or check your opinion.

Item	Column 1 How much do you agree or disagree with this statement?				Column 2 Do you feel that this is a good reason for not integrating students with handicaps?
1. There is not enough time in a regular teacher's day to deal appropriately with the needs of students with handicaps in a regular classroom	Strongly Agree	Agree	Disagree	Strongly Disagree	Yes—— No——
2. Once put into a mainstreaming program, students with handicaps are often not able to use the special services (e.g., physical therapy) which were available for them before.	Strongly Agree	Agree	Disagree	Strongly Disagree	Yes—— No——
3. Many students without handicaps tease and make fun of the student with handicaps.	Strongly Agree	Agree	Disagree	Strongly Disagree	Yes—— No——
4. Regular teachers and children without handicaps often give too much help to students with handicaps and may not give them a chance to learn by themselves.	Strongly Agree	Agree	Disagree	Strongly Disagree	Yes—— No——
5. Mainstreamed children with handicaps cannot usually use the same grading system as used for the children without handicaps.	Strongly Agree	Agree	Disagree	Strongly Disagree	Yes—— No——
6. Children with handicaps are not likely to make friends with nonhandicapped children in a regular school.	Strongly Agree	Agree	Disagree	Strongly Disagree	Yes—— No——
7. Parents of children without handicaps typically do not want children with handicaps to be in the same room as their children.	Strongly Agree	Agree	Disagree	Strongly Disagree	Yes—— No——
8. A regular school does not typically have the necessary furniture, bathroom facilities, or adaptive equipment for a child with handicaps.	Strongly Agree	Agree	Disagree	Strongly Disagree	Yes—— No——
9. Children without handicaps do not get an appropriate education and enough attention because the teacher will be occupied with the special needs of the child with handicaps.	Strongly Agree	Agree	Disagree	Strongly Disagree	Yes—— No——

Appendix 5.A. (continued)

Item	Column 1 How much do you agree or disagree with this statement?				Column 2 Do you feel that this is a good reason for not integrating students with handicaps?
10. Children without handicaps learn poor behaviors from the children with handicaps.	Strongly Agree	Agree	Disagree	Strongly Disagree	Yes—— No——
11. Children with handicaps may be tricked by other children into doing harmful or inappropriate activities.	Strongly Agree	Agree	Disagree	Strongly Disagree	Yes—— No——
12. Children with handicaps are not typically safe in regular schools.	Strongly Agree	Agree	Disagree	Strongly Disagree	Yes—— No——
13. Children without handicaps are not typically safe in the same school as children with handicaps.	Strongly Agree	Agree	Disagree	Strongly Disagree	Yes—— No——
14. Regular classrooms are already too crowded to take on the responsibility of mainstreaming.	Strongly Agree	Agree	Disagree	Strongly Disagree	Yes—— No——
Total Number out of 14	——	——	——	——	—— ——
Percentage of Total (Divide total number in each row by 14)	——	——	——	——	—— ——

Please circle the appropriate response:

1. Do you have a child with a handicapping condition?   Yes   No

2. Are you generally in favor of mainstreaming?   Yes   No

3. Is your child in a class into which children with handicaps are integrated?   Yes   No   Unsure

4. Are you: Male   Female

5. Age: _____ years

6. Years of education completed:
   Grade School   1 2 3 4 5 6 7 8
   High School   1 2 3 4
   College   1 2 3 4
   Graduate   1 2 3 more

7. Annual income level:
   5,000-10,000   20,000-25,000
   10,000-15,000   25,000-30,000
   15,000-20,000   over 30,000

Appendix 5.B.

Assessment of Parent Needs and Interests

Purpose:

Parents are sometimes overlooked by educators as a source of information while developing students' educational programs and parent training programs. The Assessment of Parent Needs and Interests was developed by VSSM staff to determine parents' views of possible instructional needs for them and their children. The results of this assessment may be used by a committee responsible for organizing parent awareness activities to plan inservice programs. Parents and educators may also find this form useful for planning goals and objectives at a child's IEP meeting.

Instructions:

In the first section, the parent assesses his/her own training needs in ten areas on a three-point scale. In the second section, the parent assesses his/her child's educational needs in four areas using a similar scale. The results may be summarized in terms of percentages for each type of response for each given area.

Appendix 5.B. (continued)

Assessment of Parent Needs and Interests

The purpose of the following section is for you to give us an idea of the areas in which you would benefit most from instruction. Read each statement and then circle the answer which best describes your feelings. There are no right or wrong answers.
Circle your answers according to this scale:
1. I need little or no extra help.
2. I have some information, but would like to know more in this area.
3. I would like to know a lot more in this area.

1	2	3	1. I know and can recognize normal developmental progress.
1	2	3	2. I can use everyday activities as learning opportunities for my child.
1	2	3	3. I can set goals for my child which are realistic for his/her abilities.
1	2	3	4. I can set rules and limits for my child's behavior and consistently enforce them.
1	2	3	5. I know where to find help or special services for (e.g., speech therapy) my child.
1	2	3	6. I understand the disability and special needs resulting from my child's handicap.
1	2	3	7. I can get other family members involved in the care and education of my child.
1	2	3	8. I can provide good health care including a balanced diet, home safety, cleanliness and medical attention.
1	2	3	9. I can teach my child skills in daily living such as dressing, eating, toilet training, and grooming.
1	2	3	10. I am aware of own feelings about my child and his/her handicaps.

The purpose of this section is for you to give us some idea of those areas in which you believe you and your child would benefit most from extra training. Please check one in each area.

	Needs *No* *work*	*Needs* *Some* *work*	*Needs* *Lots of* *work*
1. Self-help skills such as dressing, toileting, and eating.			
2. Motor skills such as walking, throwing, tying shoes, buttoning clothes, using scissors, and writing name.			
3. Language skills such as following simple commands like "Wash your hands," speaking clearly, stating wants, and naming objects.			
4. Social/Emotional skills such as getting along with others and appropriate expression of wants and feelings such as controlling temper and not biting, hitting, or hurting others.			

This checklist was adapted from the following instruments:

"Parent Self-Appraisal Inventory"
Project Kids
3801 Hershall
Dallas, TX 75269

"Parental Concerns"
Chapel Hill Training-Outreach Project
Lincoln Center
Merrit Mill Road
Chapel Hill, NC 27514

Appendix 5.C.

Options for Parent Involvement

Purpose:

Educators and other professionals are often concerned with promoting and maintaining parent involvement. The <u>Options for Parent Involvement</u> is used to assess a parent's desired level of involvement in a child's special education program. This information can be used in the development and implementation of parent preparation programs by providing educators with an estimate of the types and extent of involvement local parents want to have in their children's education. Programs promoting involvement can then be designed accordingly.

Instructions:

The <u>Options</u> consist of eight statements which describe different levels of parental involvement. After carefully reading and considering each statement, please mark all statements which describe how involved you would presently like to be in your child's educational program. Be sure to take into account such factors as your present level of involvement, the number of demands currently made on your time, etc.

Appendix 5.C. (continued)

Options for Parent Involvement

Please mark all statements that describe how involved in your child's program you would like to be:

√

	Parent receives school information, and signs consent forms and IEPs.
	Parent receives information and provides information upon request.
	Parent participates in meetings as IEP team member and/or parent/teacher conferences by contributing goals, etc.
	Parent initiates conversation or written contact with school about child and/or program.
	Parent participates in class upon request and through supportive home activities.
	Parent volunteers in class or program through direct attendance or alternate home/community activities.
	Parent participates in "parent groups." Carries out instructional and therapeutic activities within home and community.
	Parent organizes "parent groups" and parent communication programs.

Chapter 6

• • •

Identifying and Involving Preschoolers in Integration

This chapter focuses on (a) methods for identifying, recruiting, and assessing children for an integrated program and (b) methods for preparing peers without handicaps for successful integration. Figure 6.1 provides a flowchart of child preparation activities.

Child Identification and Recruitment

The identification of children to participate in an integrated preschool program includes (a) the identification of a pool of children with handicaps and (b) the identification of a pool of children without handicaps who can participate in the program.

    The recruitment of children is primarily a task of identifying and addressing parental concerns successfully, and providing a preschool program that addresses the individual needs of all participating children and their families. Since both groups are identified and accessed through different channels, each group will be discussed separately (e.g., schools have a legal requirement to educate preschoolers who have handicaps, but in most states educating preschoolers who are not handicapped is not required).

Identification and Recruitment of Children with Handicaps

All schools are required by law to have an identification and recruitment process to locate children with handicaps who have not been

147

Figure 6.1. Flowchart of Child Preparation Activities

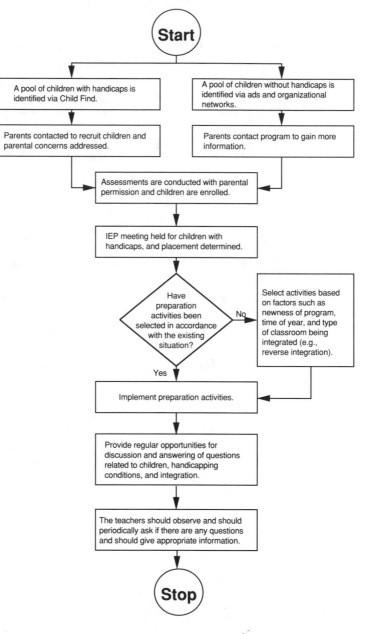

previously identified or involved in a school's special education program. This process is called child find.

Identification.   Methods for child find vary from location to location; however, they usually consist of a screening and assessment process, eligibility determination, referral to special intervention services, and development of an Individualized Education Program (IEP). Children with handicaps, by law, are to receive services in the least restrictive environment. For most, if not all, preschoolers, this means an integrated program.

In school districts the process for identifying children has been in place for some time, and the identification of children in need of special services is routine.

Recruitment.   Once a student with handicaps is identified, the process of recruitment begins. The purpose of recruitment is to encourage parents to enroll their children in the program that will best meet the needs of their child and to participate in the development of their child's IEP. During this process, the IEP team must identify and address the concerns of parents and provide emotional support as the parents are faced with the decision to enroll their child for services. It is important for staff to appreciate that this decision may be a difficult one for parents. Often, parents are facing for the first time the reality of their child's handicap. While this process of adjusting and learning to cope with this realization is just beginning, staff, eager to enroll a child in services, may overlook the parents' reactions and inadvertently alienate them. It is important that staff understand parental concerns about their child and about integration so that they can assist parents in deciding what may be best for their child. The reader is directed to Chapter 5 for a detailed discussion of procedures and materials to prepare and involve parents of children with handicaps in the process of their child's integration, and to Chapter 7 for the development of an IEP designed to guide the services offered to a child.

Identification and Recruitment of Students Without Handicaps

Reverse Integration.   The identification and recruitment of children without handicaps for a reverse integration model requires that program staff access the established channels of communication with young families in a community. One common channel in most communities is the classified advertisements section of the local newspaper. A simple text for an ad may read as follows:

The Red Rose School District has summer openings for children ages 3 to 5. Your child can benefit from individualized attention and small class sizes. Excellent preparation for children who will enter kindergarten! M–F, 8:30–11:30. Contact Betty Jones, 555-1234.

Other channels to consider include community bulletin boards, civic or church group networks, pediatricians, and displays at community functions. It is wise to develop a standard flier or brochure with the goals and a brief description of the preschool program for distribution. A flier or brochure serves to communicate important information and also presents an organized, well-prepared image of the integrated program. A sample brochure is presented in Appendix 6.A.

In developing the content of a flier or brochure, it is important that the program become identified with an upbeat, child-focused message that states the benefits of participation for children without handicaps. This message should also communicate how the program offers unique, desirable services and opportunities that may not be available or may be limited in existing community preschool programs (e.g., preparation for kindergarten, small class sizes, convenience). To this end, attention must be addressed to naming the program to reflect these goals. For example, calling a program "The Children's Playhouse" may be better accepted than "Integrated Children's Services." Attention must also be directed at assuring that the physical appearance of classrooms and play areas support the child-oriented description of the program (e.g., toys are readily accessible, materials are appropriate to a wide range of skills and interests).

Existing special education preschools that choose to desegregate their programs may find that the individualized, child-oriented philosophy used in special education is welcomed by parents of children without handicaps, and can be a critical selling point for the new program. The strategic use of small and large groups and the emphasis on enhancing all areas of development through planned, developmentally appropriate activities are features of a program that can be highlighted in recruitment advertisements or notices. A new program may only need to attend to minor expansions, such as acquiring materials for 4-year-olds who may be functioning at, or slightly above, their chronological age level. Parents may express an interest in such activities, and staff must be well prepared to enhance skills for such children.

Traditional Integration. The introduction of children with handicaps into existing programs for children without handicaps can occur in private preschools, public schools and preschools, or in a structured day-care setting. The type of setting that is most appropriate for each child is decided by the child's IEP team. Some school districts attempt to reduce costs and maximize resources by using kindergarten classes as receiving environments; however, the developmental needs of a 3-year-old and a kindergarten child are sufficiently different. Such differences discourage the provision of integrated services that are appropriate in such a setting and to the benefit of all the children. The best peer group for a preschool child is a group of other preschool children.

The identification of existing programs that can receive a group of children with handicaps is usually more difficult than reverse integration. A program must first be found in which administrative support is present and space is available to accommodate the group of new children who will be introduced into the setting. Administrative support (discussed in detail in Chapter 2) must be obtained to commit time and financial resources for modifying the environment and acquiring materials as needed. Funding such a program is usually dependent upon the contacts that the special education service providers may already have established or may need to develop within the community. Once a program is identified, staff from the special education setting must be reassigned to the new setting, and relationships must be developed to work toward a unified, single body of teachers, rather than subdivided groups of "regular" and "special" teachers. In general, this process requires a lengthy period of preparation and public relations efforts to thoroughly acquaint everyone with the intent and the particular plan for integration prior to implementing any changes. While this process is involved, many locations have successfully introduced children with handicaps into existing regular programs.

Assessment

Children identified through child find as having possible delays or handicapping conditions are referred for comprehensive assessment in areas of suspected delays as a part of eligibility determination. For those children eligible for special education and related services, the assessment information can also serve as a basis for developing appropriate programs and for establishing baseline levels of skills from which progress can be evaluated. Table 6.1 lists areas of development that should be assessed to establish baseline levels of skills, and suggested instruments for use in each area. The instruments suggested

Table 6.1. Developmental Areas to be Assessed and Suggested
Assessment Instruments

Developmental Areas	Suggested Instruments
Cognitive	- Battelle Developmental Inventory (BDI) (Newborg, Stock, Wnek, Guidubaldi, & Svinicki, 1984) (The BDI also yields scores for all of the other areas of development.) - Bayley Scales of Infant Development (Bayley, 1969)
Language	- Receptive Expressive Emergent Language Scale (REEL) (Bzoch & League, 1971) - Preschool Language Scale (PLS) (Zimmerman, Steiner, & Pond, 1979) - Program Assessment and Planning Guide (PAPG) Social Language Subtest (Striefel & Cadez, 1983b)
Social	- MESA-PK and PAPG (Social Language Subtest)
Motor	- Peabody Developmental Motor Scales and Activity Cards (Folio & Fewell, 1983) (Assessment of motor skills may be omitted for children without handicaps, since an integrated program is not expected to produce significant gain or loss of skills in this area.)

are intended to serve as examples, and do not necessarily reflect the only suitable means of assessing a specific area.

Before administering any instruments, however, informed consent for testing must be obtained from the parents. An informed consent form should be used. In this form, the purpose of the testing, the areas that will be assessed, and the rights of the parents should be explained. Specific signed consent is requested, with the option of refusing or withholding consent, pending a conference to discuss concerns or questions.

Assessments conducted and the results for every child should be organized and maintained in an easily accessible format. Information in this format should include the test administered; date of testing; name of the examiner; test scores, results, and comments; and the recommended date for retesting. The format shown in Figure 6.2 provides a simple way to organize this information in one document.

In the process of assessing children who are thought to be without handicaps, a child with a handicapping condition may be identified. If the child meets local eligibility criteria for special services, the parents should be alerted and the appropriate referral to authorities for special services in the area be made. An individualized program can be developed, and participation can be continued with the child now enrolled as a special education student.

Peer Preparation

Once children have been identified, recruited, and assessed, preparation activities should begin. Without preparation, interactions among children with and without handicaps are generally negative in nature (Gresham, 1982) or, at best, occur infrequently (Innocenti et al., 1982; Schwartz, 1984). Without systematic methods for preparing children for integration, the outcome is most likely to be unsuccessful in promoting acceptance by peers. Successful peer preparation activities are not one-time events; rather, they are systematic interventions that are incorporated into the flow of activities of an integrated program (Voeltz, 1984).

Purpose of Peer Preparation

The purpose of peer preparation is to gain the support of the children without handicaps in the program. Three goals to be achieved by peer preparation are:

Figure 6.2. Individual Test Summary

Individual Test Record						
Client: _____			**Date of Birth** _____			
Date Tested	Examiner	Test Administered	Test Scores	Test Results & Comments		Date Retest Recommended

1. To provide general information about handicapping conditions.

2. To model positive attitudes and behaviors toward children with handicaps.

3. To teach appropriate ways of interacting with children who have handicaps.

What this means practically is that the intent is to be sure that peers are not afraid of those who have handicaps and interact with them positively, that they learn to accept individual differences, that they advocate for these children, and that they develop friendships with them.

Who Should Conduct Peer Preparation?

The classroom teacher usually coordinates the peer preparation program. However, all school personnel should be familiar with ways of promoting positive attitudes and behaviors with children in the integrated classroom, since all will be involved in the integration process. Preparation activities are also a good way for people to become involved with the integrated classroom. Parents of children with and without handicaps, classroom volunteers, and older peers can be enlisted to assist in peer preparation activities.

When Should Peer Preparation Occur?

Peer preparation may differ when children without handicaps are integrated into an existing special education setting, versus when children with handicaps are integrated into an existing program for children without handicaps. The major distinctions between the two involve considerations about timing, intensity, and other details related to the preparation activities.

Generally, children with and without handicaps who begin preschool simultaneously (e.g., at the start of the academic year) require less initial preparation regarding handicapping conditions than children who are enrolled in a program during the course of the year and those enrolled in a program that is altered through an integration effort. When all children begin simultaneously, all individuals are involved in a period of adjustment in which everyone is equally disadvantaged. General, low-intensity preparation activities such as curriculum units on individual differences and making friends, books on individual differences, and audiovisual materials on individual differences may be useful at this point. As the group adjusts to the setting, more specific, intensive preparation activities may be utilized as needs arise. Intensive activities may include puppet shows, group discussions, role-playing, and audiovisual materials on specific handicapping conditions. In all cases, those conducting the preparation activity should remain sensitive to the feelings of children with handicaps who may be present in the training environment. For example, if a child appears embarrassed or uncomfortable, preparation may be better conducted in the child's absence or with the child as an active participant in the activity, instead of as a member of the audience.

Activities such as puppet shows and specific discussions are a recommended starting point when children with handicaps are to be integrated as new students into a setting in which children who do not have handicaps are already established in the classroom. Preparation activities are sufficiently different and should be interesting enough to capture children's attention and to encourage the children to learn the new ideas that form the basis for successful interactions with their new classmates.

Peer preparation activities should be an ongoing part of the integrated preschool. Generally, after integration is ongoing, peer preparation can take the form of weekly discussions and answering of questions as they arise. Periodic probes should be conducted by the teacher in the form of questions to assure that no issues concerning integration remain unresolved.

Preparation activities should be interesting and sufficiently varied to appeal to a wide range of interests in a classroom. Preparation activities include:

1. Curriculum units that emphasize the value of individual differences among people.

2. Children's reading books and coloring books about handicapping conditions.

3. Audiovisual materials about persons with handicaps.

4. Group discussions to address questions and concerns.

5. Puppet shows to communicate and practice key ideas about peers with handicaps.

These activities are detailed in Appendix 6.B. Other peer preparation activities developed by the FMS project focused on specific roles for peers, such as how to be a peer buddy. These specific roles are discussed in Chapter 9.

Appendix 6.A.

Sample Preschool Child Recruitment Brochure

Red Rose Preschool

July 1, 1985

The Red Rose Preschool is a new concept in our area. We would like you to know more about our goals.

The Red Rose Preschool is designed to:

1. Develop group activities in an integrated preschool program which address the interests and skill levels of a broad range of children.
2. Help children with and without handicaps learn how to interact.
3. Maximize the development of both groups of children in cognitive, motor, language, self-help, and social skill areas.
4. Evaluate the effectiveness of our activities through direct observation, interviews, and parent and teacher feedback.
5. Assess the effectiveness of activities designed to help nonhandicapped children feel more comfortable with their peers who have handicapping conditions.
6. Record and videotape successful techniques so other professionals can adopt similar programs.

Since you may have some questions about the program, let us provide you with some answers:

WHAT IS INTEGRATION?

Integration, in general terms, is the planned and structured education of children with handicaps in an environment with children who do not have handicaps, but which still meets each child's needs. These needs are specified by a team made up of the child's teacher(s), parents, and other instructional and specialized staff (as well as the child, if appropriate). For preschoolers with handicaps, most, if not all, of their day can be spent in regular activities because few preschool activities require sophisticated skills such as academics. Integration requires preparation of the children involved, sensitivity to the awkwardness felt by children with and without

Appendix 6.A. (continued)

handicaps as the two groups try to interact positively in new situations, communication among parents and teachers, and constant reevaluation of how things are progressing. Integration is not a one-time event; it is a process which affects all children in a program over time.

Children without handicaps will gain experiences in understanding individual differences, leadership, self-confidence, as well as specific skills that will help them when they enter kindergarten.

WHO ARE THE CHILDREN WITH HANDICAPS IN THE RED ROSE PRESCHOOL?

Eight children with handicaps will attend each classroom with 8 children who do not have handicaps. Children with handicaps have a variety of handicapping conditions, such as deafness, blindness, and/or mental retardation. They range in ages from 3 to 5 years. None of these conditions is contagious, i.e., your child can't "catch" a handicap by being around children who have handicaps.

HOW MANY DAYS WILL THE PROGRAM OPERATE?

The preschool will be conducted four mornings a week, Mondays through Thursdays, from 8:30 to 11:00. The summer session will start on July 1, 1990, and will end on August 8, 1990.

WHAT IS THE COST OF THE PROGRAM FOR PARTICIPATING FAMILIES?

A fee of $____ will be charged per quarter. No refunds will be given for illness or family vacations. No fee will be charged to parents whose children have a handicapping condition, because such children are eligible for services funded by the school system's special education program under Public Law 99-457.

WHAT IS EXPECTED OF PARENTS?

Parents who would like to visit the classroom or serve as volunteers are always welcome. However, we realize that work schedules and other obligations may prevent parents from becoming as involved as they would like. All parents will be asked to complete registration and medical emergency forms on their child, to sign releases allowing their children to be videotaped and photographed for project

Appendix 6.A. (continued)

activities, and to complete parent questionnaires about integration and about the program. Additionally, since all the children in the program need to be tested initially, parents will be asked to sign a release for gathering data through standardized tests, parent report, classroom observation, and child interview. ALL INFORMATION GATHERED ABOUT A CHILD WILL BE AVAILABLE TO PARENTS. THIS INFORMATION WILL BE KEPT IN CONFIDENTIAL RECORDS.

WHAT KINDS OF TESTS WILL MY CHILD BE GIVEN?

Children will be tested in areas of cognitive, language, academic, social, self-help, and motor development. A battery of tests including a test of intelligence, developmental scales, and behavior scales will be used.

Total testing time for any one child is not expected to exceed three hours. A second set of assessments will be conducted periodically in the class. These will be regular sociometric evaluations, in which children will be asked to identify their friends in the class, and why that person is a good friend, etc.

WHAT WILL MY CHILD'S DAY BE LIKE?

Sample Daily Schedule

Approx. Time	Activity	Content	Appropriate Microsession
8:30-8:45	Table Activities (Arrival)	Fine Motor Creativity Personal issues Social Self-Help	Fine Motor Cognitive Self-Help Social
8:45-9:00	Large Group	General concepts Theme Names, numbers Calendar Social	Cognitive Social Language
9:00-9:45 (3 Simultaneous groups- Children rotate on 15 minute intervals)	Learning Centers	Fine motor Language Social	Fine motor Occupational Therapy Language Social

Appendix 6.A. (continued)

Time	Activity		
9:45-10:00	Free Play/ Dramatic Play		Cognitive Gross Motor Fine Motor Social
10:00-10:15	Gross Motor	Dramatic Play Ad. P.E. Body Awareness Motor Planning Coordination	Gross Motor Physical Therapy
10:15-10:45	Small Group Language	Receptive, Expressive, Social Conversation Cooperative Group Story/Discussion	Receptive, Expressive and Social Language Articulation
10:45-11:00	Snack	Social Table Manners Self-Help Language	Social Self-Help
11:00-11:15	Social Play	Reciprocal Social Interactions	Social
11:15-11:30	Closing Group	Wrap-up Show-and-Tell	Self-Help

Note: Children with handicaps whose I.E.P. team members have identified special need areas which require intensive, individualized programming will be given these services at various times during the day, while still allowing them time to be with the group for the major part of the school day.

This is a basic, very general overview of the Red Rose Preschool. We hope that if you have any questions, you will feel free to call:

(Contact Persons Listed Here)

_____

Appendix 6.B
Peer Preparation Activities

1. An "Individual Differences" class unit is a method which presents handicapping conditions as another way of being different; i.e., we all have differences which make us special. Units can be easily adapted for different age levels. Examples of activities that can be part of such a unit include the following activities published by the Chapel Hill Training-Outreach Project (Heekin & Mengel, 1983).

   <u>**Correlated Activities**</u>

How Big Am I?	Behind the Screen
Hand, Foot, Finger, Toe	In the Box
My Favorite Things	Who's Under the Sheet?
Person of the Week	Our Gang
Silhouettes	Individual Differences
I Can Do It	

   It is recommended that these activities be used to show that everyone, including a child with handicaps, has differences and similarities. It should be emphasized that although children who have handicaps may not be able to do everything that other children can do, they <u>can</u> do many of the same things and they have a lot of the same likes and dislikes as other children.

2. Children's books, chosen carefully, provide additional information on handicapping conditions and demonstrate appropriate behaviors for interacting with children who have handicaps. A list of appropriate children's books may include the following titles; however, teachers are cautioned to review the books carefully before use to assure that the content is age-appropriate, of interest to the group's particular areas of concern, and relevant for the handicapping conditions represented in the integrated program.

Books About Handicapping Conditions

   <u>**Visual Impairments**</u>:

   Hunter, E.F. (1963). <u>Child of the silent night</u>. New York: Dell.

   Keats, E.J. (1971). <u>Apt 3</u>. New York: Macmillan.

   Krents, H. (1972). <u>To race the wind</u>. New York: C.P. Putnams Sons.

Appendix 6.B. (continued)

Peterson, P. (1977). Sally can't see. Day.

Rashin, E. (1968). Spectacles. New York: Atheneum.

Vance, M. (1956). Windows for Rosemary. New York: Dutton.

Wolf, B. (1976). Connie's new eyes. New York: J.B. Lippincott.

Hearing Impairments:

Charlip, R., & Anconna, M.B.G. (1975). Handtalk, an ABC of finger spelling and sign language. New York: Parents Magazine Press.

Ets, M.H. (1968). Talking without words. New York: Viking.

Greenberg, J. (1970). In this sign. New York: Avon.

Levine, E.S. (1974). Lisa and her soundless world. New York: Behavioral Publications.

Mindel, E., & McCay, V. (1971). They grow in silence. Silver Springs, MD: National Association of the Deaf.

Peter, D. (1977). Claire and Emma. Day Publications.

Mental Retardation:

Brightman, A. (1976). Like me. Boston: Little, Brown, & Co.

Byars, B. (1970). Summer of the swans. New York: Viking Press.

Canning, C. The gift of Martha. Available through Resource Development. The Children's Hospital Medical Center, 300 Longwood Ave., Boston, MA 02115.

Christopher, M. (1966). Long shot for Josh. Boston: Little, Brown, & Co.

Fassler, J. (1969). One little girl. New York: Behavioral Publishers.

Hirsch, K. (1977). My sister. Carolrhoda Books, Inc.

Larsen, H. (1974). Don't forget Tom. London: A&C Blade.

Lasher, J. (1974). He's my brother. Chicago, IL: Albert Whitman.

Ominsky, E. (1977). Jon O., a special boy. Englewood Cliffs, NJ: Prentice-Hall

Sobol, H.L. (1977). My brother Steven is retarded. New York: Macmillan Pub.

Physical Impairments:

Fanshawe, E. (1975). Rachel. New York: Bradbury.

Appendix 6.B. (continued)

Fassler, J. (1975). <u>Howie helps himself</u>. Chicago: Whitman.

Gelfand, R., & Patterson, H. (1962). <u>They wouldn't quit: Stories of handicapped people</u>. Minneapolis, MN: Lerner Publishing Co.

Stein, S.B. (1974). <u>About handicaps: An open family book for parents and children together</u>. New York: Walker & Co.

White, P. (1978). <u>Janet at school</u>. John Day.

Wolf, B. (1974). <u>Don't feel sorry for Paul</u>. New York: J.B. Lippincott Co.

Illness:

Sobol, H.L. (1975). <u>Jeff's hospital book</u>. New York: Henry Z. Walch.

Communication Disorders:

Jupo, F. (1967). <u>Ater, the silent one</u>. New York: Holiday House.

Emotional Disorders:

Gold, P. (1976). <u>Please don't say hello</u>. New York: Human Sciences Press.

A variation on the use of books is the use of coloring books that feature aspects of integration. Coloring worksheets can be adapted from children's coloring books that feature children at play, dining, sharing objects, or engaging in other appropriate social activities. These pictures should reiterate important concepts introduced during other activities, such as the puppet show described below. Pages can be distributed and used one a day over the weeks in order for the teacher to review each concept. Possible concepts to reinforce include:

"Because part of my body doesn't work right, I may sometimes look or act differently than other kids."

"But because we are mostly the same, we can still be friends."

"Having a handicap is different than being sick."

"You cannot catch a handicap like you can a cold."

"It's okay to ask someone about their handicap."

"Children who have handicaps like to play just like everyone else."

Appendix 6.B. (continued)

Another type of coloring activity may involve creative drawing, in which children can be encouraged to draw pictures of children playing together and exhibiting other socially appropriate peer interactions.

3. Audiovisual materials, (e.g., movies, videos) provide an entertaining visual format for communicating about persons with handicaps. As with any new materials, audiovisual material must be screened for appropriateness to goals, suitability for the target age group and handicapping conditions represented in the group, and should also model appropriate attitudes and methods of interactions with people who have handicaps. Examples to consider include:

American Foundation for the Blind. (1971). <u>What do you do when you see a blind person</u>? New York, NY.

California Association for Neurologically Handicapped Children. (1972). <u>A walk in another pair of shoes</u>. Los Angeles, CA.

Encyclopedia Brittanica Educational Corporation. (1978). <u>Like you, like me series</u>. Chicago, IL.

Joyce Motion Picture Co. <u>David and Goliath</u> and <u>Noah</u>. Northridge, CA.

Lawrence Productions, Inc. <u>Different from you...and like you, too</u> and <u>Special delivery film series</u>. Mendocino, CA.

Learning Corporation of America. (1976). <u>Larry, Phillip, and the white colt, Skating rink</u>, and <u>That's my name, don't wear it out</u>. New York: NY.

National Instructional Television Center. (1973). <u>Donna: Learning to be yourself</u>. Bloomington, IN.

National Foundation, March of Dimes. (1972). <u>Keep on walking</u>. White Plains, NY.

Social Studies School Service. <u>A full life for Sara</u> and <u>I'm just like you: Mainstreaming the handicapped</u>. Culver City, CA.

Stanfield Film Associates. <u>Hello everybody</u>. Santa Monica, CA.

Walt Disney Educational Films. <u>Truly exceptional people</u>. Burbank, CA.

4. Group discussions create a format which is useful when questions arise and when child-specific information needs explanation. Specific topics that may be discussed could include:

Appendix 6.B. (continued)

What are helmets, hearing aids, and other appliances used for?

Can you help a person with a handicap too much?

How can you help a peer with handicaps make new friends?

What should you do if a classmate gets aggressive?

What can you learn from your friend who has handicaps?

How can you communicate with someone who doesn't understand everything you say?

What should you do if your friend, who has handicaps, does something that may hurt him/her or someone else? What would you do if a friend without a handicap tried to do something harmful?

Are all people who have handicaps the same? Are all of your classmates the same?

How can you include students who have handicaps in your games?

How could a student in a wheelchair play softball with you? Could you include a hard of hearing student in relay races?

5. Puppet shows are an effective way to introduce information on handicapping conditions and to demonstrate appropriate attitudes and behaviors toward children who have handicaps. A sample skit developed by the FMS project is included. Puppet shows are most appropriate for children in the primary grades.

Puppet Show

Materials Needed: A puppet show script, table for the stage, required number of puppets, adults to act as puppeteers.

Time for administration:

Puppet show script   10 minutes

Questions and discussion   <u>10 minutes</u>

                            20 minutes

Target Audience: At the preschool level, a puppet show presentation is more effective with a smaller group of children. An audience of less than 20 provides more opportunities for participation by all children by allowing more discussion and individual questions. With

Appendix 6.B. (continued)

young audiences it is helpful to repeat the puppet show over several consecutive weeks to aid the children's understanding of the concepts.

General Description: Puppet shows are an excellent method for presenting basic introductory concepts about handicapping conditions, as shown in the following script. A variety of scripts can be easily developed for different and specific situations such as explaining the concept of integration, demonstrating how to welcome a child with handicaps into the classroom, and showing ways to play with a child who has handicaps.

Another advantage of the puppet show is its easy administration. Set-up simply includes a table as the stage with the puppeteers behind the table and the puppets on the table facing the audience.

Sample Script:

About Handicaps: A Puppet Show for Peer Preparation

Ages 3-6 Years

Karri:	Hi boys and girls! My name is Karri. It sure is fun being here today! I want you to meet my new friend, Kyle.
Kyle:	(Waving) Hi Karri. Hi boys and girls!
Karri:	As you can see, Kyle looks kind of different. That's because Kyle has a handicap (stated matter-of-factly).
Kyle:	Having a handicap means that part of my body doesn't work right. (turns toward audience) Boys and girls, what is a handicap?
Karri:	(With audience) A handicap is when part of the body doesn't work right.
Kyle:	The handicap I have makes me look a little different than other children.
Karri:	Is yours the only kind of handicap?
Kyle:	No, there are many kinds of handicaps. Some children who have handicaps are not able to see.
Karri:	You mean they can't see?
Kyle:	Yes, and some children can't walk.
Karri:	You mean they use a wheelchair?

Appendix 6.B. (continued)

Kyle: They might. Some other handicaps make it hard to hear or hard to do things fast.

Karri: Does that mean it's hard to do things in school?

Kyle: It might make school harder, but children who have handicaps can still go to school.

Karri: If children who have handicaps go to school, it must mean that having a handicap isn't like being sick.

Kyle: Having a handicap isn't like being sick at all.

Karri: Really?

Kyle: When a person is sick, they catch it, are sick for a while, then they get over it.

Karri: Right.

Kyle: And when a person has a handicap, usually they are born with it, and they always have a handicap. Boys and girls, is a handicap like being sick?

Karri: (With audience) No! (alone) Then you can't catch a handicap! That's good to know. That means you and I can play! Would you like to play with me, Kyle?

Kyle: I sure would! Children who have handicaps like to play just like you do. I like to play with balls and puzzles, and I like to take walks and sing and build with blocks. We sure could have a lot of fun together.

Karri: We sure could!

Kyle: Boys and girls, can children who have handicaps and children like you have fun playing together?

Karri: (With audience) Yes! (alone) Kyle, I have been asking you a lot of questions about handicaps, is that okay?

Kyle: Sure it is, I like helping you learn about handicaps, Karri. (Turn to audience) Boys and girls, I want you to learn about handicaps too! Boys and girls, if someone can't walk because of a handicap, can you catch that?

Karri: (With audience) No!

Kyle: If someone can't talk very well because they have a handicap, can you catch that?

Karri: (With audience) No!

Appendix 6.B. (continued)

Kyle:	Boys and girls, is it okay to ask someone about their handicap?
Karri:	(With audience) Yes!
Kyle:	Can you play with someone who has a handicap?
Karri:	(With audience) Yes!
Kyle:	Do children who have handicaps like to play some of the same things you do?
Karri:	(With audience) Yes!
Kyle:	Can children who have handicaps be your friends?
Karri:	(With audience) Yes! (Alone) Just like Kyle and I are friends.
Kyle:	We are friends, Karri. (To audience) Boys and girls, can you think of any questions about handicaps you would like to ask me? (Give children a chance to ask questions) If you have other questions, ask your teacher! Thanks for learning about handicaps, boys and girls.

Karri and Kyle: Bye! Bye!

6. Role-playing is an activity which teaches children specifically how to interact with a classmate who has handicaps. Role-playing allows young children to practice new interaction skills so that their proficiency in interactions can be improved in a non-threatening, training setting. Role-play activities for young children can incorporate the use of puppets, as shown in the following vignettes.

Role-play Activities

    <u>Materials Needed:</u> Puppets which fit the particular situations and the following scripts.

    <u>Time Allowance:</u> Role-play vignettes - 5 minutes apiece.

    <u>General Description:</u> Role-playing specific vignettes provides children without handicaps with exposure to specific skills and behaviors which may enable them to more easily interact with children who have handicaps.

Sample Vignettes:

Introduction to Vignettes:

    "Today we are going to play with the puppets. You're going to show us how you can be a good friend. Let's pretend that this puppet is _____ and this puppet is _____. _____, it will be your turn first." (Have other members of the group

Appendix 6.B. (continued)

watch as the first child goes through the vignettes, and allow them to coach or make suggestions throughout.)

Vignette #1:

Setting: Puppet is playing with the blocks by himself.

"Sometimes children do not know how to ask other children to play with them. Let's see if you can be a good friend and ask _____ to play."

If child hesitates, prompt, "Can I play with you?" "Let's play," etc.

The puppet should respond appropriately to the play initiation by saying "OK" and sharing the play materials.

Praise the child for his/her response.

Vignette #2:

Setting: Puppet is in the corner by himself. Give the blocks to the target child.

"Sometimes you may be playing with some toys, and one of the children from _____ class would like to play with you. Let's see if you can be a good friend and share with _____."

Make a puppet ask, "Can I play?"

Cue the child to allow the puppet to help build something with the blocks (do not just settle for giving some of the blocks to the puppet). Praise the child for his/her response.

Vignette #3:

Setting: As child is sharing the blocks with the puppet, say: "Sometimes when you are playing with _____, he/she may try to tell you something that you can't understand. (Have puppet mumble "I want the music box.") Let's see if you can be a good friend and try to find out what _____ is trying to say."

Cue the child to:

1. Ask the puppet to repeat (have puppet repeat).

2. Ask the puppet to show what he/she wants (make puppet point to or touch the music box).

When child verbalizes that he/she understands that the puppet wants the music box, have the puppet give the child a big hug and say - "I like to be your friend."

Appendix 6.B. (continued)

Vignette #4:

Setting: The puppet is trying to play with the music box, but is fumbling with it and can't get it started.

"Sometimes your friends in _____ class may need help doing things. _____ needs help turning on the music box. Be a good friend and help _____ turn on the music box."

Prompt the child when necessary, and have the puppet say "Thank you" when the child performs the desired response.

Wrap-Up:

The puppet says "I like playing with you. You're a really good friend!"

To summarize, there are six steps for developing and implementing a peer preparation program:

1.   Decide on the objectives of the preparation program (for example, providing information about handicapping conditions generally, or providing information on a particular handicap; modeling accepting behaviors toward persons with handicaps, etc.).

2.   Select one or more activities to meet these objectives.

3. Train individual implementors to carry out these activities and have them practice the presentations.

4.   Develop a schedule for and conduct activities on an ongoing basis throughout the school year.

5. Evaluate the impact of the activities. (For example, observe the number of social interactions between children with and without handicaps, ask children about their reactions to the preparation activities, and assess children's attitudes about handicapping conditions.)

6. Encourage peers, parents, community volunteers, and other school staff to become involved in the preparation program.

Footnote

Appreciation is expressed to Connie Nelke for her assistance in developing this puppet script.

Chapter 7

. . .

The Individualized Education Program

Implementation of P.L. 99-457 is resulting in more children 3 to 5 years of age entering the public schools than ever before. The influx of students is already under way in most states. As more preschoolers with handicaps enter the schools, the need for addressing the IEP decision-making process becomes paramount, especially when school staff attempt to comply with the intent of P.L. 99-457 to provide a free, appropriate education for each child in the least restrictive environment. The philosophy espoused herein is in total compliance with P.L. 94-142 and P.L. 99-457 and emphasizes that all preschool children with handicaps can be educated in environments with their peers who are not handicapped.

P.L. 94-142 states that

> ... to the extent appropriate, handicapped children ... are educated with children who are not handicapped, and that special classes, separate schooling, or other removal of handicapped children from the regular educational environment occurs only when the nature or severity of the handicap is such that education in regular classes with the use of supplementary aids and services cannot be achieved satisfactorily. (Education for All Handicapped Children Act of 1975, 1976, p. 7)

It is assumed, based on information provided in earlier chapters, that school administrators, teachers, and selected services staff are committed to educating preschoolers in the least restrictive environment. In so doing, preschoolers with handicaps should already be riding the

171

regular school bus, entering the building through the same door as their peers, eating in the same lunchrooms at the same time as their peers, and having playtime with their peers. The purpose of this chapter is to provide administrators, principals, teachers, and related services staff with a rationale and sequential process for developing IEPs.

Required Components of an IEP

The required components of an IEP as specified in P.L. 94-142 include:

1. A statement of the present levels of educational performance of a child.
2. A statement of the annual goals and short-term instructional objectives.
3. A statement of the specific educational services to be provided and the extent of involvement in regular education.
4. The projected start date, duration, objective criteria and evaluation procedures, and progress review schedule for each objective (Education for All Handicapped Children Act of 1975, 1976).

Additional components often include a signature block for parental permission for placement which can be used to document parent participation, designation of persons responsible for each goal and objective, and a summary of testing information.

The IEP Decision-Making Process

The sequence of steps in the IEP decision-making process is shown in figures 7.1 through 7.4.

Initiating the Process

The IEP decision-making process is initiated (Figure 7.1) through the identification of a preschool child as having a handicap based on an assessment and eligibility determination. The recruitment, identification, and assessment process are discussed in Chapter 6 and again

Figure 7.1. Flowchart for Conduct of IEP Meeting

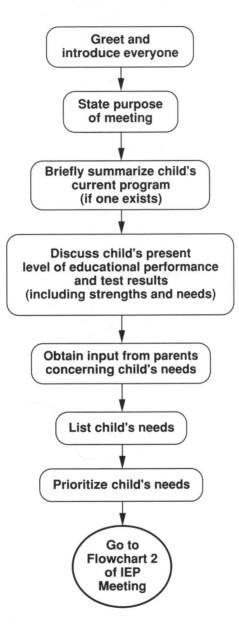

in Chapter 8; thus, they will not be discussed here. Once the assessment process has been completed, the IEP meeting can be scheduled and an IEP can be developed. Arrangements should be made to have all assessment information and forms available for the meeting, and for parents to be briefed in terms of bringing information concerning their child's strengths, needs, and possible goals.

The IEP is developed by a child study team that includes parents, the program administrator or designee, a representative teacher(s), related service personnel, sometimes the child, and an advocate or someone else deemed appropriate for participation. For the initial IEP, the examiners who determined the child's eligibility must also be present. Care should be taken to assure that persons essential to the development of the IEP are in attendance, but care should also be taken to not overwhelm parents with the sheer number of people in attendance. Parents are to be considered equal partners in the IEP process, and they often provide valuable information.

The IEP Decision-Making Meeting

A variety of tasks and considerations must be addressed during the IEP meeting. It is the IEP decision-making process that provides the essential mechanism for integrating preschoolers into classrooms with peers who are not handicapped. Appendix 7.A provides information that is useful in conducting the IEP meeting, including a self-evaluation checklist of dos and don'ts. The IEP document becomes the plan that guides program implementation and child integration.

The meeting starts out with the child study team leader/facilitator assuring that everyone has been made to feel welcome, has been introduced to everyone else, and has been provided with a comfortable place to sit. Other creature comfort amenities, such as a place to put one's coat and obtaining a cup of coffee, are also addressed.

Thereafter, the leader states the purpose of the meeting, for example, "We are here to develop an IEP for Sally Jones." A brief summary of the child's current program, if one exists, is then presented with child study team members participating as appropriate. A person is designated to be the recorder of information at the beginning of the meeting.

Present Level of Performance.   The first substantial task for the child study team is to determine the child's present level of educational performance. To accomplish this, all of the relevant assessment information collected is reviewed to determine the child's strengths and needs. It is essential to obtain input from the parents in terms of strengths and needs. Discrepancies in information should be resolved and a summary or list of the child's strengths and needs should be written. The needs should be prioritized based on a consensus by the child study team members. Needs in all five common preschool domains—cognitive, self-help, language and communication, social, and motor—should be addressed. The social area is often overlooked.

Needs. Not all identified needs are appropriate for being addressed in the school setting (Figure 7.2). Thus, the child study team must decide, "Should any of the identified needs be met in a nonschool environment?" Needs that should be addressed in other environments are those that are typically the responsibility of some other community or state agency, or a private provider. Such needs include dental services, general medical care, financial resources, needs of the family per se, and other family needs such as marital counseling. It must be remembered that some medical conditions will be addressed as part of a school program (e.g., giving medication prescribed by the family physician or feeding a child using a gavage tube). If non-school-related needs have been identified, the team leader should clarify for the parents and other team members that these needs are not within the jurisdiction of the school, and the parent should be assisted or referred to sources where such needs can be addressed (e.g., the family physician). These needs would be removed from the prioritized needs list.

Strengths. The child study team should then review the preschool child's strengths to determine which of these strengths can be enhanced or used to address the child's needs. It is important that these strengths include more than just a list of test scores. Examples of strengths that could be used to address other needs include:

1. Good pointing skills can be used to enhance object labeling.

2. Good self-help skills can be used as a context for language training.

3. Good picture identification skills can be used as a consequence (reward) for engaging in a task the child is not good at (e.g., toileting).

Goals and Objectives. A child's annual goals and short-term instructional objectives should address specific child needs identified through standardized and criterion-referenced assessment. Observable, measurable terms should be used to word goals and objectives. Moreover, care should be taken to assure that the terminology used encourages rather than discourages integration. For example, the goal, "Billy

Figure 7.2. Flowchart 2 of IEP Meeting

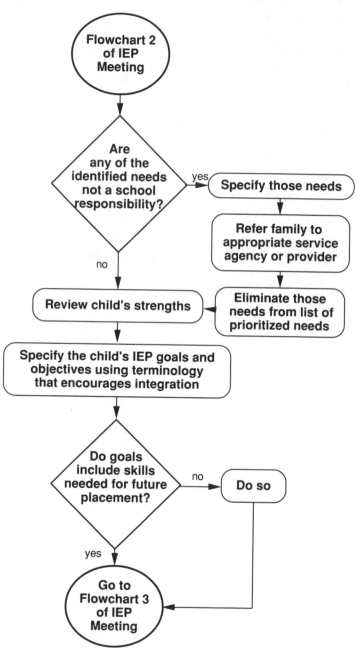

will count all objects from 1 to 10 correctly on 3 random trials. He will do so by taking turns with peers who are not handicapped," encourages integration, whereas the goal, "Judy will not hit any other child for 30 days as a condition for moving from a self-contained to an integrated classroom," discourages integration.

If the goals and objectives do not include skills that will be needed for future placement, the child study team should consider adding such goals based on when the child might transition to that next environment (e.g., the FMS model begins transition planning when the child enters the program). Goals for the future also include being ready for doing what a child will be expected to do when he or she is 1 year older (e.g., sitting in a chair and raising one's hand to be recognized).

Serious Behavior. The traditional approach in regular education programs has been to place children who act out (e.g., are aggressive) into self-contained classrooms (Gaylord-Ross, 1988). Many rationales have been used to justify such placements. The most common rationale is that the appropriate resources are not available in the regular classroom. This is often an accurate description of classroom reality; yet in fact, at the preschool level it is difficult to justify placement of the child outside of the regular integrated preschool classroom. Preschool-age children (with and without handicaps) often display aggressive behavior as a part of normal development. Aggression often serves the function of obtaining teacher or other student attention for children whose language and/or social skills have not yet developed adequately. Preschool teachers regularly teach children alternative ways of interacting.

Consider for a moment a child who is extremely aggressive, engages in life-threatening behavior, or who is medically or physically fragile. The assumption supporting removal from the regular classroom is that doing so will prevent injury, will prevent interference with other children's programs, or will result in access to more resources. Often preschool teachers underestimate the resources available to them (e.g., other children). In reality, most teachers can readily handle a child with problems such as aggression in a regular integrated preschool classroom because

1. The child is small.

2. The child's behavior is not as severe or likely to result in injury as is the behavior of an older and larger child.

3. Preschool student-to-teacher ratios are usually small.

4. The same resources are needed in either an integrated or a self-contained classroom to change the child's behavior.

The advantages in keeping such a child in an integrated classroom are that

1. Classmates are generally mobile and can remove themselves from the situation if a child is aggressive toward them. Such may not be the case in a self-contained classroom.
2. Classmates generally have sufficient language skills to inform an adult if a problem arises. Not all children in the self-contained classroom are able to do so.
3. Classmates can defend themselves if necessary, whereas some children with handicaps may be unable to do so.
4. Classmates can be told about the child's problems so that they can participate in controlling the problem behavior and/or learn how to avoid the situation. Again, some children with handicaps may be incapable of understanding a verbal explanation.

In addition, can one justify placing children who have handicaps at jeopardy when they are in greater need and at greater risk of injury? We doubt it.

If, in fact, the problem behavior is extreme (e.g., life-threatening), it will take the same type of human resources, equipment, and/or materials to control or eliminate the problem behavior in either the integrated or self-contained classroom. In summary, the real issue is deciding what resources are needed and assuring that they are available (Figure 7.3) in all settings.

Integrated Services. After each annual goal and short-term instructional objective has been specified, decisions must be made concerning the services that will be needed to address each goal and objective. The focus should be on how an integrated service can be used to achieve each goal and objective. If integrated services are not directly considered for achieving each goal and objective, it is likely that staff will rely on old habits to determine the services needed. Relying on old habit patterns will probably result in the preschool child with handicaps being served in a segregated setting. Direct attention to integrated services allows for creativity on how to achieve specific goals and objectives. Some integration service options include (a) training the skill in an integrated group, (b) using a peer tutor, (c) using a peer who

Figure 7.3. Flowchart 3 of IEP Meeting

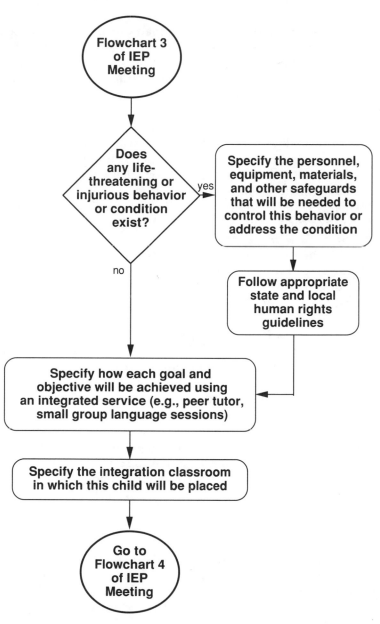

is not handicapped as a model, and (d) using a within-class microsession that includes one peer.

Selecting the Classroom.   If more than one integrated preschool class-room is available within a school, the next task for the child study team is to select the classroom in which the specific child will be placed. This can be done on the basis of available slots for children, person-alities, parent preference, or other variables, as long as the child's needs are addressed in the least restrictive environment.

Other IEP Tasks.   Once a classroom assignment and teacher have been agreed on, the child study team can specify how each goal and objective will be monitored, when services for each goal and objective will be initiated, the duration of service, and when progress will be reviewed. Formal reviews at the preschool level typically occur twice per year because of the rapid progress possible. Formal review information is added to the IEP document.

Other concerns of team members are also addressed at this point (Figure 7.4). Parents should be an integral part of all IEP development activities, because they will often be involved in conducting home pro-grams. See Chapter 5 for more information on parent involvement.

Finalizing the IEP.   The only IEP task remaining is to assure that all of the information is on the IEP document, that team members sign the document, and that team members (especially parents) know how to contact each other. Parents should be provided with a signed copy of the IEP. Striefel and Cadez (1983a) review additional information relevant to IEP development.

Sample IEP.   A partially completed sample IEP is shown in Figure 7.5. The goals are worded to encourage integration. Appendix 7.B includes a copy of the instructions and blank IEP forms.

Straw Men

Those who wish to avoid integrating preschool children into integrated classrooms have created many straw men. A straw man, as used here, is an excuse or rationale that is not in keeping with the intent of P.L. 94-142 and/or P.L. 99-457. These straw men include:

1. "I don't have the skills needed to work with that child." The lack of skills is not a justifiable reason for relegating a child to a

Figure 7.4. Flowchart 4 of IEP meeting

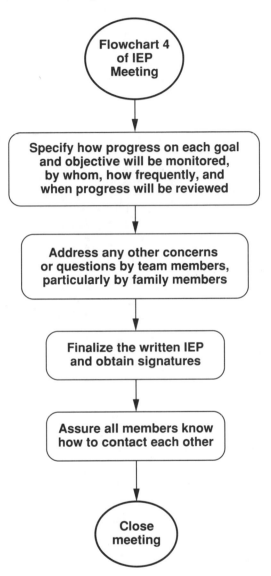

Figure 7.5. Sample Completed IEP Forms

IEP FORMS

Mountainland **School District**
Individualized Education Program (IEP)

Handicapping Condition: Preschool Handicapped
Referral Date: Aug. 8, 1988
Initial Classification Date: 8/3/88

Demographic Information

Student: Judy Smith Birthdate: Aug. 1, 1985 Parent/Guardian: Harold & Mary Smith Primary Language: English

Address: 512 Integration Avenue, Logan, UT Phone: 750-1100

School: Johnson Elementary Grade: Preschl Initial IEP Date: 8/30/88 Mid-Year Review Date: 2/1/89 End of Year Evaluation Date: 5/29/89

Testing and Assessment

Test/Assessment	Date administered	Results	Examiner
Batelle Developmental Inventory	8/12/88	Overall Functioning at 18-21 month level.	Bob Clark
Peabody Motor Development Scales	8/12/88	Gross Motor Skills at about 32 months and Fine Motor Skills at 20-24 month level	Molly Motor
Program Assessment and Planning Guide	8/15/88	Functioning at 2 year level on dressing and feeding; Her expressive language skills are at 20-30 month level	Sue Brooks
Sequential Inventory of Communication Skills	8/22/88	Receptive language at 30-32 month level, Expressive language at 20-24 month level	Lori Carson

Justification for Placement Overall functioning 12-15 months below chronological age level, with some highs and lows in some skill areas; needs intensive intervention to remediate developmental delays, and formal social interaction training with peers who are not handicapped.

Present Levels of Social and Academic Performance Judy does not initiate social contact but responds to initiations by others. She attends well and can work in large groups. She follows simple directions, and has a vocabulary of about 10 words. Judy's fine motor skills are about 1 year delayed, and she is non-aggressive. She lacks many self-help skills.

Figure 7.5. (continued)

Student _____ Judy Smith

Strengths and Needs

Student's Strengths   Attends to others' directives and materials, is cooperative and does fine in groups, responds to social initiations, smiles at others, can walk, is toilet trained and has good gross motor skills, imitates gross motor behaviors. Has no aggressive, disruptive, or offensive behaviors

Student's Needs   Lacks skills in tying shoes, buttoning, feeding, personal hygiene. Needs to learn additional vocabulary items and to combine words. Needs to initiate social contact. Evaluation for possible seizures.

Prioritized Needs	Is need a nonschool responsibility?	If Yes, Referrals for nonschool needs / If No, Child's strengths that can be used to improve need areas
1. Evaluation for seizures	(Yes)/ No	Refer to family Pediatrician.
2. Learning additional vocabulary	Yes /(No)	Cooperativeness, willingness to follow instructions, imitation skills.
3. Self feeding	Yes /(No)	Attending, gross motor, and imitation skills.
4. Dressing skills	Yes /(No)	Attending, gross motor, and imitation skills.
5. Initiation social contact	Yes /(No)	Willingness to follow instructions, respond to initiation by others.
6. Personal hygiene	Yes /(No)	Attending, gross motor, and imitation skills.
7. Combining words	Yes /(No)	Existing vocabulary, imitation skills.
8.	Yes / No	
9.	Yes / No	
10.	Yes / No	
11.	Yes / No	
12.	Yes / No	
13.	Yes / No	
14.	Yes / No	
15.	Yes / No	

Does the prioritized list of needs include skill development for future placements?   (Yes)/ No

If not, include needs that address skill development for future placements.

Figure 7.5. (continued)

Annual Goal No.* __1__ **which assesses prioritized need number** __2__

Person(s) Responsible Sue Brooks

Goal Judy will increase her vocabulary from 10 words to 60 words. She will use these words correctly to label objects and make spontaneous requests, and will do so in the presence of her peers.

Is the goal worded to encourage mainstreaming? (Yes) / No   If no, reword.

Special Services and Adaptive Equipment Needed Language therapy and occupational therapy. No adaptive equipment needed.

Mainstreaming Placements Where The Goal Can Be Accomplished Any of three integrated preschool classrooms in the school.

Most appropriate placement for this goal __Ms. Brooks' classroom__ Is it an integrated placement? (Yes) / No
If not, give justification why an integrated placement was not made.

Short-Term Instructional Objectives	Criteria	Dates Started	Dates Mastered	Schedule and Evaluation Procedures
1- When presented with the following objects and an exaggerated verbal model of its label, Judy will imitate the words correctly: arm, hand, boy, girl, shoe, dress, milk, coke, bed, ball, cup, doll, chair, eye, and 36 other words from objectives 53 & 55 of PAPG.	Correct imitation of all 50 words on 5 separate days, across 3 trainers.	9/1/88	12/1/88	Weekly probe of all words.
2- When presented with the objects from objective 1 above and asked "What is this?" Judy will label each item correctly.	Correct labeling of all 50 objects on 5 separate days, across 3 trainers.	12/2/88	3/1/89	Weekly probe of all objects.
3- In the presence of objects listed in objectives 1 & 2 and asked questions such as, "What do you want?" or "What do we drink?" Judy will correctly identify the desired or appropriate object.	Correct responding to questions related to each object on 5 separate days, across 3 trainers.	3/2/89	in progress	Weekly probe of all items.
4-				

* A separate sheet is used for each goal.

Figure 7.5. (continued)

Mid-Year Progress Notes

Obj. 1-
Judy correctly imitated the labels for all 50 objects designated
by this goal and spontaneously began imitating others' words.

Obj. 2-
Judy correctly labeled 37 of the objects specified in this
objective and spontaneously labels other objects in her
environment.

Obj. 3-
No training on this objective has occurred yet.

Obj. 4-

End of Year Evaluation

Obj. 1-
See mid-year notes, continue weekly/monthly maintenance probes.

Obj. 2-
Judy correctly labels all 50 objects specified for the objective
and spontaneously labels at least 40 other objects.

Obj. 3-
Judy responds correctly to questions concerning 47 of the 50
objects. It is anticipated that she will master the 3 remaining items
within a week.

Obj. 4-

Figure 7.5. (continued)

Signature Section for IEP Team

IEP Team Members

Name	Title	Phone #	Initial IEP Signature	Date	Mid-year Review Signature	Date
Harold Smith	Parent/Guardian	753-3706	*	8/30/88	*	2/1/89
Mary Smith	Parent/Guardian	753-3706		8/30/88		2/1/89
Sue Brooks	Teacher	753-4020		8/30/88		2/1/89
Bob Clark	Psychologist	753-4020		8/30/88		2/1/89
Lori Carson	Language Therapist	753-4020		8/30/88		2/1/89
Molly Motor	Occupational Therapist	753-4020		8/30/88		2/1/89
Larry Carpenter	LEA Representative	752-4021		8/30/88		2/1/89

Summary of Mid-year IEP Review and Evaluation Meeting

Judy is making good progress in all goal areas. She has learned to button, to feed herself, to use verbal labels, to initiate social contact, and to combine words. She has made several friends who interact with her in the preschool, and Mrs. Smith reports that the children invite Judy to participate in neighborhood sports.

* Note in a completed IEP all team members listed would have signed in this section.

self-contained program. School districts are responsible for assuring that their staff receive the training they need to educate the children in their classroom and/or access to technical experts in the form of consultants.

2. "I don't have enough staff, or the right kind of staff." The lack of sufficient members or types of staff (e.g., a physical therapist) is not recognized in the law as a justifiable reason for not meeting a child's needs. The school is responsible for hiring the staff or using volunteers to assure that the child receives a free, appropriate education.

3. "This child will hurt other children in my classroom." This excuse implies that it is okay if a child with handicaps injures another child with handicaps but not okay if a child who is not handicapped is injured. In reality, appropriate resources and safeguards should be available to prevent injury to all children.

4. "This child's behavior will disrupt the education of the other children in the class." Whereas it is true that a new child may disrupt the flow of classroom activities temporarily, the disruption is generally no different whether a child does or does not have a handicap. Again, it is discriminatory to assume it is okay to disrupt the education of other children who have handicaps but not the education of those who don't have handicaps. Moreover, children who are not handicapped are usually less subject to distraction and can be kept on task via verbal instructions to do so.

5. "The child who has handicaps will have no friends, or will be ridiculed or endangered by the activities of the other children." In fact, the available data show that this seldom happens, especially at the preschool level. When it does occur, it is often due to the teacher not educating the students on how to interact appropriately with others. Informing students as to the teacher's expectations and then following problem behaviors with specific consequences typically eliminates such problems rapidly.

6. "The behavior or appearance of the child who has handicaps will shock the other children." Part of an educational process is to prepare individuals to deal with their environment and those in it. Exposure to individual differences in appearances and behavior, even when extreme, provides an opportunity to educate children on accepting such differences as a fact of life. Preventing children from having such contacts leads to many misunderstandings and the development of prejudices about those who are different.

Teachers are models and model appropriate behavior and prepare children for the entry of a child who is different in advance of the child's arrival in the classroom.

7. "My classroom is inaccessible, has insufficient space, and/or is inadequate in some other way." Such a statement is at best indicative of a lack of administrative support and is a violation of Section 504 of The Rehabilitation Act of 1973.

8. "My class is already too large. I can't have a child like this added." Class size is a real problem in many schools. Yet, schools commonly add one more student to a class rather than start a new class because of financial factors. Excluding a child who has handicaps when a child who is not handicapped would be accepted is discrimination. The best solution would be to have fewer children per class. For cost reasons, that is generally not likely to occur. A second potential solution is to integrate children who have handicaps into the classroom and send an aide with them. So doing would provide additional assistance in the classroom not only for the child who has handicaps, but also for the other children.

9. "The dollars or services needed to educate this child are not available." The lack of dollars or services is not acceptable. The law mandates that all children who have handicaps will receive a free, appropriate education in the least restrictive environment. Thus, services must be created, and the dollars located within the local or state education agency.

Appendix 7.A.

The Mainstream I.E.P.

A Training Program for Administrators,
Teachers, and Other Specialists

Introduction

On the following pages, you will find an outline of basic ideas that promote the concept of educating children with handicaps in integrated preschool classrooms (least restrictive environment). Integrated education may consist of educating children who are not handicapped in the regular or reverse mainstreaming (special education) classroom.

It is suggested that you, the reader, first respond to the questions on the Self-Evaluation Checklist, then compare your responses to the ideas raised in the brief discussion following each question.

The questions and discussions herein are designed to help the concerned professional in his or her efforts to encourage parents to become active, informed participants at the I.E.P. meeting. With the support and contributions of parents who feel that they are welcome and valued members of their child's team, the decisions made at the team meetings are certain to increase the likelihood of benefiting the child. This training is also aimed at guiding educators and parents in the IEP decision-making process by examining a child's program in individual need areas. Preschool children with handicaps have a wide range of skills, and can and should be integrated into classrooms with children who do not have handicaps for all of the school day. Any child with sufficient skills deserves a chance to be integrated and thus to become more independent.

Discussion

Before the Meeting ...

Remember the feeling of returning to class after a long absence, or the feeling of being the new kid in class? That feeling of being left out, or of having less information about what is happening, is a feeling that many parents share at I.E.P. time. The rest of the IEP team often have test results and they discuss the child's progress regularly in less formal settings. However, the parents do not have this information unless they are sent copies of evaluation reports. Informed parents are not only equipped to develop goals and objectives, but they also become more understanding of the job of the educator or specialist.

One way to structure parent preparation and participation is by sending home copies of evaluation reports and by sending a form on which parents can write goals and/or objectives they would like their children to achieve. Parents should be asked to bring these written goals and objectives to the IEP meeting.

At the Start of the Meeting ...

Very few sensitive professionals introduce themselves to parents by title only. Using a title, or leading an introduction with one's title, immediately sets the professional apart from the parent, and places the professional in a position of authority that the parent cannot share.

Appendix 7.A. (continued)

One suggested way to work around the name/title issues while assuring that the parent knows everyone's role at the meeting would be to lead an introduction with first and last name, then state one's relationship to the child. For example, "I am Mary Jones, Tommy's occupational therapist (speech and language pathologist, teacher, etc.)." This format allows the parent to share a position of equality with others in the team.

We often assume that everyone knows why the meeting is being held. However, this may not always be the case, and parents are not always the only team members who need this information. Administrators from other agencies and teachers who may be representing a potential integrated setting are not necessarily as well versed in special education procedures and terminology as those who use this expertise daily. A feeling of teamwork can be created by briefly reviewing the purpose of the meeting for all present, and then encouraging their active participation throughout the meeting by directing questions to different individuals at different times, and by having everyone contribute something early in the meeting. Talking early in a meeting sets a pattern of participation for the rest of the session.

During the Meeting ...

Every agency that serves children with handicaps establishes a routine which is comfortable for people in that system. In reviewing your own procedures, keep these thoughts in mind:

A "Round Robin" system of reporting information is one where each team member reports information while others wait quietly for their turn. Although this system is orderly and quick, it creates a fragmented, piecemeal picture of a child. It also places the parent in a lesser position since the parent does not have a neatly organized, formal report and presentation during his or her "turn." An alternative approach is for the team leader to introduce an area (for example, communication skills) and have all the team members contribute information concerning the child's communication within their domain, such as how the child understands instruction during a motor activity. In this situation, the language specialists would still provide the bulk of progress and test data, but others would be expected to contribute to a total view of the child's use of functional communication skills.

In reporting test results, it is important for all team members to know why a test was chosen. A brief statement would be sufficient for this purpose, and shows that careful thought was given to the assessment of the child as an individual.

It is more meaningful to a person who is not familiar with testing to hear results as ranges of ability, such as, "He recognized single words which I read to him about as well as a two-and-a-half-year-old child," rather than using precise numbers and technical terms such as, "He is functioning at a 2.6 age equivalent in receptive language." By stating results in common language, we avoid having to explain our terms and avoid inadvertently placing parents and others in the group in the lesser position of having to be educated in special education terminology. The explanation of terms, although commonly considered a courtesy, can actually backfire by emphasizing the parents' lack of knowledge and setting them further apart from the team.

Although we are commonly told to speak directly to parents, this courtesy can also work against team functioning. In a team, it is important that the speaker address everyone in the group. By targeting one individual and directing reports and questions to that person, we imply by our actions that the individual is the one who needs our information and everyone else either is uninterested or already has the information

Appendix 7.A. (continued)

being provided. Even if this is so, it is advisable to scan the room and make eye contact equally with all members in order to foster a feeling of involvement.

It is a well-known fact that questions which can be answered with yes or no do not encourage active participation. It would be more helpful to parents and other team members if questions were phrased so that responses required some thought. Open-ended questions often provide the most information about a particular child since they stimulate people to respond. They also give parents more flexibility for contributing information from the perspective of someone who knows the child intimately well in the home setting, a setting which professionals often do not see. An example of open-ended questions could be, "What questions or concerns do you have about these test results?" instead of, "Do you understand these test results?"

Never refer to a parent as "Mom" or "Dad" unless all other team members are equally addressed by role, such as "Teacher," "Occupational Therapist," "Psychologist," etc.

At the End of the Meeting ...

It is almost impossible in a large group to assimilate all of the information as it is presented in the meeting. For this reason, it is imperative that someone summarize the child's program and progress at the end of the meeting. In so doing, this person presents a total picture of the child. This summary should include current placement, overall progress, recommendations, and changes in future placement.

Although communication with parents is often left to the teacher, every professional in the room should be accessible to the parent. It is important for parents to feel that they can contact any team member with the same ease that people within the same building can communicate with each other. One suggested way to accomplish this is to list names, specialty areas, and phone numbers for the parent and for any other team member who wishes this information. This list can be generated by circulating a sign-up sheet at the meeting, or by writing telephone numbers by the signatures on the I.E.P. and giving a copy of the I.E.P. to the parent. It is also particularly useful to identify one key person on the list for the parent to use as a general contact. This person will generally be the teacher, although another contact can serve the purpose just as well, as long as the person is well acquainted with the child's program.

Appendix 7.A. (continued)

The I.E.P. Process: A Self-Checklist

Circle the appropriate letter for each item. Y = yes, N = no.

Before the Meeting ...

Y   N   Do I send the parent enough test, program, and progress information so the parent can develop goals and objectives?

Y   N   Do I give the parent a form for recording goals and objectives and for bringing them to the I.E.P. meeting in written form?

At the Start of the Meeting ...

Y   N   Do I introduce myself to parents using first and last name, followed by relationship to the child?

Y   N   Do I know the parents' first and last names?

Y   N   Do I assure the parents that their input is essential and is welcome?

Y   N   Do all team members know the reason(s) for the meeting?

During the Meeting ...

Y   N   In reporting test results, program data, and other child information, do all members contribute information in each area rather than reporting individually (one person at a time) while others wait in silence for their turn?

Y   N   When I report age or grade equivalents, do I use phrases such as, "Talking like most two-year-olds"?

Y   N   Do I speak and make eye contact with all team members?

Y   N   Do I explain the reason(s) why I chose a specific test?

Y   N   Do I ask the parent to add information from home that relates to the information given about school performance?

Y   N   Do I avoid referring to the parents as "Mom" or "Dad"?

Y   N   Do I check with the parents during the meeting to assure that they understand what is being said or decided?

Y   N   Do I ask open-ended questions?

At the End of the Meeting ...

Y   N   Do I, or another appointed person, summarize what was decided?

Y   N   Do I make provisions for follow-up communication with the parent?

Appendix 7.A. (continued)

Individualized Education Program
Parental Involvement in Goal Setting
VSSM

Dear

Your child's IEP (Individualized Education Program) is being developed or revised. The term "individualized education program" means a written statement of instruction especially designed to meet the unique needs of your child. You, as a parent, are an important part of the IEP development. We need your participation in developing goals for your child.

To help you think about your child's strengths and needs, there is a brief description of the six areas of a child's development and some examples of goals in each area.

We'll share our ideas at the IEP meeting on _____
at _____
It would be extremely helpful if you could return this form before the IEP meeting. If you are unable to do so, please be sure to bring it with you when you attend.

A.   **Gross Motor:** Your child's ability to move his body (e.g., walking up stairs, running, throwing and catching a ball). Example of a gross motor goal: My child will be able to catch a ball.

     1. _____
     2. _____
     3. _____
     4. _____

B.   **Fine Motor:** Your child's ability to use his hands (e.g., turn pages, handwriting, cutting figures with scissors). Example of a fine motor goal: My child will be able to write his name.

     1. _____
     2. _____
     3. _____
     4. _____

Appendix 7.A. (continued)

C. **Self-Help:** Your child's ability to care for himself (e.g., toileting, dressing, brushing teeth, eating). <u>Example</u> of a self-help goal: My child will be able to brush his teeth by himself.

    1. _____

    2. _____

    3. _____

    4. _____

D. **Language/Speech:** Your child's ability to understand and respond to people around him or her. This does not necessarily refer to only talking, as there are other ways children do communicate (e.g., activity stops when hearing "NO," responds to own name, speaks clearly). <u>Example</u> of a language/speech goal: My child speaks clearly so that strangers can understand him.

    1. _____

    2. _____

    3. _____

    4. _____

E. **Social/Behavioral:** Your child's ability to interact and get along with other people (e.g., plays with other children, follows rules, complies with adult requests). <u>Example</u> of a social/behavioral goal: My child will play cooperatively with other children.

    1. _____

    2. _____

    3. _____

    4. _____

F. **Cognitive:** Your child's ability to think and figure out how to do things by himself (e.g., matching objects, working with numbers, reading). <u>Example</u> of a cognitive goal: My child will be able to count to 20.

    1. _____

    2. _____

    3. _____

    4. _____

Which of the above areas do you feel are most important?

_____

Appendix 7.B.

Instructions and IEP Forms

Gary Percival, Sebastian Striefel,
Brooki Sexton, & Joel Allred

Rationale

The FMS model outlines a specific process for conducting an IEP meeting. Specific information is needed during this process and can be recorded on the IEP Forms. The purpose of this process is to identify the services that will allow the child with handicaps to be placed in an integrated preschool classroom while meeting the needs of the child with handicaps and without detracting from the education of the child's peers.

Instructions

The following steps outline the information that is to be recorded on the attached IEP forms.

Step 1: Demographic Information

Demographic information for the student, family, and school should be listed in the appropriate spaces provided. Starting from the top of the first page of the IEP Form, the demographic information should be listed as follows: a) the student's handicapping condition, b) the date the student was referred to special education (referral date), c) the student's inital classification, d) the name of the school district which the student attends, e) the student's name, f) the student's birthdate, g) the student's parent or guardian, h) the primary language spoken by the student, i) the student's address and address of the student's parent or guardian if different from the student, j) the student's home phone number and phone number of the student's parent or guardian if different from the student, k) the name of the school that the student attends, l) the student's grade level, and m) the date that the IEP meeting takes place. The Mid-Year review date and the End of the Year Evaluation should be added in the space provided when these meetings occur.

Step 2: Testing and Assessment

A list of all formal and informal assessments that were completed on the student should be recorded in the space provided along with the date of the assessment, the results of the assessment, and the person who conducted the assessment.

Step 3: Justification for Placement

The justification for the child's placement should be recorded on the IEP forms. This information will help direct the IEP team in formulating appropriate goals and objectives for the student. It will also allow the IEP Team to justify any decision made during the IEP Meeting.

Appendix 7.B. (continued)

Step 4: Student's Social and Academic Performance

From the testing and assessments completed, the student's current social and academic preformance should be summarized in the space provided. This information will help in explaining the results of the testing to the student's parents/guardians. It will also help the IEP Team in identifying services that will enable the student to maximize his or her progress.

Step 5: Student's Strengths and Needs

From the testing and assessment results, input from the IEP Team and the student's parents/guardians, the student's strengths and needs should be determined. Determining the student's strengths is important because all too often strengths are overlooked and allowed to degress. Also student strengths can be used to motivate the student to work on need areas. Record the strengths in the space so labeled.

The student's needs should be determined, recorded, and then prioritized. The list of prioritized needs should include skill development for future placements. Most students have many need areas and it is impossible to work on all needs within the course of one school year. It is important to prioritize the student's needs so the most important need areas can be identified and remediated. Once the needs are identified and prioritized it is essential to identify the needs which are not a school responsibility. The parents or guardians should be referred to the appropriate service agency for meeting the non-school needs. For each of the remaining needs any of the student's strengths that can be used to help remediate the need area should be listed. This will help the IEP Team to develop goals and objectives that will work on the student's deficit areas, using and maintaining strength areas wherever possible.

Step 6: Goals and Objectives

The IEP Team should now develop and record IEP Goals and Objectives on the IEP forms. The Goals should address at least one of the prioritized needs and should be worded to encourage integration. The person or persons responsible for the completion of the goal should be determined and listed.

Once the goal is identified any special services and/or adaptive equipment that the student needs to complete the goal should be determined and listed. A list of all mainstreaming options where the goal can be accomplished should be listed and the most appropriate placement should be determined. If the most appropriate placement is not an integrated placement then justification should be given for not making an integrated placement.

Once the placement is determined the short-term objectives, criteria, and evaluation procedures should be determined and listed. These objectives should break the IEP goal into steps that can be accomplished in the specified placement. If the specified placement is not an integrated placement then the objectives should develop skills that will allow the child to be placed in an integrated placement in the future.

Appendix 7.B. (continued)

Step 7: Signatures

All members of the IEP Team should sign and date the IEP Form for the inital IEP meeting. IEP Team members should also provide their position/title and phone number so that future contacts between IEP Team members are possible.

Step 8: Mid-Year and End of the Year Evaluations

A Mid-Year IEP Evaluation Meeting of the IEP Team should be conducted. On the back of each IEP goal sheet there is space provided to indicate progress toward each objective and to make any needed changes in the goals or objectives. A summary of the mid-year IEP meeting should be recorded on the IEP forms and signatures of the IEP members should be obtained for the mid-year review.

The End of the Year Evaluation is the beginning of the testing and assessment for the next year's IEP. Progress toward each goal should be noted on the back of each IEP goal sheet from the initial IEP meeting. No signatures of the IEP Team members are required as they will be obtained on the inital IEP form for the next year.

Appendix 7.B. (continued)

IEP FORMS

School District
Individualized Education Program (IEP)

Demographic Information

Student _____ Birthdate _____ Parent/Guardian _____

Handicapping Condition _____
Referral Date _____
Initial Classification Date _____

Primary Language _____

Address _____

Phone _____

School _____ Grade _____ Initial IEP Date _____ Mid-Year Review Date _____ End of Year Evaluation Date _____

Testing and Assessment

Test/Assessment	Date administered	Results	Examiner

Justification for Placement

_____
_____
_____

Present Levels of Social and Academic Performance

_____
_____
_____

Appendix 7.B. (continued)

Student _____

Strengths and Needs

Student's Strengths _____

_____

Student's Needs _____

_____

Prioritized Needs	Is need a nonschool responsibility?	If Yes, Referrals for nonschool needs If No, Child's strengths that can be used to improve need areas
1.	Yes / No	
2.	Yes / No	
3.	Yes / No	
4.	Yes / No	
5.	Yes / No	
6.	Yes / No	
7.	Yes / No	
8.	Yes / No	
9.	Yes / No	
10.	Yes / No	
11.	Yes / No	
12.	Yes / No	
13.	Yes / No	
14.	Yes / No	
15.	Yes / No	

Does the prioritized list of needs include skill development for future placements?   Yes / No

If not, include needs that address skill development for future placements.

Appendix 7.B. (continued)

Annual Goal No.* _____ which assesses prioritized need number _____

Goal _____

Is the goal worded to encourage mainstreaming?   Yes / No   If no, reword.

Special Services and Adaptive Equipment Needed _____

Mainstreaming Placements Where The Goal Can Be Accomplished _____

Most appropriate placement for this goal _____   Is it an integrated placement?   Yes / No

If not, give justification why an integrated placement was not made. _____

Short-Term Instructional Objectives	Criteria	Dates Started	Dates Mastered	Schedule and Evaluation Procedures	Person(s) Responsible
1-					
2-					
3-					
4-					

* A separate sheet is used for each goal.

Appendix 7.B. (continued)

End of Year Evaluation

Obj. 1-

Obj. 2-

Obj. 3-

Obj. 4-

Mid-Year Progress Notes

Obj. 1-

Obj. 2-

Obj. 3-

Obj. 4-

Appendix 7.B. (continued)

Signature Section for IEP Team

IEP Team Members

Name	Title	Phone #	Initial IEP Signature	Date	Mid-year Review Signature	Date
	Parent/Guardian					
	Parent/Guardian					

Summary of Mid-year IEP Review and Evaluation Meeting

Chapter 8

●　●　●

The FMS Integrated Service Delivery Model

The following six steps have been used successfully by staff implement-ing the FMS model to achieve effective functional groupings in inte-grated settings using a combination of developmental curricula and special education intervention.

1. Assess children for instructional program needs and demands of future environments.

2. Develop IEPs to determine individual goals, objectives, and teach-ing intensities or groupings of students for instruction.

3. Develop microsessions.

4. Plan coincidental teaching opportunities.

5. Organize daily and weekly schedule.

6. Design and implement systematic peer interventions.

Step 1: Assessment

Assessment in preschool special education serves many purposes including child find, determining eligibility, instructional program development, and evaluation (Behl, 1988). Typically, child find and eligibility assessments are conducted using standardized instruments by examiners who are unfamiliar with the child and the child's family. Young children in novel settings are often difficult to test for a variety of reasons including apprehension to interact with strangers, inadequate levels of expressive and receptive language, and a general disinterest in the testing situation. Few standardized assessments detail the specific task-analyzed sequences of behaviors that are needed for establishing individualized instructional programs for children. As a result, the need for additional criterion-referenced assessments by classroom staff is critical. In the FMS model, criterion-referenced testing goes beyond assessment of a child for deficits in general areas of development to include identification of the demands and skills needed for increasing success in children's future least restrictive environments and for transition planning.

Traditional Criterion-Referenced Testing

Criterion-referenced testing is conducted in all areas of general skill development, including cognitive, motor, language, self-help, social/ emotional, and behavioral domains, to identify child deficits and strengths. Criterion-referenced tests typically used include the *Brigance Diagnostic Inventory of Early Development* (Brigance, 1978), the *Program Assessment and Planning Guide for Developmentally Disabled and Preschool Children* (Striefel & Cadez, 1983b), *Developmental Programming for Infants and Young Children* (Schaefer & Moersch, 1981), and the *Peabody Developmental Motor Scales* (Folio & Fewell, 1983).

Assessment of the Demands of Future Environments

Assessing the demands of future environments is conducted with the MESA-PK, *The Mainstreaming Expectations and Skills Assessment–Preschool and Kindergarten* (Killoran, Striefel, Quintero, & Yanito, 1986), found in Appendix 8.A. The MESA-PK provides educators involved in integration with a global picture of a child's skill level and the demands of potential future placement. It can also be used as a guide for identifying and training those child skills that are critical for successful functioning in normalized environments for IEP development and for identifying areas in which teachers need technical assistance and support.

Step 2: Reviewing IEPs and Developing Instructional Groups

IEP development, as discussed in Chapter 7, is consistent with current best practice. It stresses with equal emphasis remediation of present deficits, as well as teaching skills for transition and success in future settings. Criterion- and future-referenced assessment data are used to identify specific goals and objectives, intervenors, and settings, and to identify the intensity or grouping in which each skill will be taught.

The FMS model uses three specific grouping techniques for delivering instruction in integrated classrooms: large group instruction, small group instruction, and microsessions. In addition, incidental and coincidental teaching is used throughout the day to teach new skills and to generalize and transfer previously learned skills to new settings and trainers. The teaching intensity or grouping to be used for each short-term objective is identified and coded as large or small groups, microsessions, or to be taught coincidentally. General concepts, attending skills, classroom survival skills, readiness skills, and social activities are initially introduced and taught in large groups. Small groups are used to facilitate specific skill development and acquisition, usually in an identified deficit area that is not being achieved in large groups. Large and small group instruction are conducted as integrated activities with nonhandicapped peers serving as models, tutors, and buddies.

If a child is not progressing at acceptable rates in a particular skill in group instruction, or if the child's IEP team has determined an immediate need, the child is moved to special instruction referred to as microsessions. Microsessions are conducted within the classroom rather than in separate therapy rooms or isolated settings. Nonhandicapped peers are used as tutors and models within microsessions as often as possible.

Large Group Instruction

In large group instruction (16 children), all children work on similar activities using similar materials and methods within the group. An example would include opening circle, when calendar skills, names, and other general concepts are taught. However, instruction for students with handicaps is individualized in the large group to include varying cues, responses, and reinforcers for children, introducing skills as task-analyzed steps rather than general concepts and using incidental teaching and direct instruction techniques as needed. Data are collected through nonobtrusive pre-/posttests, probes, anecdotal recording, and checklists on a weekly basis or as testing naturally occurs throughout the school year.

Skills taught within individualized large groups are coded on a child's IEP as LG. Instruction is delivered through a developmental group approach such as unit-based themes, which are commercially available or teacher made. Commercially prepared direct instruction programs such as *DISTAR Language* (Englemann & Osborn, 1976) or the *Peabody Early Experiences Kit* (Dunn et al., 1976) may also be used. Incidental/coincidental instruction is used to teach new and previously learned skills in nonstructured time such as large group free play. Progress is monitored through unobtrusive pre-/posttests, checklists, and weekly probes.

Small Group Instruction

Children with handicaps are also taught specific skills identified on their IEP in integrated individualized small groups of two to six children (coded on the IEP as SG), in which children without handicaps also share learning experiences appropriate to their developmental levels. Children with handicaps who are developmentally similar are placed into groups where their abilities correspond with the abilities of their nonhandicapped peers within the group. Instruction is presented incidentally, through discrete trial training and/or direct instruction. Data probes are collected on a regular basis by rotating the skills and/or the children on whom data are being collected during that particular training session. Fewer trials are sampled than in microsessions, but enough information is collected to make decisions on a child's progress and the need for instructional program revision. Skills most often taught in small groups include cognitive, fine motor, language, readiness, transition, and self-help skills. Although groups are established around a particular skill, each child's instruction is individualized. For instance, in a self-help group two children may be working on fastening, one on taking off a shirt, one on putting on shoes, and two serving as models or tutors. In a cognitive group, two children may be matching letters, one identifying letters by pointing, two copying letters independently, and one child may be writing his or her name independently.

Step 3: Developing Microsessions

Microsessions, originally conceptualized by the Social Integration Project (Stowitschek, Striefel, & Boswell, 1981), are typically used (a) with children who are making insufficient progress toward IEP goals and objectives in group instruction; (b) when an individual child's skill deficit is so severe the IEP team determines the need for immediate intensive instruction; or (c) when particular intervention, such as toileting, may be inappropriate or intrusive to deliver in a group setting.

Microsessions are defined as individual or small group (2) instructional sessions, usually lasting only 5 to 10 minutes. They use a planned instructional sequence to address specific short-term objectives identified within the student's IEP. An advantage of microsessions is that they employ traditional behavioral special education components, including assessment, identification of specific stimuli or cues, identification of specific child responses desired, correction procedures, reinforcement procedures, and ongoing child progress monitoring for instructional decision-making. Skills to be taught in microsessions are coded as MS and reflect critical skill deficits that demand immediate and intensive behavioral special education. Instructional decisions (e.g., changing a child's reinforcers or schedule of reinforcement) are made at the end of each training session for immediate implementation within the next session. Microsessions are used to teach a child's most critical deficits and have most often been used for articulation, gross motor, feeding, and cognitive programming. Nonhandicapped peers are frequently used as peer tutors and models during microsession training.

A second advantage in the use of microsessions is that the procedure has been designed as a means of systematically training professionals, instructional aides, and paraprofessionals in validated techniques and can be used to transfer instructional programs from teachers and consultants to paraprofessionals and volunteers. This training is conducted during the regularly scheduled teaching session with the specific child for which the microsession was developed and requires only weekly supervision by the classroom teacher when the training and transfer procedures are completed. Developing microsessions and training paraprofessionals in their implementation are specifically described in the *Microsession Training and Transfer Procedural Manual* (Killoran et al., 1987) developed by the Social Integration Project, which may be obtained by contacting the second author.

The first step in developing a microsession is the completion of a Program Data Sheet (Figure 8.1). This form is the actual program and data collection system that the teacher will utilize when implementing the microsession. This program/data sheet is composed of six parts:

1. Setting/materials—Describes where the program should be conducted and lists all materials needed for implementation. The developer should build in generalization of the skill whenever possible.

Figure 8.1. Program Data Sheet

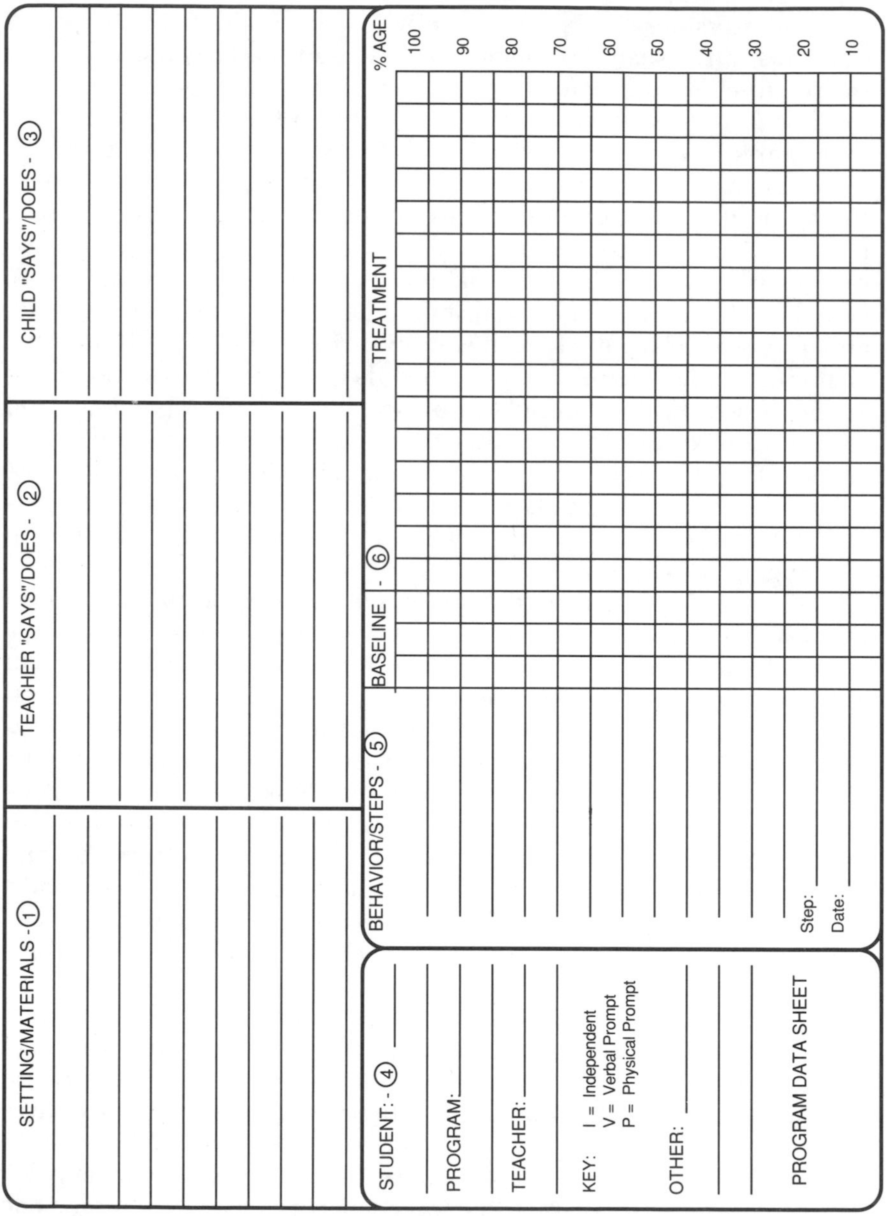

2. Teacher Says/Does—States exactly what the teacher says to the student and what the teacher does with materials, correction procedures, and so on.

3. Child Says/Does—Utilized for listing all acceptable student responses. Again, the teacher should strive for generalization.

4. Demographics—Includes student, teacher, and program names; keys for scoring student responses; and miscellaneous information.

5. Behavior/Steps—Converts all subobjectives of the skill to be taught during the microsession to verbal prompts. Verbal prompts should be succinct statements, calling for a single response. When chained together, they lead to acquisition of the short-term objectives.

6. Data System—Used to record a student response as (a) independent, (b) verbally prompted, or (c) physically prompted. Independent responses are graphed directly over daily data, allowing a quick and easy visual analysis of the student's progress.

Step 4: Incidental and Coincidental Teaching

Incidental teaching refers to the spontaneous teaching of skills to a child during the times of the day when that skill naturally occurs. An example of incidental teaching would be teaching children to button their coats as they are getting ready to go outside for free play. Skills to be taught incidentally are coded IN on the IEP.

In contrast, in coincidental teaching, staff plan and structure specific activities during the times of the day when they naturally occur. Specific prompting and praising procedures are then used to teach targeted children. Incidental teaching is spontaneous in contrast to coincidental teaching, which is planned and structured into the classroom's daily routine. Since incidental and coincidental teaching utilize materials and events that occur naturally in the environment and throughout the child's daily routine, they are not only useful for teaching new skills, but extremely beneficial in generalization training. CO is used to code skills in the IEP that will be taught coincidentally. For example, a teacher may structure Andy's arrival so he can practice independently unzipping and hanging up his coat while greeting and socially initiating to a peer. Or, after a snack, the teacher may prompt him to independently clean his area, then potty, wash his hands, and then brush his teeth. Data may be collected for specific task-analyzed behaviors or for less-specific chains of behaviors.

Incidental and coincidental teaching techniques are also advantageous because they are easy to implement, and they do not disrupt scheduled activities in the classroom.

When using coincidental teaching, one must first list all activities that occur during the preschool day on the Coincidental Teaching Planning Form (Figure 8.2). Programs are then matched with the times of day at which the skill naturally occurs. The teacher can often schedule and teach several objectives in one opportunity, such as sharing, self-help, and language skills during snack. When this has been completed, the teacher has now identified opportunities for coincidental teaching.

Both incidental and coincidental teaching rely on graduated prompting and praising as their primary intervention techniques. Killoran et al. (1983) present the following guidelines for the use of graduated prompting and praising.

Graduated Prompting

Graduated prompting is an intervention strategy designed to provide the student with the least amount of assistance needed to complete a skill. It refers to the verbal and physical guidance a teacher gives to the child. The essential point to remember when using graduated prompting is to provide only the minimum amount of help needed to have the child complete a task.

Initially, a child is prompted verbally. A *verbal prompt* is simply telling the child what to do. If the student does not respond or responds incorrectly to the verbal prompt, the teacher then *models* the task to the child while repeating the prompt. Modeling is simply demonstrating or showing the student what to do. If modeling is also unsuccessful, the teacher must then *physically guide* the student through the task. For example:

1. The teacher has just given Johnny the verbal prompt, "Share your crayons with Susie." He does not respond. The teacher must now;
2. repeat the original command while showing Johnny how to share the crayons. If he still does not respond correctly;
3. the teacher must now repeat the verbal prompt while simultaneously grasping his hand and guiding him to pick up the crayons and then give them to Susie.

Physical prompting has a major limitation in respect to verbal responding. That is, it is not possible to physically prompt speech! If

Figure 8.2. Coincidental Teaching Planning Form

Teacher _____   Date(s) _____
Class _____   _____

Daily Activities	Coincidental Skill Opportunities	Target Student
8:00 - 8:30		
8:30 - 9:00		
9:00 - 9:30		
9:30 - 10:00		
10:00 - 10:30		
10:30 - 11:00		
11:00 - 11:30		
11:30 - 12:00		
12:00 - 12:30		
12:30 - 1:00		
1:00 - 1:30		
1:30 - 2:00		
2:00 - 2:30		
2:30 - 3:00		

the teacher prompts, "Say hi to Susie," and the child says nothing, the teacher cannot physically force the child to speak. If a child does not follow a verbal prompt on a skill that cannot be physically prompted, it is sometimes effective to ask a different child to complete the skill. When that child responds, he or she should be enthusiastically praised for completing the skill. It may also be possible to substitute and physically prompt a motor response, such as waving to Susie.

Praising

Praising is used to reinforce the child for responding appropriately. A common type of praising used is social-verbal praise. There are four rules for praising the preschool-age child: (a) Be specific, (b) be immediate, (c) be enthusiastic, and (d) be sincere.

When praising, tell the child exactly what he is doing that you like. "Good sharing the crayons!" is much more effective than "Good boy." Praise the child as soon as he completes the skill, but be careful! Don't be caught praising Johnny for hanging up his coat as soon as he stands up. He may walk right past the coat rack!

Verbal praise should be coupled with social praise. Hugs, pats, and smiles should come from the student's peers as well as teachers. Initially, praise the child each and every time he or she completes a prompt. As the skill becomes mastered and part of the child's repertoire, systematically fade the rates of praise. Be generous in the use of praise. Good attempts deserve praise, as do skilled responses. Quiet sitters and listeners deserve praise as much as active participants. Alternate praise of individuals in a group with praise of the group as a whole.

Praise should be given immediately after the child attempts or completes the desired skill. Praise should be contingent, that is, it should be given when the child does the skill, and it should not be given when he or she doesn't do it. Praise statements should be given sincerely, and the form should vary. The same thing said over and over again becomes boring and loses its effectiveness.

It *is* possible to overpraise. If the child does something on his or her own, that skill should be praised less than a skill that is still developing. Lessening the amount of praise given to an acquired skill actually serves to strengthen that skill. If praise interrupts an ongoing behavior and the child focuses his or her attention on the adult, the adult is probably overpraising. A final note: When in doubt—praise—immediately after the child does what you want.

Step 5: Organizing the Daily and Weekly Schedule

After identifying the groups that are needed to address children's needs, daily and weekly schedules are planned to accommodate various learning centers. The FMS model includes at least two periods each day where two or three learning centers (small groups) are planned. Children rotate from one group to another at 15-minute intervals. Fifteen minutes was selected due to the short attention span for young children. The groups typically address different skills. For example, one group may address cognitive matching skills, another a fine motor art activity, and another role-playing social skills. Teachers report that the variety of groups allows them to address many different skill areas every day. Also, the makeup of the groups can be recombined for different activities. See Appendix 6.A for the daily schedule used in the FMS classrooms for a typical half-day (3-hour) session.

The daily schedule is not intended to be inflexible and rigid, but is to provide a general guide for the classrooms. When a daily schedule has been developed, the classroom team begins lesson planning.

Weekly lesson plans are based on concepts using developmental approaches. Weekly lesson plans are individualized by the child's study team in one of two ways. For children who are nonhandicapped, plans are individualized according to the curriculum-based assessment that has been conducted on that child. For children with handicaps, the weekly lesson plans are individualized to provide training and intervention in the IEP goals and objectives that have been established for that particular child.

The FMS Lesson Planning Forms comprise three components: the Weekly Lesson Summary, Individualization Summary, and the Suggested Goals for Small Group Language and Motor Activities sheets.

The Weekly Lesson Summary (Figure 8.3) is used to plan weekly theme activities for (a) opening circle and table activities, (b) small group language activities, and (c) learning centers. Learning centers incorporate instruction in social skills, daily living skills, fine and gross motor skills, and cognitive skills as well as additional language intervention. Learning centers use large and small group individualized instruction.

The Individualization Summary (Figure 8.4) allows the child study team to prioritize IEP objectives as maintenance, current, or generalization objectives; identify data collection methods and number of trials that data will be collected; and identify any curricula modification and materials needed for each child in the class.

Figure 8.3. Weekly Lesson Summary

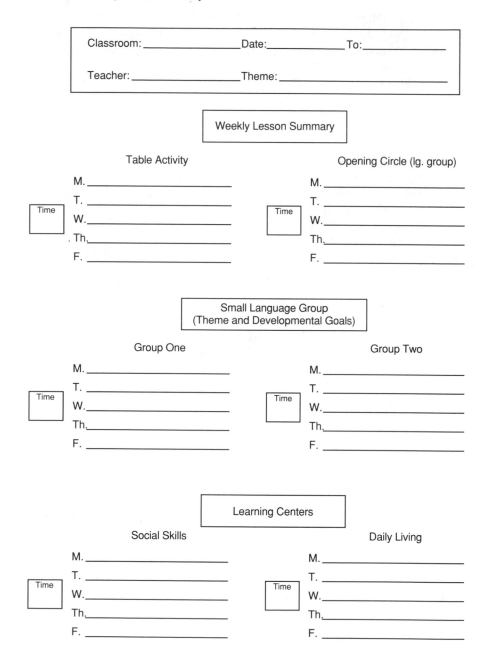

Figure 8.3. (continued)

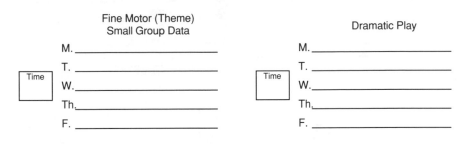

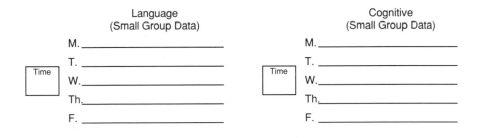

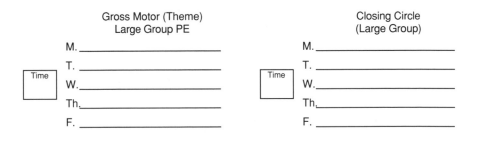

Figure 8.4. Individualization Summary

Classroom: _____ Reporting Therapist: _____

Date: _____ To: _____ Receiving Teacher: _____

Child	Objective	Data Points	*M, C, G	#Trials/ Frequency	Available Materials
1.					
2.					
3.					
4.					
5.					
6.					
7.					
8.					

*M = Maintenance   C = Current Goal   G = Generalization

Figure 8.4. (continued)

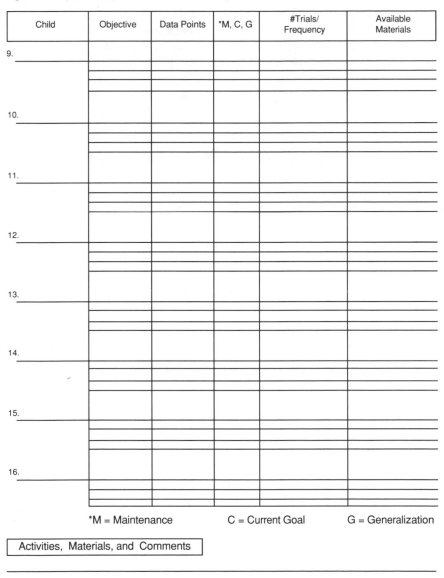

Child	Objective	Data Points	*M, C, G	#Trials/ Frequency	Available Materials
9.					
10.					
11.					
12.					
13.					
14.					
15.					
16.					

*M = Maintenance   C = Current Goal   G = Generalization

Activities, Materials, and Comments

The Suggested Goals for Small Group Language and Motor Activities sheets (Figure 8.5) may be used by consultants to provide suggestions to classroom staff for incidental training throughout the day. The lesson planning forms are completed by the classroom team weekly, for implementation the following week. The planning process entails approximately 1½ hours per week and should be planned into, rather than added to, staff work loads. By maintaining a master file of lesson plans, the classroom team can enhance planning activities.

Step 6: Systematic Peer Intervention

Step 6 in implementing the FMS model, designing and implementing systematic peer interventions, is the basis of Chapter 9.

Figure 8.5. Suggested Goals for Small Group Language and Motor Activities

**Suggested Goals for Small Group
Language and Motor Activities**

Classroom: _____ Reporting Therapist: _____

Date:_____ To:_____ Receiving Teacher: _____

_____

_____

_____

_____

_____

_____

_____

_____

_____

_____

_____

_____

_____

_____

_____

Comments

_____

_____

_____

_____

_____

_____

_____

_____

Appendix 8.A.

Instruction Manual

MESA-PK

Mainstreaming Expectations and Skills Assessment–
Preschool and Kindergarten

John Killoran M.Ed., Sebastian Striefel Ph.D.,
Maria Quintero Ph.D., and Trenly Yanito M.S.

Introduction

The Mainstreaming Expectations and Skills Assessment–Preschool and Kindergarten (MESA-PK) provides educators involved in mainstreaming with a global picture of a child's skill level, the regular classroom teacher's expectations of their students, and allows comparison of a child's skill levels and teacher expectations on each item. It can also be used as a guide for identifying and training those child skills which are critical for successful functioning in normalized environments and for identifying areas in which teachers need technical assistance and support.

The MESA-PK is designed to provide a child study team (composed of teachers, parents, administrators, and specialists) or other individuals involved in mainstreaming preschool and kindergarten children who have handicaps into normalized settings with the following information:

1. A description of behaviors characteristic of the child, that needs to be remedied or trained if the child is to achieve success in the mainstream classroom;

2. Specific goals and objectives to train critical skills needed in normalized environments;

3. Areas in which the regular classroom teachers may require assistance if the mainstreaming experience is to be successful for everyone in his/her classroom;

4. Information to help an administrator determine which teachers are better suited for teaching a particular child who is being mainstreamed and information on the numbers and types of mainstream settings needed;

5. Information about children's current level of functioning and the challenges that mainstreaming will provide for the children and parents;

Specific behaviors required for a successful mainstreaming experience can be identified by a child study team. This team is responsible for selecting the behaviors needed in various normalized environments, and for training the child in those behaviors.

Appendix 8.A. (continued)

Rationale

It is speculated that efforts to match teacher expectations with an incoming child's skills can facilitate the mainstreaming process by increasing the likelihood of mainstreaming a child whom a teacher is willing or prepared to teach (Striefel & Killoran, 1984b). If a teacher is not willing, but has no choice because of administrative decisions, completing the MESA-PK may provide information which will help the regular teacher know the child's level of functioning, and identify the technical assistance and support needed for increasing their effectiveness in teaching a mainstreamed child.

Mainstreaming a child with handicaps into a classroom where a teacher is willing and prepared to teach that child increases the chances for successful mainstreaming. By identifying a teacher's expectations and technical assistance needs, as well as the target child's actual skill level, both teacher and child may be prepared before and during the mainstreaming process.

Target Population

The MESA-PK is designed to facilitate mainstreaming for the preschool- and kindergarten-age child (3-6 years of age), who is mildly to severely handicapped and is currently being served in a special education class for all or part of the day. It may also be used to help determine initial placement for children who have not been previously served or who are being initially referred for services.

The special education teacher and/or child study team of the particular child are asked to assess the target child's skill level. It is suggested that the child study team review the child's most recent assessment information and observational data before completing the MESA-PK. If current information is not available, it is suggested that the MESA-PK not be completed until progress assessments are conducted. Current assessment information will increase the likelihood of successfully identifying student needs, teachers' technical assistance and support needs, and provides the receiving teacher with more accurate information on what kinds of activities will be needed to teach the target child.

The regular classroom teacher being considered as a potential mainstreaming teacher is asked to code his or her expectations of the target child who may participate in regular class activities for part of the day.

Materials Needed

The MESA-PK manual and protocol, recent child assessment information, recent observational data, and IEP planning forms (when applicable).

Time for Administration

Special Educator - Skill Profile -   10 Minutes
Regular Educator - Expectations Profile -   +10 Minutes = 20 Minutes Total

Appendix 8.A. (continued)

General Description

The MESA-PK contains five categories of items which describe child behaviors typically demonstrated in the school setting.

1. Classroom Rules - e.g., replacing materials and cleaning work places.
2. Work Skills - e.g., recognizing materials which are needed for tasks.
3. Self-Help - e.g., eating lunch with minimal assistance.
4. Communication - e.g., following group directions, and
5. Social Behaviors - e.g., social amenities.

Specific Instructions for the Special Educator

For each item, indicate the target child's skill level by circling the appropriate code - (A) Acceptably Skilled, (L) Less than Acceptably Skilled, or (CL) Considerably Less than Acceptably Skilled, in the column to the right of each item.

(A) **Acceptably Skilled** means that the child displays the skill at a level consistent with your standards, or for 90% or more of opportunities.

(L) **Less than Acceptably Skilled** means the child is deficient in the skill and demonstrates the skill from 50 to 89% of opportunities.

(CL) **Considerably Less than Acceptably Skilled** indicates that the child demonstrates the skill on less than 50% of opportunities to do so.

Specific Instructions for the Regular Educator

You have been presented with a behavior profile of a child with handicaps who is being considered for mainstreaming and may be placed in your classroom. This assessment should identify those behaviors which are important to you in your classroom and on which training can begin before and after the child's placement. As you circle each item, remember to keep in mind the activity for which the child's placement is being considered. Circle the appropriate letter in the columns to the left of each item to indicate if the item is (C) Critical, (D) Desirable, or (U) Unimportant in your classroom.

(C) **Critical** indicates that you will not accept the child in your classroom unless the child is acceptably skilled (the child demonstrates the behavior on 90% of opportunities to do so).

(D) **Desirable** means that you would like the student to demonstrate the behavior but you will accept a child who is less than acceptably skilled.

(U) **Unimportant** indicates that the behavior is unimportant for the student to demonstrate upon first entering your class.

Appendix 8.A. (continued)

Technical Assistance (TA) Requests by Regular Educators

Technical assistance refers to training and materials which may be provided to teachers to address specific needs which arise when teaching children who are handicapped. Technical Assistance can include a) demonstration via modeling, b) discussion, c) feedback, d) reading materials, and e) provision of curricula. **Indicate by checking in the appropriate column, those behaviors which you would be willing to train in your classroom if TA were available to you.**

Scoring the MESA-PK

A profile of a child's training needs and a teacher's TA needs can be generated by coding the "match" between child skill level and teacher expectation for each item. In the column marked, "Priorities by Child Study Team," using this coding system, child training need and teacher technical assistance needs can be identified. The following code is recommended:

I. Child Training Needs.

If child is rated:	And the potential receiving teacher marked:	Then score in the Child Study Team priority column is:
CL	C	1
L	C	2
CL	D	3

The Child Study Team (CST) should first address items scored "1," since these items are most likely to interfere with successful integration and transition to future integrated settings. Items scored "2" should be addressed secondarily, since the teacher considers these skills critical, and the child is not fully proficient on them. Items marked "3" merit consideration, but need not be considered urgent.

II. Teacher Technical Assistance Needs

Review the form and note TA needs checked by the receiving teacher. These items should be discussed by the child study team to provide solutions. Any materials or training needs should be referred to the principal or agency director who can access such resources.

Appendix 8.A. (continued)

Student Protocol

MESA-PK

Mainstreaming Expectations and Skills Assessment–
Preschool and Kindergarten

John Killoran, M.Ed.
Sebastian Striefel, Ph.D.
Maria Quintero, Ph.D.
Trenly Yanito, M.S.

Child _____	**Sex** _____	**Age** _____
Present Placement _____	**Date of Birth**	_____
Present Educator _____		
Potential Educator _____	**Class/Grade Taught**	_____
Date _____		

The MESA-PK was adapted from the EnTrans-Transition Skills Assessment developed by Teaching Research Associates, Monmouth, Oregon

Appendix 8.A. (continued)

Skill Level of Child	Present Placement Code A = Acceptably Skilled L = Less than Acceptably Skilled CL = Considerably Less than Acceptably Skilled	Potential Placement Code C = Critical D = Desirable U = Unimportant	Expectations of receiving/ future setting	Technical Assistance	Priorities by Child Study Team
	Classroom Rules				
A L CL	1. Follows established class rules.		C D U		
A L CL	2. Moves through routine transitions smoothly.		C D U		
A L CL	3. Uses appropriate voice volume in classroom.		C D U		
A L CL	4. Uses appropriate signal to get teacher's attention when necessary (i.e., raises hand).		C D U		
A L CL	5. Waits appropriately for teacher response to signal.		C D U		
A L CL	6. Replaces materials and cleans up own work space.		C D U		
A L CL	7. Recognizes and stays within area boundaries in classroom.		C D U		
	Work Skills				
A L CL	1. Does not disturb or disrupt the activities of others.		C D U		
A L CL	2. Produces work of acceptable quality given his/her skill level.		C D U		
A L CL	3. Asks for clarification on assigned tasks when initial instructions are not understood.		C D U		
A L CL	4. Follows one direction related to task.		C D U		
A L CL	5. Occupies self with age-appropriate activity assigned by an adult.		C D U		
A L CL	6. Recognizes materials needed for specific task.		C D U		
A L CL	7. Selects and works on an activity independently.		C D U		
A L CL	8. Recognizes completion of task/activity, indicates to adult that s/he is finished and stops activity.		C D U		
A L CL	9. Works on assigned task for 5 minutes.		C D U		
A L CL	10. Self-corrects errors.		C D U		
A L CL	11. Recalls and completes task demonstrated previously.		C D U		
A L CL	12. Uses crayons and scissors appropriately without being destructive.		C D U		

Appendix 8.A. (continued)

Skill Level of Child	Present Placement Code A = Acceptably Skilled L = Less than Acceptably Skilled CL = Considerably Less than Acceptably Skilled	Potential Placement Code C = Critical D = Desirable U = Unimportant	Expectations of receiving/future setting	Technical Assistance	Priorities by Child Study Team
	Self-Help				
A L CL	1. Monitors appearance, e.g., keeps nose clean, adjusts clothing, uses napkin.	C D U		
A L CL	2. Locates and uses a public restroom with minimal assistance in the school.	C D U		
A L CL	3. Puts on/takes off outer clothing within a reasonable amount of time.	C D U		
A L CL	4. Eats lunch or snack with minimal assistance.	C D U		
A L CL	5. Independently comes into the classroom or house from bus or car.	C D U		
A L CL	6. Goes from classroom to bus or car independently.	C D U		
A L CL	7. Knows way and can travel around school and playground.	C D U		
A L CL	8. Responds to fire drills as trained or directed.	C D U		
A L CL	9. Seeks out adult for aid if hurt on the playground or cannot handle a social situation, e.g., fighting.	C D U		
A L CL	10. Follows school rules (outside classroom).	C D U		
A L CL	11. Stays with a group according to established school rules, i.e., outdoors.	C D U		
A L CL	12. Recognizes obvious dangers and avoids them.	C D U		
	Communication (Includes gesture, sign, communication board, eye pointing, speech, and other augmented systems).				
A L CL	1. Attends to adult when called.	C D U		
A L CL	2. Listens to and follows group directions.	C D U		
A L CL	3. Communicates own needs and preferences, e.g., food, drink, bathroom.	C D U		
A L CL	4. Does not ask irrelevant questions which serve no functional purpose or are not task related.	C D U		
A L CL	5. Stops an activity when given a direction by an adult to "stop."	C D U		
A L CL	6. Attends to peers in large group.	C D U		
A L CL	7. Responds to questions about self and family, i.e., personal information.	C D U		
A L CL	8. Responds appropriately when comments/compliments are directed to him/her.	C D U		
A L CL	9. Responds to questions about stories.	C D U		

Appendix 8.A. (continued)

Skill Level of Child	Present Placement Code A = Acceptably Skilled L = Less than Acceptably Skilled CL = Considerably Less than Acceptably Skilled	Potential Placement Code C = Critical D = Desirable U = Unimportant	Expectations of receiving/ future setting	Technical Assistance	Priorities by Child Study Team
	Communication (Cont.)				
A L CL	10. Protests appropriately.	C D U			
A L CL	11. Requesting assistance from adult or peer, e.g., help in cafeteria, bathroom, mobility.	C D U			
A L CL	12. Responds without excessive delay.	C D U			
A L CL	13. Uses intentional communication (speech, sign, or gesture).	C D U			
	Social Behaviors				
A L CL	1. Uses social conventions, e.g., help in cafeteria, bathroom, mobility.	C D U			
A L CL	2. Complies to teacher commands.	C D U			
A L CL	3. Takes direction from a variety of adults.	C D U			
A L CL	4. Separates from parents and accepts school personnel.	C D U			
A L CL	5. Follows specified rules of games and/or class activities.	C D U			
A L CL	6. Makes choice between preferred items or activities.	C D U			
A L CL	7. Initiates interaction with peers and adults.	C D U			
A L CL	8. Plays cooperatively.	C D U			
A L CL	9. Respects others and their property.	C D U			
A L CL	10. Defends self.	C D U			
A L CL	11. Shows emotions and feelings appropriately.	C D U			
A L CL	12. Responds positively to social recognition and reinforcement.	C D U			
A L CL	13. Interacts appropriately at a snack or lunch table.	C D U			
A L CL	14. Expresses affection toward other children and adults in an appropriate manner, i.e., is not overly affectionate by hugging, kissing, and touching.	C D U			
A L CL	15. Refrains from self-abusive behavior, e.g., biting, cutting, or bruising self, head banging.	C D U			
A L CL	16. Refrains from physically aggressive behavior toward others, i.e., hitting, biting, shoving.	C D U			
A L CL	17. Does not use obscene language.	C D U			
A L CL	18. Discriminates between edible and non-edible toys and objects.	C D U			
A L CL	19. Uses play equipment in an age-appropriate manner during unstructured activities with limited adult supervision.	C D U			

Chapter 9

* * *

Designing and Implementing Systematic Peer Interventions

A major premise for integrating children who are handicapped into the normal environments is to prepare them as much as possible for independent functioning—presently, as well as in the future. Integration is an ongoing process that should prepare children, with and without handicaps, to interact to the maximum extent possible in normal preschool settings. Integration should be the preparation phase for later transitioning to school, into the community, and for independent living and/or competitive employment (Adams, Striefel, Frede, Quintero, & Killoran, 1985). Since successful functioning in school and the community rely heavily on social interaction skills, integrated settings must promote positive interactions between children with handicaps and those without. These interactions must be planned and systematic, since spontaneous interactions that do occur between children with and without handicaps who are in physical proximity generally are infrequent and negative (Gresham, 1982), and may actually foster negative attitudes toward individuals with moderate and severe handicaps (Mott et al., 1986). Unfortunately, most integration efforts have fallen short in using planned systematic peer intervention in the mainstreaming process to enforce interactions between students (Taylor, 1982).

Peer interaction systems are promising methods for enhancing positive interaction, since children with handicaps often have difficulty developing social relations with peers (Walker, 1983). With systematic planning and implementation, a peer interaction system may foster positive attitudes and development of friendships, increase academic skills in both groups of students, and reduce the demands on the teacher to provide one-to-one instruction (Striefel & Killoran, 1984a, 1984b).

In addition to teacher prompting, praising, and grouping of children, the FMS project has relied on the use of two specific peer-implemented interaction systems in its model: buddies and tutors. Buddies refer to children who are helpers and assist their peers who are handicapped. In contrast, tutors are used as instructional agents. We have found that buddies rather than tutors are most often used in the preschool setting.

Peer Buddies

The use of peers as an educational resource presents a valuable tool for classroom teachers (Schwartz, 1984; Voeltz, Keshi, Brown, & Kube, 1980). Peers provide individualized attention, which teachers can rarely provide without sacrificing attention for the group (Jenkins & Jenkins, 1982), and they can enhance generalization of skills (Johnson & Johnson, 1981; O'Connor, 1972). More importantly, interventions that increase interactions between children with and without handicaps must be developed, since children with handicaps in a mainstream setting do not spontaneously imitate the desirable social behaviors of their peers (Gresham, 1982; Walker, 1983). The structure of a buddy system provides a format for establishing and encouraging interactions among children.

What Is a Buddy?

A buddy is a child who accompanies and/or guides another child (called a companion in this program) in nonacademic and unstructured activities. A buddy is an equal and a friend, but if a potentially harmful situation arises or if the companion assigned to the buddy engages in inappropriate behavior, a buddy must be able to exert authority, take control of the situation, or access a readily available adult. Buddies can be used for any activity at any time if needed, when the product of that activity is not being used to evaluate a student's skill level. Examples of possible activities in which to use buddies could include lunch, recess, assembly, putting on coats and shoes, going to class or bus, library time, group art, field trips, and music.

Basically, buddies are used to increase the number and level of social interactions between handicapped and nonhandicapped children within the context of normal daily preschool routines.

Establishing a Buddy System

The implementation of a buddy system involves six basic steps: (a) identifying a companion, (b) identifying a pool of buddies, (c) preparing potential buddies, (d) assigning specific buddies, (e) training specific buddies, and (f) implementing and evaluating the buddy system (Figure 9.1).

Step 1: Identifying a Companion. The first step in establishing a buddy program is to identify children with handicaps who could benefit from having an assigned buddy and to designate the specific purpose for pairing each child with a buddy. The purpose should state the activities in which the buddy will assist the companion. Repetitive practice in these activities may well result in the companion acquiring some specific skills. For example, in repeatedly being assisted by the buddy in going through the lunch line, the companion may learn to engage in that activity without assistance.

Theoretically, all children with handicaps could benefit from a buddy system. However, some children may already have developed friends who serve the same purpose, and some children may exhibit behaviors that must first be controlled before a buddy can be used. These behaviors include aggression (physical or verbal), noncompliance, running away, tantrums, and inappropriate touching (of self or others).

Step 2: Identifying a Pool of Buddies. This pool may be peers within the classroom or members from another class. Children in any prospective pool of buddies will react to the activity in response to the demonstrated behaviors of adult leaders in the group (e.g., teacher or group leader). Consequently, the adult leader must first demonstrate support of the buddy system activity and exhibit a positive attitude toward students with handicaps.

The following guidelines should be kept in mind when buddies are selected:

1. *Solicit Volunteers.* While any child could potentially be a buddy, those who want to be a buddy are likely to try harder to do a good job. Volunteers should be solicited. No child should be coerced into being a buddy. Although the ultimate goal of a buddy system is to

Figure 9.1. Flowchart of Peer Buddy System

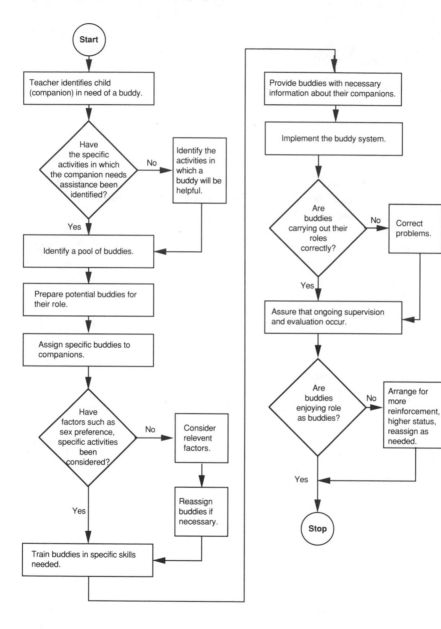

encourage and structure interactions among children with and without handicaps, teachers should not limit the identification of buddies to children without handicaps. An occasional buddy from the set of children with handicaps provides an excellent opportunity to enhance the social status of that person and to demonstrate that handicapping conditions are not necessarily constraints to assuming responsibility in the class. In addition, there are often children who do not have handicaps who could use a buddy to get them from place to place, to get them involved in play activities, or to show them where things in a classroom are located.

2. *Observe for Children Who Are Positive Toward Peers with Handicaps.* Children who demonstrate an interest in children with handicaps by asking questions about them, or attempting to interact with them, are likely to be good buddy candidates.

3. *Select Outgoing, Verbal Buddies.* A child who is verbal and outgoing is a good candidate for increasing the success of initial buddy pairings. Shy, quiet children have been successfully used as buddies with children who have handicaps, resulting in significant positive changes in the shy child. However, the initial selection of a child who is not viewed by peers as a "leader" can create a stigma for buddy programs, by presenting the program as an activity for children with difficulties.

4. *Use Children Who Have Relatives or Friends with Handicaps.* Some relatives of a child with handicaps make excellent candidates for being buddies due to their experience with unconditional acceptance and recognition of the abilities of a child with handicaps. However, it is important to watch for the burnout from existing responsibility in the home or school. If this is noted, the child being considered as a buddy should not be expected to bear the added responsibility of being assigned as a buddy to a child with handicaps.

5. *Check for Dependability and Good Attendance.* Any potential buddy must be reliable in completing assigned tasks and must have regular attendance.

Step 3: Preparing Potential Buddies. The third step in establishing a buddy system is the preparation of the pool of buddies. This preparation is best started through handicap awareness activities such as puppetry, role-playing, and discussions.

Introducing the buddy concept to a class should begin with an explanation of why the children are going to be assigned such an important task. It is helpful to enhance the status of buddies by indicating how being a buddy is a responsible and desirable role. Although buddies are to help their peers with handicaps, this idea should not be overemphasized to the point that children with handicaps come to be perceived by their classmates as helpless.

The puppet show activity described in Chapter 6 can be used to educate the class about children with handicaps in a fun and non-threatening manner that they can understand. This same puppet show can explain and introduce the general use of buddies to the class by explaining that (a) a buddy accompanies a handicapped child during recess, lunch, in the hall, or whenever the teacher might need some extra hands to help the child if he or she needs the help; (b) being a buddy means being a helpful friend to the child with handicaps; (c) the teacher really likes and appreciates buddies who are good friends and helpers; and (d) stickers, specific praise, buddy badges, or special privileges are earned by being good buddies. A buddy should also be a friend. A friend is someone whom one knows well and whom one is fond of, and who is helpful, supportive, and reliable.

Step 4: Assigning Specific Buddies.   After preparing the group, individual buddies should be identified for assisting specific companions in specific activities. The following items should be considered in assigning buddies:

1. *Select Buddies Who Exhibit the Behavior in Which the Child with Handicaps Needs Assistance.* A potential buddy must also possess at least age-level play skills, display age-appropriate levels of social interaction with peers, and possess the skills needed to assist the companion in the activities targeted for assistance.

2. *Observe the Buddy's Leadership Ability.* Some potential buddies might be more natural and patient in demonstrating some tasks in guiding peers or in commanding attention as a result of previous experiences with sibling care-giving duties or other relevant experiences. Although the presence or absence of this skill may not be a limiting factor in the selection of buddies, a child who demonstrates leadership skills would be easier to use as a buddy.

3. *Check for Sex Preferences.* If a child has a preference for a buddy or companion of the same sex, these preferences should be noted. Although research literature varies on the impact of buddies of the same and opposite sex, it may prevent discomfort if a child's preference is met. If no preference exists, a buddy for the situation should be assigned based upon the goal of the buddy activity (e.g., assisting to and from the bathroom versus helping during art activities).

Step 5: Training Specific Buddies. Individual buddies must be trained in specific skills (e.g., drawing and maintaining a child's attention, using special communication techniques, and praising). Buddy training may sound extensive, but in reality it can be effectively introduced in 10 minutes, then shaped during actual buddy/companion interactions.

Certain specific information is needed by all buddy candidates. Buddies need to know the following about their companion with handicaps:

1. The name of their companion.

2. The handicapping condition and a *brief* background of why the child has a handicapping condition. (For example, "Don has Down syndrome, which is a condition he was born with.")

3. Awareness that the handicap is not contagious.

4. How to communicate with the companion (e.g., selected manual signs).

5. The companion's likes and dislikes.

6. Any unusual behavior the companion exhibits, and how to handle it.

7. Specific ways of interacting with the companion. Role-playing can be a useful technique for practicing ways of interacting until such time as the buddy is comfortable with the new skill. For example, one may role-play how to initiate and maintain interactions with children who are often unresponsive, or limited in their social interaction skills. In such role-playing, eye contact, voice inflection techniques, and physical prompting may need to be practiced, depending upon the buddy's skills and age. One may role-play how to give praise and reinforcement for appropriate behavior and noncritical feedback and correction for inappropriate behaviors. Initially, adults will need to intervene and prompt these behaviors with statements such as, "John (buddy), let Mike (companion) know what a neat tower he's building with those blocks." One can also role-play what action to take if a situation arises in which a buddy is not sure of what to do. Under these circumstances, the buddy should always ask for help from the teacher or another available adult. Clearly, buddies should always operate in a supervised environment.

8. When a companion refuses the buddy's advances or behaves inappropriately (e.g., tantrum), it does not necessarily mean that

the companion dislikes the buddy; rather, it is likely that the companion does not know how to play (e.g., paint, run) correctly. A buddy must know what to do when rejected (e.g., persist, seek an adult).

It is important to acknowledge that some children with handicaps lack the skills needed to reinforce a buddy for his or her efforts; therefore, external (teacher-provided), specific, and potent reinforcers might be needed, such as stickers, specific praise, or privileges. These items can help to make being a buddy a desirable activity for the buddy and other class members who may be future buddies.

Step 6: Implementing and Evaluating the Buddy System. The best way to evaluate the effectiveness of a buddy system is to see if it is meeting the purposes for which it was designed. The purpose(s) outlined for each handicapped child should be reviewed periodically to document changes in behavior. These changes may include an increase in the number of positive interactions and a decrease in the number of negative interactions. Also, one may examine if the child with handicaps has developed more contacts with peers outside of school. This can be measured through parent and child feedback. Additionally, the reactions of buddies can be recorded daily by asking if they had an "easy, so-so, or hard day" at the end of the session, and recording this information along with the supervising adult's rating of the day's interaction.

When a child with handicaps is initially assigned a buddy, other peers may be curious and may provide too much attention to the companion. The system may appear to be confusing and unsuccessful, when, in fact, several peers may be attempting to be "good buddies" by directing help and attention toward the companion. The child with handicaps may try to relieve this attention through aggression or running away from peers. At this point, the teacher may need to instruct all of the children to treat the companion a little more like they treat any other friend and not help the child unless it is needed. It is important to monitor the feelings of satisfaction or dissatisfaction of buddies to prevent burnout. Where dissatisfaction is due to specific problems (e.g., not knowing how to address a specific situation), a correction should occur. When dissatisfaction is due to being with the same child, rotating buddies once a week, or even daily, may lessen buddy burnout. Rotating buddies can also lessen the disruption of natural friendships that may exist between peers and foster more friendships between the various buddies and the companion. However, when buddies prefer to remain with a specific companion or an ongoing friendship is developing, it is best to leave the pair together.

The eventual goal of the program is to fade out the use of assigned buddies as a child with handicaps is assimilated more and more into being just another member of the class. One way to test the continued need for buddies is for the teacher to announce that buddies are not specifically being assigned for the day. The adults should observe the result of the withdrawal of specifically assigned buddies. If social interactions and play behaviors continue smoothly, the point may have been reached where specific buddies can be faded out. If the desired behavior is not demonstrated, buddies may still be needed.

Assuming that positive outcomes occurred when no specific buddies were assigned for a day, then buddies can be assigned every other day, or be discontinued altogether. Careful behavioral observations will need to be conducted to insure that desirable interaction levels are maintained as the buddies are gradually eliminated. A specific timetable to use in fading out buddies would be difficult to determine in advance. Each situation is unique, and the fading will have to proceed as the situation allows.

Peer Tutoring Systems

Simply stated, peer tutoring is the provision of instruction by a fellow student. The FMS peer tutoring system (Appendix 9.A) provides specific instructions for implementing a peer tutor program in integrated settings. In this program, peer tutors assume the role of teacher or supervisor. The tutor's role is structured with specific skills being taught to the tutor in a directed manner. The system is designed to introduce effective strategies for designing and implementing a systematic peer tutoring system. The procedures are particularly suitable for use in integrated settings and to increase social interaction between students. Figure 9.2 provides a flowchart of the peer tutoring system, and Figure 9.3 provides a data sheet useful for peer tutors in recording data.

The use of systematic peer interventions is critical in integrated settings, since children with and without handicaps will not naturally interact based only on location or physical proximity. The FMS model has found the buddy and tutoring systems to be excellent vehicles for increasing the probability of positive, spontaneous interactions between students with and without handicaps.

Figure 9.2. Flowchart of Peer Tutoring System

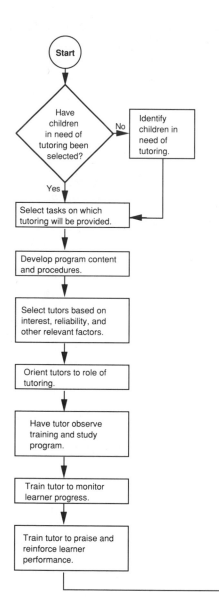
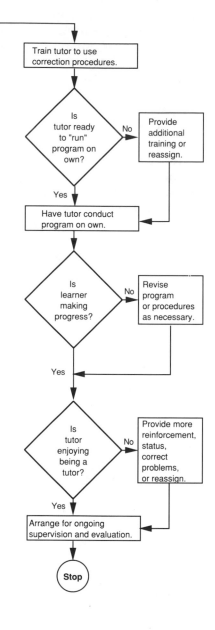

Figure 9.3. Data Sheet

Multi-Behavior/ Step/Students DATA SHEET	Behaviors/Steps Students	Conditions	%										Object.	Date	Percent.	Comment
			100													
			90													
			80													
			70													
			60													
			50													
			40													
			30													
			20													
			10													

Student: _____

Data Collector: _____

Program: _____

_____

_____

_____

Key:
+ : **CORRECT**

O : **INCORRECT**

____ : __

____ : __

Graph Legend: _____

Other: _____

| Objective |
| Date/Year |
| Percentage |
| Comments |

Formula: % correct = no. correct ÷ total no. of trials x 100

Appendix 9.A.

The Mainstreaming Teacher's Guide To

Designing and Implementing A Peer Tutoring System

John Killoran, Joel Allred, Sebastian Striefel, & Maria Quintero

The purpose of the peer tutoring system is to introduce effective strategies for designing, implementing, and evaluating a systematic peer tutoring system. Whereas most peer tutoring systems concentrate on training students with severe and multiple handicaps in a variety of self-help and basic skills, the procedures we describe are particularly suitable for use in mainstreaming activities and for increasing social interaction between students.

Rationale

A major premise of mainstreaming children who have handicaps into the regular school environment is to prepare them as much as possible for independent functioning; presently as well as in the future (Striefel, Killoran, & Quintero, 1984). Mainstreaming is an ongoing process that should prepare children, with and without handicaps, to interact to the maximum extent possible in normal settings. Mainstreaming should be the preparation phase for later transitioning from the school into the community for independent living and/or competitive employment (Adams, Striefel, Frede, Quintero, & Killoran, 1985). Since successful functioning in school and the community relies heavily on social interaction skills, mainstreaming must promote positive interactions between children. These interactions must be planned and systematic since spontaneous interactions that do occur between children who are handicapped and nonhandicapped are generally infrequent and negative in nature (Gresham, 1982), and may actually foster negative attitudes toward individuals with moderate and severe handicaps (Mott, Striefel, & Quintero, 1986). Unfortunately, most mainstreaming efforts have fallen short in using planned systematic decision making during the mainstreaming process to enforce interaction (Taylor, 1982).

Peer tutoring systems are promising methods for enhancing positive interactions since children with handicaps often have difficulty developing social relations with peers (Walker, 1983). With systematic planning and implementation, a peer tutoring system may foster positive attitudes and develop friendships, increase academic skills in both students, and reduce the demands upon the teacher to provide one-to-one instruction (Striefel & Killoran, 1984a, 1984b).

Peer Tutoring Defined

Simply stated, peer tutoring is the provision of instruction by a fellow student. To be effective, peer tutoring systems (1) should be cost effective; ultimately saving time for the teacher and allowing the teacher to spend more time with individual or smaller groups of children; (2) should increase the skills of both the tutor and the learner and (3) should enhance the social interactions of students.

Appendix 9.A. (continued)

In this program, peer tutors assume the role of teacher or supervisor. The tutor's role is structured with specific skills being taught to the tutor in a directed manner. Tutors are usually non-handicapped students although recent investigations using students with handicaps as tutors indicate that they can also be effective tutors (Scruggs, Mastropieri, & Richter, 1981).

Tutors can volunteer, or they can be selected by the teacher. They can be of the same sex and age as the learner, or can vary in sex or age from the student to be tutored (Scruggs et al., 1981; Krouse, Gerber, & Kauffman, 1981).

Target Audience

This manual is intended for use by a variety of professionals including regular and special educators who are involved in the process of mainstreaming children who have handicaps into less restrictive settings. It is designed to be used to train tutors to teach and interact with children having mild to severe handicaps.

Materials needed

Preselected programs including all materials and data systems and the Peer Tutoring Checklist will be needed.

Location

The location where the tutoring will take place does not seem to be a critical factor in the success of the program. However, some issues should be kept in mind when determining the location. Peer tutors need supervision, especially when tutoring sessions first begin. If the regular classroom or special education teachers cannot provide the supervision needed, then either a paid aide or trained volunteer should be present for the first sessions. One potential setting is in the special education classroom. An advantage of bringing tutors to the special education classroom is that it relieves the regular classroom teacher of students, and since the classroom is relieved, an exchange can take place to allow another child who has handicaps to be mainstreamed during this time. One disadvantage of conducting peer tutoring in a self-contained setting is that the child who has handicaps does not have the opportunity to interact with non-handicapped peers other than the tutor, nor to observe and perhaps learn from the behaviors of children in a regular classroom. In addition, the children in the regular classroom do not have the opportunity to learn to interact with the child who has handicaps. Ideally, peer tutoring should be conducted within the regular class since the regular class represents most children's least restrictive environment. However, a systematic process of transfering training from the self-contained setting to the regular classroom will be needed for more severely involved students.

Peer Tutoring Training Checklist

The key element in the training paradigm is the Peer Tutor Training Checklist. This checklist outlines basic steps to transfer the implementation of a program from the trainer (teacher) to the tutor and allows for long-term supervision and monitoring of the tutoring. As a task is completed, or the tutor masters the behaviors under each step of

Appendix 9.A. (continued)

the checklist, the trainer enters the dates and progresses to the next training step. See the Peer Tutoring Checklist located at the end of the Manual.

Rate of Transfer

The rate at which the tutor will demonstrate the behaviors operationalized under each step of the checklist will be dependent upon several factors including the severity of the handicap of the learner, the skill being trained, and the skills of the tutor. As such, the number of sessions to be conducted for each step cannot be predetermined. The tutor should be trained on each step until he/she demonstrates each of its operationalized behaviors. At that time, the tutor progresses to the next step in the training paradigm. It is important to be patient during the initial training of a tutor since success will enhance the skills and enthusiasm of the tutors. In contrast, rushing through the initial program transfer may result in failure and frustration for all involved. Approximately three thirty-minute training sessions have been found sufficient for tutors seven years of age or older. Four to five sessions are recommended for children under six.

Handshaping

A handshaping procedure is used to train the tutor. This handshaping procedure is an adaptation of the <u>Microsession Training and Transfer Procedure</u> (Killoran, Killoran, Rule, Innocenti, Morgan, & Stowitschek, 1987) which contains teaching techniques demonstrated as effective in mainstream classes (Rule, Killoran, Stowitschek, Innocenti, Striefel & Boswell, 1985). Handshaping consists of : (a) demonstration of the program to the tutor, (b) graduated transfer of the program to the tutor using demonstration, shaping, and feedback, and (c) systematic fading of supervision by the trainer. These procedures are sequentially applied within each of the five checklist steps on which the tutor is trained. The training should be done with the child who is to be tutored rather than in a role-play setting. In handshaping, the trainer:

1. Demonstrates the program to the tutor, emphasizing the steps being trained during that specific session.

2. Asks the tutor to explain the step being trained and answers all questions.

3. Again demonstrates the program and then has the tutor implement the step with the learner.

4. If the tutor makes an error, the trainer physically guides the tutor to correct the error, concentrating on the step being trained and refining previous steps as needed, while providing descriptive feedback and praise.

5. Initials the peer tutoring checklist beside each of the operational behaviors mastered by the tutor during the training session, and records the date of mastery for each step.

Appendix 9.A. (continued)

The following section discusses the steps of the Peer Tutoring Checklist.

Step One: Choosing the Child to be Tutored (Learner)

Theoretically, all children with handicaps can benefit from a peer tutoring system. However, some children may exhibit behaviors which must be first controlled before peer tutoring can be used. These behaviors include: aggression (physical or verbal), noncompliance, running away, tantrums, and inappropriate touching (of self or others). If a child demonstrates these behaviors, it will prove beneficial to obtain verbal behavior control (responding to verbal cues and commands) over them before implementing the tutoring system. Learner behaviors which will enhance the success of a tutor program include:

1. Attending Skills
    a. Establishing and maintaining eye contact with trainer.
    b. Establishing and maintaining eye contact with presented objects.
    c. Sitting upon verbal/signed commands.
    d. Maintaining sitting position.

2. Ability to follow simple verbal commands, e.g.:
    a. point to......,
    b. touch the......,
    c. pick up the object......,

3. Ability to imitate simple motor tasks, e.g.: "Do this" (imitate modeled motor movements).

Step Two: Program Selection

The first task in program selection is to determine the tasks or activities for which the child with handicaps will have a tutor. Children whose IEPs contain objectives for attaining social and academic or self-help skills are good candidates for tutoring because tutoring is a method that can foster the learning of social skills while increasing skills in other areas.

Criteria for Program Selection

The following components enhance a program or activity selected for tutoring:

1. Behavioral objectives for the skill to be trained should be stated and the behavior task analyzed into steps appropriate for the target student.

2. The program should outline systematic direct teaching procedures including the presentation of a stimulus, child responses, and appropriate consequences; i.e., praise and specific reinforcement and correction procedures.

Appendix 9.A. (continued)

3. The program should include methods for measuring the child's acquisition or mastery of the skill on a daily or weekly basis.

4. The skill must be simple and sufficiently task analyzed into small, sequential steps to be taught by a peer.

5. The program must be one in which the safety of the students may not be jeopardized (for example, it would not be appropriate to have a peer run a motor program such as walking a balance beam or a leisure program such as bike riding or swimming).

If when selecting a program one of the criteria is lacking, the program should be modified before training the tutor. As a general rule, children with increasingly severe handicaps will require programs with more systematic direct teaching strategies. For example, an extremely individualized task analyzed program with daily data collection may be needed for a child with severe handicaps. In contrast, a published curriculum with weekly probes may be used to teach the same skill to a child who is moderately handicapped.

Step Three: Selecting the Tutors

The selection of a tutor should be made by the regular and special educator in accordance with the needs of the children (both handicapped and non-handicapped), the needs of the teacher, and the demands of the activity. Generally, a tutor of the same age is most appropriate. However, cross-age tutoring has been demonstrated to increase social contacts with elementary-aged students (Asper, 1973). Sex of the tutor does not seem to affect the success of a program (Krouse et al., 1981). In a structured and supervised tutoring program, children learn regardless of whether or not the learner has handicaps (Scruggs et al., 1981). When choosing the tutor, it is important to consider how the tutor will benefit from the activity. The following guidelines are important considerations for selecting peer tutors:

1. The tutor should have a good attendance record.

2. The tutor should display positive, unprompted social initiations toward other children during free play.

3. The tutor must respond positively to social invitations from other children.

4. The tutor must reliably follow adult directions (Strain, Hoyson, & Jamieson, 1985).

5. It has also been found during field-testing of the checklist that the tutor should be able to physically prompt the learner through a task if required.

Communication with the parents of the tutors is also a factor when selecting tutors. The regular classroom teacher should contact the parents of the potential tutor and explain the purpose of tutoring and the benefits the child is expected to gain. Parents should be encouraged to visit the special education classroom to observe a

Appendix 9.A. (continued)

tutoring session with another child or a training session with the teacher. Having the parents' support at home can help the tutors maintain positive attitudes about their experiences. It is imperative that the regular classroom teacher assure that parental informed consent has been obtained and that the participation as a tutor does not disadvantage a child by significantly decreasing his/her own instructional time.

Orientation - Once peer tutors are selected and informed consent is received (see parent permission forms in this appendix), an orientation meeting is held. The orientation meeting should be held informally and incorporate a highly reinforcing activity (e.g., an ice cream social). The following topics are discussed during the orientation:

1.   The need and importance of peer tutoring.

2.   The need for punctuality and high attendance.

3.   The benefits received as a tutor.

4.   The amount of available teacher support.

5.   An overview or brief description of the children who will be tutored.

The orientation should close with a visit to the classroom in which students will be tutoring. The purpose of the visit is to introduce the children to one another and to familiarize the tutor(s) with the classroom in which they will be working.

Step Four: Study and Observe

In step four, the tutor studies the program to be trained and observes the implementation of the program as demonstrated by the trainer. The trainer explains the program, emphasizing program preparation and set up; asks the tutor to explain the program; and the tutor is verbally quizzed on his/her knowledge of the program. The trainer should also provide feedback and redirection as needed.

Step Five: Progress Monitoring

Progress monitoring refers to the method(s) used to record the learner's performance during a tutoring session. This measurement may be as simple as anecdotal reports or as complex as discrete trial response recording. In Step Five, the trainer explains and demonstrates the program to the tutor while the tutor collects and records progress data. Throughout the session, the trainer provides feedback to the tutor.

Step Six: Praise and Reinforcement

Reinforcement most often consists of social verbal praise, coupled with a tangible or edible item for severely involved children or others who do not respond to praise alone. All reinforcement should be individualized for the learner. Praising, tangibles, and edibles are used to reward the learner for a correct response. Verbal social praise is an easy and often effective form of reinforcement. When praising it is important to

Appendix 9.A. (continued)

remember to be: (1) specific in your praise, (2) enthusiastic while delivering it, and (3) immediate. When being praised, the child should be told by the tutor exactly what s/he is doing that is correct, e.g., "Good reading that sentence" is much more effective than "Good boy." The learner should be praised by the tutor as soon as s/he completes a task. The tutor should be enthusiastic and sincere when praising the learner (Killoran, Striefel, Stowitschek, Rule, Innocenti, & Boswell, 1983).

Verbal praise may be coupled with other social attention (that is age appropriate) such as hugs, pats, and smiles from the tutor. Initially, the learner should be praised each and every time s/he responds correctly. Praise should also be provided to the tutor on a regular basis for his/her work. As the skill becomes mastered and part of the learner's repertoire, the tutor should systematically fade the rates of praise. The trainer will need to monitor the amount of praise and have the tutor fade or systematically decrease the amount of praise given when appropriate. The tutor should be generous in the use of praise; good attempts deserve as much praise as skilled responses (Killoran et al., 1983).

Step Seven: Correction

Correction refers to the procedures which the tutor will follow if the child responds incorrectly. An easy way to train and use a correction procedure is graduated prompting. Graduated prompting is an intervention strategy which is designed to provide the child with the least amount of assistance needed to complete a skill (Killoran et al., 1983). It refers to the level of guidance the tutor will give to the child. There are three levels of guidance used: verbal, visual, and physical. The essential point is to train the tutor to provide only the minimum amount of guidance needed to have the learner complete a task.

Initially, the tutor should prompt the learner with a verbal command. A verbal command is simply having the tutor tell the learner what to do. If the child does not respond or responds incorrectly to the verbal command, the tutor then demonstrates (visual prompt) the task to the learner while repeating the verbal command. Demonstrating is simply having the tutor show the student what to do. If the visual prompt is also unsuccessful, the tutor must then physically guide the student through the task. For example:

1. The tutor has just given the learner the verbal command, "Touch the letter A." The learner does not respond.

2. The tutor must now repeat the original command "Touch the letter A," while touching the letter himself/herself. If the learner does not respond correctly,

3. The tutor must repeat the verbal command, "Touch the letter A," while simultaneously grasping the learner's hand and physically guiding the learner to touch the letter A.

Physical prompting can guide the learner through every part of the task or may be just touching the learner's arm to initiate movement. Again, the tutor must be trained to provide the least amount of help needed for the learner to complete the task. When using a physical prompt, the tutor must be trained to couple physical prompts with the original verbal command, then to repeat the verbal command while giving the child an opportunity to perform the skill alone.

Appendix 9.A. (continued)

Graduated prompting has a major limitation when applied to verbal responding because it is not possible to physically prompt speech. In such cases when a child does not follow a verbal prompt on a skill which cannot be physically prompted, the tutor may be able to substitute and physically prompt a motor response (Killoran et al., 1983). For example, although children cannot be physically prompted to say "cat," they can be physically prompted through a manual sign for "cat."

The tutor must be able to describe and implement the graduated prompting procedures to be used in the tutoring session. During step seven, the trainer conducts the entire program while the tutor reinforces and corrects. Upon completion of the session the tutor is given feedback and the trainer initials all operationalized behaviors mastered.

Step Eight: Independent Direct Teaching

Direct teaching refers to the tutor conducting the program. It includes program implementation, recording progress data, reinforcement, and correction. Simply stated, this step is "running the program." When operationalized behaviors within Step Eight are mastered, the tutor will be able to independently run the tutoring session and should need only occasional supervision.

In Step Eight, the trainer demonstrates the entire program to the tutor, emphasizing the direct teaching aspects of the program; observes and handshapes the tutor's implementation of the program; and initials operational behaviors as appropriate. Step Eight is to be repeated until the tutor demonstrates all behaviors during two consecutive training sessions.

Step Nine: Reliability Checks, Supervision and Monitoring

Supervision begins when the tutor begins the system and continues even after the tutor has mastered Step Eight and runs all aspects of the direct teaching procedures. Having someone available to observe sessions, forestall problems and unexpected situations, answer questions, and handle emergencies is important, especially during the first few tutoring sessions. It is suggested that daily supervision be gradually faded out over four half-hour sessions.

Once the tutor is running the tutoring system independently, the trainer need only monitor the tutor and conduct reliability checks. Initially, weekly monitoring is suggested. Although the tutor is recording child progress during tutoring sessions, overall responsibility for progress monitoring and program changes is accorded to the trainer. Tutors should be encouraged to talk to the trainer as soon as any questions or problems occur. Appendix 9.B. provides an evaluation system for determining peer satisfaction.

Step Ten: Comments

Step Ten is really a part of ongoing monitoring. The Peer Tutoring Checklist includes a space for the tutor to record comments concerning problems and mastery of a skill. The supervisor should check for such comments on a regular basis and make appropriate adjustments in the turoring program as necessary.

Appendix 9.A. (continued)

Tutors as Trainers

One drawback to peer tutoring systems is the amount of time an adult must spend in training and supervising the tutors. An alternative is to have experienced tutors train new tutors. This can be expedited by training tutors in the use of the checklist. Periodic supervision by teachers is still necessary, and young tutors are not always successful tutor trainers. However, it is a viable method for eliminating the need for some staff time. Rotating tutors every six weeks can also be beneficial in that the learner with handicaps establishes relationships with more peers and skills generalize more for both tutors and learners. In addition, more non-handicapped children may have planned systematic interactions with children with handicaps.

Summary

The use of peer tutoring has many valuable benefits for the classroom teacher. Among these benefits are increased ability to individualize instruction and increased opportunities for social interaction. The system which has been described is not specific to a content area. Rather, it has proved useful in teaching a wide variety of skills to students who are severely and multiply handicapped and has provided a variety of opportunities for social interaction which have been too often overlooked.

Appendix 9.A. (continued)

Peer Tutoring Checklist
Validated Strategies for School-Age Mainstreaming (VSSM) Project
Developmental Center for Handicapped Persons
Utah State University

Tutor _____ Program_____

Tutor's Teacher_____ Location_____

Learner_____ Date Began _____

Adult Trainer_____ Date Completed_____

Step One
Selection of Child to be Tutored (The Learner)
A. Under Verbal Stimulus Control for   A. _____
   Disruptive Behavior
B. Follows One-Step Academic Commands   B. _____
C. Imitates Simple Motor Behaviors   C. _____
D. Select Learner   D. _____

Step Two
Program Selection for the Learner
A. Task Analyzed Behavior Objective   A. _____
B. Systematic Direct Teaching Procedure   B. _____
C. Child Progress Measure   C. _____
D. Appropriate for Peer Instruction   D. _____
   1. Simplicity   1. _____
   2. Safety   2. _____
E. Parent Permission for Child to be Tutored E. _____

Step Three
Tutor Selection and Orientation
A. Completion of Tutor Job Description   A. _____
B. Tutor Criteria Checklist   B. _____
   1. High Attendance   1. _____
   2. Socially Initiates   2. _____
   3. Socially Reciprocates   3. _____
   4. Follows Adult Directions   4. _____
   5. Ability to Physically Prompt   5. _____
   6. Parent Permission to Tutor   6. _____
C. Select Tutor   C. _____
D. Tutor Orientation   D. _____
   1. General (i.e., Puppet Show, etc.)   1. _____
   2. Introduction to Learner and Program   2. _____
   3. Child Specific Preparation   3. _____

Step Four
Study and Observe
A. Observe Program Implementation   A. _____
B. Describes Direct Teaching   B. _____
   1. Presentation   1. _____
   2. Child Response   2. _____
   3. Praise/Reinforcement   3. _____
   4. Correction Procedures   4. _____
C. Describes Child Progress Monitoring   C. _____
D. Describes Material and Setting   D. _____

Step Five
Progress Monitoring
A. Prepares Materials and Settings   A. _____
B. Observes Data Collection   B. _____
C. Collects   C. _____
D. Scores and Records Data with   D. _____
   90% Agreement with Trainer

Step Six
Praise and Reinforcement
A. Prepares Materials and Settings   A. _____
B. Collects and Records Appropriate
   Child Progress Data   B. _____
C. Praises Correct Responses Per   C. _____
   Identified Reinforcement Schedule
D. Pairs Praise with Identified Reinforcers   D. _____

Step Seven
Correction Procedures
A. Prepares Materials and Settings   A. _____
B. Collects and Records Appropriate
   Child Progress Data   B. _____
C. Praises and Reinforces as Trained   C. _____
D. Recognizes/Intercepts Errors
   Independently   D. _____
E. Conducts Stated Correction
   Procedures to the Trainer   E. _____

Step Eight
Independent Direct Teaching
A. Prepares Materials and Settings   A. _____
B. Gains Child's Attention   B. _____
C. Presents Appropriate Command/   C. _____
   Request
D. Waits for Child Response   D. _____
E. Praises and Reinforces as Trained   E. _____
F. Recognizes/Intercepts Errors
   Independently   F. _____
G. Conducts Stated Correction Procedures G. _____
H. Maintains Attending Behavior   H. _____
I. Records Appropriate Child Progress   I. _____
   Data

Appendix 9.A. (continued)

Step Nine
Trainer and Tutor Reliability Checks

Reliability Checks on Data Collection Between Tutor and Trainer

1. Date: _____	% Agreement: _____	9. Date: _____	% Agreement: _____
2. Date: _____	% Agreement: _____	10. Date: _____	% Agreement: _____
3. Date: _____	% Agreement: _____	11. Date: _____	% Agreement: _____
4. Date: _____	% Agreement: _____	12. Date: _____	% Agreement: _____
5. Date: _____	% Agreement: _____	13. Date: _____	% Agreement: _____
6. Date: _____	% Agreement: _____	14. Date: _____	% Agreement: _____
7. Date: _____	% Agreement: _____	15. Date: _____	% Agreement: _____
8. Date: _____	% Agreement: _____	16. Date: _____	% Agreement: _____

Step Ten
Comments

1. Date: _____
    Notes: _____
   _____
   _____

2. Date: _____
    Notes: _____
   _____
   _____

3. Date: _____
    Notes: _____
   _____
   _____

4. Date: _____
    Notes: _____
   _____
   _____

5. Date: _____
    Notes: _____
   _____
   _____

6. Date: _____
    Notes: _____
   _____
   _____

7. Date: _____
    Notes: _____
   _____
   _____

8. Date: _____
    Notes: _____
   _____
   _____

Appendix 9.A. (continued)

Tutor/Buddy Participation
Parent Permission Form

Child's Full Name _____

Dear Parents:

Students in your child's class have the opportunity to learn to become tutors and buddies to children with handicaps. If you and your child agree to participate, potential benefits to your child such as (1) developing an understanding and tolerance for individual differences among all people, (2) learning about different handicapping conditions, and (3) learning how to interact with children who have handicaps may occur.

If you decide to participate, your child will be under the ongoing supervision and guidance of school personnel to ensure program success and child well-being. Since the activities your child would be involved in are very common in the school setting, we anticipate that no harm to your child as a function of participation will occur.

In addition, your child's progress in his/her regular classes will be supervised by his/her teacher to ensure that s/he is not missing any valuable classroom time or activities. If, however, for any reason or at any time you or your child decide not to continue participation in this program, you may do so upon request without penalty.

To determine whether or not your child is benefiting from the program, information regarding social interactions and attitudes toward persons who have handicaps will be obtained (1) by talking with your child and (2) by having him/her complete a questionnaire. Photographs and/or videotapes may also be taken of your child during interaction to serve as data records and/or to train other students in the program. Any information which is collected will be available to parents in the form of group summaries upon request.

If you have any questions or concerns regarding this project, feel free to contact your child's teacher. But regardless of whether or not you decide to allow your child to participate, please sign below the appropriate question and return this form to your child's teacher by _____.

I <u>do not</u> grant permission for my   or   I <u>do</u> grant permission for my child
child to participate in this activity.   to participate in this activity.

_____   _____
       Parent Signature   Parent Signature

Thank you for your time and consideration.

Appendix 9.B.
Peer Tutoring Session Evaluation
VSSM Project
Recommended for Children 3-7 Years of Age

Joel Allred, John Killoran, Sebastian Striefel

When evaluating the success of a tutoring system, it is often helpful to know the feelings of both the tutors and the learners regarding their sessions together. Whether the tutor/learner felt good, bad, or indifferent to the session can have a significant effect on the overall quality of their present and future interaction. If the tutor and/or learner express dissatisfaction with the tutoring session, remedies should be devised to prevent animosity and/or apathy from developing within the tutor-learner relationship. For this reason, peer tutoring evaluation forms and procedures have been developed and will be presented in the following sections.

Session Evaluation

Upon completion of the peer tutoring session, the trainer will ask the tutor to describe how the session went. The question is phrased in general terms as opposed to specific questions about the learner, the program, etc. An example of how the question should be asked is: "How did the session go, Tony?" After the question, the trainer provides the tutor with the opportunity to respond. The **Peer Tutoring Session Evaluation 3-7** is used at this point to allow the tutor to select the face which most resembles how the session went for that specific tutoring session. The tutor expresses his attitude toward the session by pionting to or touching the face which represents his/her feeling and attitude for that session.* The faces which represent the three (3) global feelings are as follows:

*The placement of the faces on the demonstration sheet does not follow an equal progression in degrees of happiness (i.e., the first face is average, the next face is happy, the next face is sad). In the field-testing it was observed that tutors consistently selected the face located on the same side of the demonstration sheet regardless of the day or session. The ordering of the faces was therefore randomized to ensure that the tutors looked at all the faces before making a selection.

Appendix 9.B. (continued)

1. <u>Smiling face</u> - This face denotes a satisfied feeling toward the session, day, learner, program, etc. The expression on the face shows a half circle turned upward where the mouth is located.

2. <u>Average face</u> - This face denotes an average attitude (so-so) toward the session, day, learner, program, etc. The expression on the face shows a horizontal line where the mouth is located.

3. <u>Sad face</u> - This face denotes an unhappy, concerned, and/or sad attitude toward the session, day, learner, program, etc. The expression on the face shows a half circle turned downward where the mouth is located.

Another option for the tutor to demonstrate his/her feeling toward the session may involve coloring the face of choice. The trainer may also cut out the faces and randomly place them before the tutor and allow him/her to select the face s/he wants.

The key to the **Peer Tutoring Session Evaluation 3-7** is to allow the tutor a chance to express his/her feelings toward the session in order that the trainer may evaluate the session and make adjustments in the programming for the learner, the tutor, the instruction, future tutor placements, etc. The global question allows continuity, reliability, and validity over time as opposed to specific questions about the learner, the program, and the fact that the learner did not want to work. Keeping the question in general terms allows the tutor to decide how the session went and how the learner responded. His/her rating is more likely to be based upon all variables within the tutor/learner session if asked in global terms rather than in specific instances of behavior. Moreover, giving the same question each time provides a standardized procedure across all tutors and learners.

Data System
A comparison between tutor feeling and teacher/trainer observation toward the session over time may result in helpful hints regarding future placement, programming, etc. For this reason, the **Peer Tutoring Data System (3-7)** has been developed to record tutor responses and trainer observation checks. The tutor response may be checked or colored in (a red or blue felt-tip pen allows for more coverage and a better overall look) depending on the preference of the teacher/trainer. We have found it

Appendix 9.B. (continued)

useful to color in the face after each tutoring session and visually observe a larger and brighter pattern over time. After each session the trainer observes, s/he checks the face which corresponds with her/his feeling toward the tutoring session (i.e., Happy, Average, Sad). A space is also provided for comments about the session. The trainer may note any relevant observations or comments made by the tutor. These comments may also prove useful when studying observations made in sessions long past, which do not correspond or which need clarification. Not to be confused with the **Peer Tutoring Checklist,** which also has a section for comments, the **Peer Tutoring Data System's** (3-7) comments section is for noting comments regarding peer tutoring. The **Peer Tutoring Checklist's** comments section is for noting specifc data regarding the training of the peer tutor and his/her progress in program training mastery.

Appendix 9.B. (continued)

Peer Tutoring Data System 3-7
FMS/VSSM Projects

Date	Tutor	Learner	Time	Tutor/Learner Response	Observer Check	Comments

Appendix 9.B. (continued)

Peer Tutoring Session Evaluation 3-7
FMS/VSSM Projects

Chapter 10

· · ·

Transition for Kindergarten

The passage of Public Law 99-457 greatly enhances the interdisciplinary planning and programming elements for transition of handicapped infants, toddlers, and preschoolers and broadens the concept of transition. Since many agencies are involved in the planning and implementation of service delivery to preschool handicapped children, P.L. 99-457 attempts to clarify the roles of interagency service providers participating within this transition process. Most states will use multiple agencies in the provision of early intervention services. This multiplicity in service providers creates an increased need for smooth and well-defined transition strategies that cause little disruption in students' progress and families' lives (Killoran, 1988b).

Transitional Steps

Transition in preschool special education is accomplished through (a) transdisciplinary teaming, (b) parent involvement and training, (c) assessment and curricula, (d) interagency cooperation, (e) individual transition planning, and (f) program evaluation.

Transdisciplinary Teaming

Transdisciplinary teaming is a critical element in preschool special education. With the wide variety of health, developmental, and educational needs manifested by preschoolers who are handicapped, the expertise of many team members is needed to plan efficient and comprehensive assessment, intervention, and direct services. Each team member must incorporate a transition focus into his or her program and philosophies. This increased consistency across providers results in substantial child gains and also eases the difficulties of transition faced by children and parents.

Parent Involvement and Training

Parent involvement and training are also key aspects of transition planning. Parents who are actively participating and demonstrating responsibility in the transition process are more fully informed of the steps in transition and are most likely to feel in control of the process.

Assessment and Curricula

The use of appropriate assessment and curricula is essential to the achievement of one of the major goals of transition planning, which is to prepare children for placement in their next environment. This focus on preparing a child for future placements is especially evident in early childhood programs where students are receiving services for only 1 to 2 years. In essence, the entire preschool experience can be considered a transition process in terms of preparing parents as well as children for longitudinal school-age programs. Appropriate assessment and curricula can help prepare the child for future placements.

Interagency Cooperation

Interagency cooperation is essential in early childhood transition planning. At any single point in time, several agencies are likely to be providing services to preschool children with handicaps. These agencies include social, health, and educational agencies. The goal of interagency cooperation should be to strive for comprehensive planning and coordination of services to children.

Individual Transition Planning

Individual transition planning is essential for a child's success in both the preschool and future environments. The planning for each child needs to be based on the individual child's skills and deficits and on the skills needed in the next most likely environment (e.g., kindergarten). The planning must include a transdisciplinary team, as well as staff from other agencies, if the ultimate transition is to occur with minimal or no problems.

Program Evaluation

Ongoing program evaluation will measure the success of transition plans that have been developed. Evaluation information will contribute to effective transition planning by identifying the curricula needs in future environments, the most effective ways to meet those needs, and the type and intensity of parent training that will be necessary to be successful (Killoran, 1988b).

A Model for Transition Planning

Transition planning begins on the first day of the child's entrance into the integrated preschool and entails much more than the mere physical transfer of students and their records. In the FMS model, transition planning is conducted as a four-phase process (see Figure 10.1) which includes (a) interagency planning, (b) transdisciplinary staff preparation, (c) parent preparation, and (d) IEP-driven service delivery to the child. The process is simultaneous rather than sequential; that is, all phases may be addressed concurrently, rather than one after another.

Interagency Planning

Interagency planning refers to the planning conducted by sending and receiving agencies to transition children between agencies with no disruption in the service the child receives. Specifically, this planning includes:

1. Identifying case managers and transition coordinators in the sending and receiving agencies.

2. Jointly developing and disseminating interagency policies dealing with:

Figure 10.1 Flowchart of Transition Process

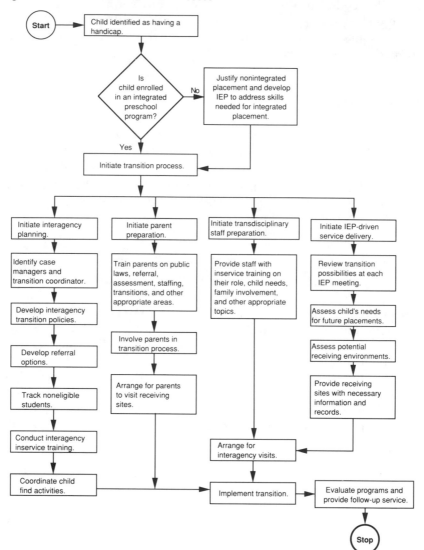

a. eligibility requirements (e.g., age at entry or exit),

b. referral of noneligible students,

c. funding responsibilities,

d. functional information to be forwarded and procedures for transfer of documents, and

e. plans and schedules for joint inservice activities.

3. Identifying and compiling a directory of referral options for students needing services, but no longer qualifying for special education.

4. Developing and implementing a system for tracking noneligible students to assure that they receive needed services and to monitor for future special education eligibility.

5. Jointly developing and conducting identified inservice activities (e.g., P.L. 99-457, Part B eligibility requirements).

6. Coordinating community child find activities and referral networks.

Transdisciplinary Personnel Preparation

This preparation is focused on providing staff with inservice training related to their role in the transition process, receiving agency eligibility criteria, family reactions to transition, and follow-up activities. Specific steps include inservice training of:

1. Professionals on their role in the transition process

2. Professionals regarding families as equal partners in the transition process.

3. Early intervention and preschool staff in eligibility criteria and interagency transition policies and procedures.

4. Professionals regarding the individualized special needs of technology-dependent children and how to effectively address them within the classroom/intervention setting.

5. Professionals on family/professional reactions to transition and positive coping with changes.

6. Professionals on appropriate follow-up activities.

The brochure, Questions Teachers Often Raise About Mainstreaming, presented in Chapter 3, may also be used with the staff in receiving agencies to answer the most common questions and concerns of teachers.

Parent Preparation for Transition

Parents need training concerning the different environments that their child might enter; P.L. 99-457 and P.L. 94-142; and the referral, assessment, and staffing procedures of the school that their child will attend. Since so few programs are presently integrated, parents must be prepared to encounter resistance from staff, students, and other parents as they attempt to insure continued integrated services for their child. Parents entering traditional school systems must be trained to be advocates for their child; therefore, they must receive information to use in discussing the benefits of integration. One such resource is a brochure entitled Facts About Integration: Answers for Parents (Appendix 10.A). This brochure can be distributed to parents as an informational resource. Additionally, it can serve as the basis for future parent training sessions about transition into kindergarten. Parent preparation for transition should begin upon a child's entry into an integrated program. At this initial point, transition preparation involves low-intensity general discussion about the program and goal of preparing children for their next placement.

At the beginning of a child's final year of preschool, medium-intensity preparation involves receiving a child's MESA-PK and examining the information to identify skills to be trained during the final year in preschool. Parent preparation involves reviewing the characteristics of the projected receiving environment and giving parents a person to contact in the district (e.g., the director of special education) who can answer specific questions and address concerns. The brochure Facts About Integration can be reintroduced at this point for general information. In the last quarter of a child's preschool program, high-intensity preparation of parents may involve structured meetings, a review of plans for their child, a review of their child's records and progress, and visits to the potential receiving school and classroom.

IEP-Driven Service Delivery

The IEP-driven service delivery to children is the most important aspect of transition planning and includes:

1. Orienting the family to transition procedures at each IEP review including eligibility criteria and transition activities specific to the child. The IEP should also address generic skills needed for success in the student's next possible placement (least restrictive environment).

2. Within 6 months before expected entry into school services, the child is assessed according to the eligibility requirements for school-age special education and related service, and a transition coordinator is assigned.

3. A transition planning meeting is held to:

   a. identify potential receiving classrooms and other intervention settings so parents and staff can visit,

   b. establish transition dates and time lines,

   c. provide prior notice for transfer of records,

   d. initiate a formal referral for services, and

   e. complete a child profile (Appendix 10.B), which is designed to provide a receiving teacher with an overview of a child's history and strengths.

4. Staff arrange site visits to potential receiving settings within the LEA to become familiar with the nature of each program and to become acquainted with the staff.

5. Conduct site visits using the Classroom Environment Observation Profile (Appendix 10.C), which was designed to obtain information related to expectations needed for success in the potential settings.

6. Receiving agency conducts observation in preschool setting.

7. Parents and representatives from the sending and receiving agencies meet to develop the child's IEP and to determine the child's appropriate placement, including starting date of service, or child is placed in a local education agency program based on existing IEP with the next IEP to be developed within 30 days of placement.

8. Transition goals and objectives, based on generic skill assessment that addresses specific needs for successful placement in the next least restrictive environment, are added to the IEP for the remainder of the child's preschool services.

Preparation for Future Environments

In recent years, there has been much discussion of the need before transition to identify and train survival skills that will be demanded in a child's next environment (Carta, Sainato, & Greenwood, 1988; Hains, Fowler, & Chandler, 1988; Rule, Fiechtl, & Innocenti, 1990; Walter & Vincent, 1982). Examples of these survival skills include following directions, independently completing tasks, or working in large groups. Preparing students for these demands will help them function in mainstreamed kindergartens or first grades (Carta et al., 1988; McCormick & Kawate, 1982; Rule et al., 1990).

Rationales for teaching future-referenced survival skills to preschoolers with handicaps include handicapped children's inability to spontaneously imitate the actions of their nonhandicapped peers without systematic instruction, as well as dichotomous learning conditions between preschool and school-age settings, such as decreased teacher attention, praise, and correction procedures (Rule et al., 1990).

To be successfully mainstreamed into integrated kindergarten classrooms, children must (a) work independently, (b) participate in groups, (c) follow varied directions, and (d) use varied materials. It is clear that to teach children these future-referenced survival skills, preparation must be initiated upon initial entry into the preschool rather than immediately prior to the actual transition to kindergarten.

Skills for School Success Curriculum

The *Skills for School Success* curriculum (Fiechtl, Innocenti, & Rule, 1987), developed by the Preschool Transition Project at Utah State University, addresses nine activities that frequently occur in mainstreamed kindergartens and first grades. These activities include:

1. Entry routines (hanging up coat, selecting toy, and playing until the teacher announces the next activity).

2. Sequenced individual tasks (individually completing a series of tasks announced daily).

3. Pledge of Allegiance.

4. Group circle activities (e.g., discussion of calendar or weather).

5. Individual tasks (manipulative or paper-and-pencil tasks from commercially available sources).

6. Large group activity (instructional activities using commercially available curricula).

7. Workbook.

8. Quiet time (child-selected, child-guided activity).

9. Classroom transition (getting coat and materials to take home, lining up, walking in line through the building).

Each activity is analyzed into component skills or tasks, and performance criteria describe the speed and competence necessary for completing each task (Rule et al., 1990).

The curriculum is used for a short duration daily beginning in January of the year before children enter kindergarten or first grade. More difficult activities, such as workbooks, are introduced in the last 2 to 3 months of the school year. Teachers provide assistance as necessary, but teacher attention is carefully faded to assure that children are not dependent on assistance and approval. To assure that children attend to daily directions and tasks, rather than learning routines, instruction and location of materials are varied (Rule et al., 1990).

The *Skills for School Success* curriculum provides an efficient and cost-effective method for initiating longitudinal transition planning in integrated preschool settings. (For further information on the Skills for School Success curriculum, contact Sallie Rule, Outreach Development and Dissemination, Developmental Center for Handicapped Persons, Utah State University, Logan, UT.)

Appendix 10.A.

Facts About Mainstreaming and Integration:

Answers for Parents

With the passage of Public Law 94-142, and the recent amendments in Public Law 99-457 -- The Education of Handicapped Children Acts -- more and more children with handicaps are being integrated into regular education classrooms. The changes brought about by integration have raised many questions by parents. The purpose of this brochure is to answer many of the most common questions that parents have asked.

1.   What is integration?

Integration is the process of serving all children, with and without handicaps, in the same setting, to the maximum extent possible. A program for children with handicaps that is separate from programs for other children is a restrictive environment. All children need an opportunity to interact with others, whether they have a handicap or not. By law every child has the right to be in the least restrictive environment. A self-contained program may be the least restrictive environment for a few children; for most it is not.

2.   What is mainstreaming?

"Mainstreaming" and "integration" are often used interchangeably. They are not the same. Mainstreaming is defined as placement (grouping) of children with and without handicaps, without planned/structured involvement in common social and instructional activities. Integration is defined as the process of placing (grouping) children with and without handicaps in the same setting with planned/structured involvement in common social and instructional activities. Most schools, however, do not use the term *integration*. Since schools usually use the term *mainstreaming*, this term will be used in this brochure to facilitate communication within traditional school systems.

3.   Does this mean that special education programs will be dissolved, and all children with handicaps will return to regular programs?

No. For a child with handicaps, mainstreaming may involve a range of activities, from full-day placement in a regular class to short periods of mainstreaming at play times. The rest of the time, the child may be in a self-contained program. The extent to which a child is mainstreamed is based on the child's individual needs. These needs are determined by the child's parents and the professionals that work with that child.

Appendix 10.A. (continued)

4. *Who decides when and how to mainstream a child?*

Children with handicaps have a child study team made up of the child's parents, teachers, the administrator, and specialists (speech therapists, motor specialists, etc.). This team develops the child's goals and objectives -- the individualized education program or I.E.P. -- and decides on the amount of mainstreaming which is appropriate. Based upon the child's social, cognitive, self-help, motor, and academic skills, a decision is made on whether a child would benefit from receiving services in a program alongside classmates without handicaps. These decisions are made individually for each child with handicaps, and her/his progress is reviewed periodically.

5. *How much of a say do I have in my child's placement?*

Each child with special needs is required to have parental approval of his/her IEP. By law, the IEP must list: (a) the child's present level of performance, (b) short- and long-term educational goals for the child in the coming year, (c) how progress toward these goals is to be measured, (d) the educational services the child is to receive including any special services, (e) the extent the child is to be mainstreamed, and (f) the date the services are to begin as well as the length of time the services are to be provided. Parents must also be given written notice of any proposed changes in the child's placement. If there is a disagreement between the parents and the school over the child's placement which cannot be resolved, the problem may be settled through administrative channels. Administrative procedures may include informal mediation or a formal hearing. Contact your state educational agency for further information.

6. *How can I get involved in my child's education?*

There are a variety of ways and levels in which you can get involved. Joining parent groups such as the PTA, volunteering in the classroom, and attending parent workshops and in-services are several possibilities. Advocating for mainstreaming by becoming part of a school committee for public awareness, participating in local school board meetings, or by talking to other parents are also ways of getting involved.

Working with your child at home involves you in your child's growth, especially working on your child's programs and discussing the topics covered in class. Informal exchanges with the teacher also count. Any input you can give, such as progress you are seeing at home or distinct behaviors that you are observing, will help the teacher and ultimately will benefit your child.

7. *What benefits are there for taxpayers when children are mainstreamed?*

A person with handicaps who learns to function alongside persons without handicaps is a tremendous tax savings for the community. For example, it costs several times as much of our annual tax dollars for residential care for a person with handicaps, compared to one year of self-contained public education for that same person who can later join the work force and contribute to the tax base. Additionally, a mainstreaming program, once begun, is far less expensive than a self-contained program. Less monies spent for special services means more monies to improve the quality of services for all children.

Appendix 10.A. (continued)

8. *What kinds of children with special needs are mainstreamed?*

Children who are mainstreamed have a variety of handicapping conditions, ranging from mild to severe disabilities, such as intellectual handicaps, social deficits, and language and/or motor delays. No matter what the handicapping condition is, one important thing to remember is that children with handicaps are just like all other children. They like to play with the same kinds of games and toys, they like to have friends, and they need to be loved and accepted.

9. *Will my child pick up any of these handicapping conditions like she/he would a cold?*

No. Handicapping conditions are not contagious. It is important for parents to reassure their children that they will not become handicapped if they play with or work next to a child with a handicap. Remember, children model their parents' attitudes and biases.

10. *Will my child see or learn strange behaviors from the children with handicaps?*

Sometimes children with handicaps exhibit unique, repetitive movements called stereotypic behaviors. At worst, these may include twirling, flapping hands, or waving arms. It is possible that a young child without handicaps will imitate these behaviors once or twice to try out something new. However, unless adults specifically praise or give positive attention for these behaviors, the child will stop because these behaviors are not acceptable at home, in the classroom, or with friends. Parents need not worry that their child will learn permanent strange behaviors.

11. *Who decides in which mainstreamed classroom a child with handicaps will be placed?*

At present, the most common way to decide where to place a child is by asking for teachers to volunteer to take the child in her/his class. A teacher is in the best position to decide if her/his classroom can accommodate a new student. However, the selection of teachers should be systematic rather than haphazard. Factors such as age, gender, developmental level, teacher skills and expectations, and environmental limitations are considered.

12. *Will my child lose the special services now offered to her/him?*

Teachers use several ways of making sure each child receives the attention that she/he needs. For example, peer buddies and peer tutoring allow the children to interact positively within a structured, supervised program, while giving the teacher more time to provide concentrated attention to others in the class who need it.

The teacher is not expected to teach a child in areas of need that are beyond the scope of her/his training, such as speech therapy or motor services. But this does not mean that children coming into the program should lose special services that are needed. If a child has an area of need, the agency should provide the most appropriate service for that need. If this service is not available in the classroom, a different placement may be needed.

Appendix 10.A. (continued)

Before mainstreaming, it is important to specify who will be working with the child and in what areas she/he will be working, e.g., physical therapy, small group activities, etc. Specialists/therapists may choose to conduct one-to-one sessions with the child as the child's team deems necessary. Teachers, aides, and volunteers can also be trained to provide these services under the supervision of the therapist.

13. Will the children and the teacher help my child too much and reduce her/his independence?

Well-meaning people may have a tendency to step in and help too quickly at times. By keeping well informed about the program and serving as a class volunteer or visiting the class occasionally, a parent can see if this problem is occurring and can consult with the teacher on alternatives to increase, not decrease, the independence of the child.

14. Will my child get the same amount of attention even though the teacher has to tend a child with extra needs?

A well-planned mainstreaming program actually results in more individualized attention for all students. A teacher who learns to spot "special" needs in one child also learns to spot "special" needs of other children. By grouping children and designing individualized lessons, teachers actually can do a better job of meeting the needs and interests of all children.

15. What about activities my child can't do because of her/his handicapping condition?

For rare situations like this, there are other activities that the child can engage in. All children, with and without handicaps, need to receive appropriate services and therefore, must be treated equally in the classroom. This means that a child should not automatically be limited by age and/or handicapping condition. Each child should be allowed to try every activity, with encouragement and formal teaching, if needed, to do the best that she/he can.

16. Will my child be safe in the same program as children with special needs?

The idea that persons who are intellectually handicapped, or retarded, are violent or aggressive is an incorrect and unfortunate myth. There are persons with handicaps who are aggressive, just as there have always been class "bullies." However, a child who is physically aggressive and is a danger to himself or others, handicapped or not, would not be enrolled in a mainstreamed classroom until her/his behavior can be controlled under adult supervision.

17. How are children without handicaps prepared to interact with children with handicaps?

Children and adults will make fun of different things that they do not understand. By explaining handicaps as individual differences, and by actually helping children learn to play together within the limits of one child's handicap, teachers and parents

Appendix 10.A. (continued)

can help children learn tolerance and respect for the feelings of others.

When a teacher has prepared classmates to receive a new child who has some limitations in ability, the students will be unlikely to injure the new child. This type of preparation may consist of talking about the new student, doing puppet skits about mainstreaming situations, and practicing ways to be a "buddy" to the new student. Other concerns about playground, bus, or other settings should be addressed directly to the school and plans must be made jointly with them to assure the child's safety.

Besides peer preparation, peer buddies will also help the child adjust to the new situation. But as with all new children, it may take a few days for her/him to establish a place in the social structure of the class.

If your child tells you that she/he is unhappy or feels left out, you should bring it to the teacher's attention right away.

18. How will other parents react to my child's presence in the classroom?

Again, people tend to question things they don't understand. In this case, parents who are unfamiliar with mainstreaming may have doubts about it at first. By having their questions answered and by seeing a successful mainstreaming effort, they tend to become strong supporters of mainstreaming. Most importantly, parents should remember that there are more similarities than differences among parents of children with and without handicaps.

19. What possible benefits will mainstreaming have for _my_ child?

1. Most importantly, mainstreaming teaches children without handicaps about tolerance and understanding of individual differences in all persons.

2. Children without handicaps in mainstreaming programs have shown more socially mature behaviors than without mainstreaming, such as the development of leadership skills.

3. The language level, plus the rate of social interaction, of children with handicaps in a mainstreaming program is higher than those involved in segregated programs.

4. Teachers in a mainstreamed classroom learn skills to identify the needs of children and teacher techniques that increase the quality of individualized attention.

In this brochure, we are trying to show that although there are differences between children with and without handicaps, there are also similarities. These similarities also exist among parents, no matter if their child has handicaps or not. The ultimate concern that is shared by all parents seems to be that their child will receive quality services and gain a positive classroom experience at the same time. Quality services for all children, giving them equal opportunities to learn, play, and grow together to the maximum extent possible, is our ultimate goal.

Appendix 10.B.

Child Profile

Sebastian Striefel, Maria Quintero, & John Killoran

Purpose:

The Child Profile is designed to provide a receiving teacher in a mainstream setting with an overview of the child's educational and medical history along with existing strengths in various areas. The information on the profile can be very useful in forwarding information from one academic setting to another when mainstreaming is occurring, and can be used by the child's study team (IEP team) to plan the child's IEP. The profile can also be used as a "check-up" to monitor the child's improvements. It can be used by the regular education teacher as a working record of the child's skills, any medical conditions (e.g., seizures, diabetes, etc.), and behavior management programs.

Description:

The Child Profile has twelve information sections in which brief summaries of a child's handicapping condition, educational history, academic skills, social skills, communication skills, motor skills, and medical history are recorded. The first five sections provide demographic data. The remaining seven sections each contain a brief statement about the child's skills, qualities, and needs. The completed Child Profile should provide the Child Study Team with more knowledge and a better understanding of the child and the child's skills so that they will be aware of any steps which need to be taken to facilitate mainstreaming.

General Instructions:

The teacher, in conjunction with the child's parents and other members of the Child Study Team, should complete the Child Profile. Accuracy is critical, so it may be necessary to obtain some of the information from primary sources such as the child's school and medical files. This profile should be placed in the child's file to safeguard its confidentiality.

Appendix 10.B. (continued)

Child Profile

I. Child's Name: _____ Child's Nickname: _____

II. Age: _____ Date of Birth: _____

III. Sex: _____

IV. Exceptionality (check one):

IH	———	Hearing Impaired-Deaf	———	Physically Handicapped ———
SIH	———	Hearing Impaired-Hard of Hearing	———	Communication Disordered ———
SMH	———	Visually Impaired-Blind	———	Behavior Disordered ———
SMH-Autistic	———	Visually Impaired-Partially Sighted	———	Learning Disabled ———
SMH-Deaf/blind	———			Other (Specify) ———

V. Educational History

	Hospital Instruction	Homebound Instruction	Special Day School	Self-Contained Full day	Self-Contained Part day	Resource Room Full day	Resource Room Part day	Regular class Full day	Regular class Part day	Other - Specify
Current Placement: (check all that apply)										
Placement during previous year: (check all that apply)										

VI: Readiness Skills (Check all that apply)

Please indicate programs in progress with "P".

Identifies simple objects and their functions _____

Identifies major body parts: receptively _____
                                                 expressively _____

Identifies objects as big or little _____

Appendix 10.B. (continued)

Appendix 10.B. (continued)

Recognizes first name _____

Identifies colors: receptively _____
                    expressively _____

Identifies shapes: receptively _____
                    expressively _____

Counts objects to: _____
Rote counts to: _____
Recognizes numerals: _____

Discriminates same and different _____

Matches ABC's _____
Identifies ABC's: receptively _____
                   expressively _____

VII. Social Skills:

How does child initiate play with peers? Check all that apply:
—— Gestures with objects (hands, objects, etc.)
—— Joins in ongoing play without prompting
—— Appropriately calls peers to join him/her without prompting
—— Child does not engage in appropriate play with peers
—— Other _____

In a group situation, the child   mostly:
—— Participates in cooperative play with peers
—— Plays only alongside peers (parallel play)
—— Plays alone (isolate play)

How does child respond when another child initiates play or speaks to
     him/her?
—— Responds appropriately by handing toy/sharing/engaging in verbal
     exchange (if child has verbal skills)
—— Ignores peers
—— Demonstrates physical/verbal aggression
—— Overtly refuses to interact (says "no," runs away, etc.)
—— Other: _____

Appendix 10.B. (continued)

VIII.   Communication Skills:

How does child make needs/wants known? _____

_____

For communication, child uses (check all that apply):

Manual sign language _____   Single words only _____
Communication board _____   Short phrases _____
Written communication _____   Full sentences _____
Other (specify) _____

According to most recent testing, the child's language skills are:

Receptive language age equivalent   _____
Expressive language age equivalent   _____

IX.   Motor Skills:

Child can (check all that apply:)   _____ Walk with support
                                        _____ Go up/down stairs alone
                                        _____ Walk alone

Child uses hands for: _____ Coloring   _____ Cutting
                                        _____ Feeding self _____ Pre-Writing
                                        _____ Picking up small objects

Child uses the following: _____ Wheelchair   _____ Walker
                                        _____ Other (specify) _____
                                        _____

(If applicable) Child can:

_____Propel wheelchair independently
_____Transfer own body independently from wheelchair to seats, etc.

Child can toilet self: _____ yes _____ no

Child can dress self: _____ yes _____ no

For what motor activities, if any, does the child need help?

_____

_____

Appendix 10.B. (continued)

Note any restrictions to physical activity.

_____

_____

X. Medical Notes:

Is child on medication?   _____ yes   _____ no
Is medication administered during school hours?   _____ yes   _____ no
If yes, indicate name of medicine   _____
    Dosage _____
    Time of day when administered   _____
    Physician's name   _____
    Physician's telephone number   _____
    Indicate side effects of medication (sleepiness, lack of appetite, etc.)

    _____

    _____

Does child have seizures?   _____ yes   _____ no
If yes, what does the child do during a seizure (e.g., fall to the floor,
    stare, etc.)?   _____

_____

_____

_____

Indicate procedure to be followed when child has a seizure   _____

_____

_____

_____

Does child have vision or hearing problems?   _____ yes   _____ no
If yes, indicate type of problem   _____

Does child use a hearing aid?   _____ yes   _____ no
Does child wear glasses?   _____ yes   _____ no

Does the child currently have tubes in his/her ears?
                _____ yes _____ right   _____ left   _____ no

Does the child need a catheter or colostomy bag?   _____ yes   _____ no
If yes, indicate procedure to be followed.   _____

_____

_____

Appendix 10.B. (continued)

Does the child have food allergies or intolerances? _____ yes _____ no
If yes, please indicate. _____

_____

Does the child have feeding problems? _____ yes _____ no
If yes, please indicate. _____

_____

Does the child have cardiac problems? _____ yes _____ no
If yes, please indicate. _____

_____

Does child have other medical difficulties? _____ yes _____ no
If yes, please indicate. _____

_____

_____

XI. Service Needs
Please complete each area:

Therapy	Goals of Therapy	Frequency/Duration of Therapy	Name of Therapist
Communication			
Occupational Therapy			
Physical Therapy			
Behavior Therapy			
Nutritional Programming			
Adaptive Physical Education			
Other			

Appendix 10.B. (continued)

XII. Behavior Management

Check reinforcers which are effective and describe conditions for which they are used regularly:

———— edible; specify _____

———— points/chips; specify _____

———— stickers; specify _____

———— free time; specify _____

———— verbal praise; specify _____

———— physical attention (hugs, etc.); specify _____

———— other; specify _____

What procedures are effective? _____

_____

_____

When are they used? _____

_____

_____

Appendix 10.C.

Instruction Manual

**CEO Profile
Classroom Environment Observation Profile
for Mainstreaming (CEO)**

Maria Quintero, Sebastian Striefel,
John Killoran, & Joel Allred

Purpose:

The Classroom Environment Observation (CEO) Profile for Mainstreaming is designed to be used by teachers and other members of a child's study team when they observe a potential receiving environment to determine the appropriateness of that environment as a placement for a student who is to be mainstreamed. This information can be used to:

1. Modify the special education environment to more closely approximate the regular setting so that the child to be mainstreamed can adjust more easily to the transfer.

2. Identify potential areas of difficulty in the receiving environment (e.g., physical barriers) which can be addressed before the child's change in placement.

3. Identify skills a child needs in order to be successful in the observed environment, so those skills can be trained prior to placement.

It is acknowledged that the CEO Profile is not all-inclusive; every setting poses unique problems and presents unique strengths which can be missed by an attempt to be all-encompassing. The CEO Profile is best viewed as a list of reminders for an observer to assure that limited observation time is used efficiently to gather important relevant information.

Description:

The CEO Profile is composed of six sections:

Section 1:
Teacher Instructions or Cues - In this section an observer will check and list the types of directions, methods of presentation of materials, attention cues, and behavior management techniques typically used by the teacher in the observed setting.

Section 2:
Children's Skills - By observing the group attending skills of the classroom children, an observer will note how children in that setting respond to instructions from the teacher, and how they are expected to attend and interact in groups and individual activities.

Appendix 10.C. (continued)

Section 3:
   Peer Systems and Grouping Techniques - Since group activities are common in many settings, in this section, an observer will note the size of groups used in the observed setting, the nature (cooperative, competitive, individualized, independent) of group activities, and the existing use of peers as facilitators of learning (e.g., as buddies or tutors).

Section 4:
   Resources - The personnel and material resources in a setting can be critical factors to be considered in mainstreaming. Section 4 requests that an observer record the number of adults who work in the setting, the physical arrangement, and any potential structural limitations of the receiving environment.

Section 5:
   Curriculum - When considering mainstreaming which involves academic activities, it is important to know if the target student can function within the curricula used in the receiving setting. On Section 5, an observer will note the curricula used in a number of academic areas, as well as teacher instructions which may be specific to the task. For example, the instruction, "Follow along with your eyes while Mary reads," can be very confusing to a student who has not previously participated in group reading activities. Prior training, or alerting the teacher to a child's limited understanding, can prevent confusion and/or behavior problems.

Section 6:
   Classroom Diagram - In this section, the observer will sketch the physical layout of the setting to note work areas, physical barriers, etc. Such a diagram would be particularly useful in mainstreaming students with motor or sensory disabilities, since these students may require more space or special seating arrangements in order to participate effectively.

General Instructions:

   An observer should use the CEO Profile as a guide, or a set of reminders, for what to observe when visiting a potential receiving environment. Whenever possible, notes and examples should be used to supplement the checklist sections which are indicated on the CEO Profile. The applicable sections of the checklist should be used during observations of the work times, transition periods, in-class leisure time, and non-academic school activities (lunch, recess, etc.) which are proposed for mainstreaming. A separate CEO Profile should be used for academic and nonacademic activities to identify pertinent physical characteristics, staff/pupil ratios, and resources in different situations. At first inspection, the observation of several environments may seem overwhelming; however, in reality, functional mainstreaming is rarely conducted as a total removal of a child from one setting to place him/her full-time in another setting. Gradual mainstreaming, which allows a student to adapt to increasing levels of integration, would require that observations be conducted only in those settings/activities being considered for the target child's immediate mainstreaming.

Appendix 10.C. (continued)

Specific Instructions:

When observing a potential receiving site, an observer should:

1. Complete the relevant demographic and informational items on page 1 of the CEO Profile.

2. Complete Sections 1 through 3: (1) **Teacher Instructions or Cues**, (2) **Children's Skills**, and (3) **Peer Systems and Grouping Techniques**, by carefully observing the class and noting the items indicated on the CEO Profile.

3. Observe the classroom and the school settings indicated in Sections 4 and 6, **Resources** and **Classroom Diagram**, to identify physical characteristics and people resources.

4. Interview the teacher to obtain information for completing Section 5, **Curriculum**.

Appendix 10.C. (continued)

CEO Profile
Classroom Environment Observation Profile

Maria Quintero
Sebastian Striefel
John Killoran
Joel Allred

Observer _____ Date _____

Classroom _____ Teacher _____

Activity/Setting _____

Time Start _____ Time End _____

Appendix 10.C. (continued)

Section 1	Section 2
Teacher Instructions or Cues **(Verbal or Nonverbal)**	**Children's Skills**

The teacher in this setting uses (check and give examples): 1- step directions _____ example: _____ _____ _____ 2- step directions _____ example: _____ _____ 3- step or longer directions _____ example: _____ _____ _____	For each item, check some, most, or all. Some ___ Most _____ All _____ Children follow 1 step instructions Some ___ Most _____ All _____ Children follow 2 step instructions Some ___ Most _____ All _____ Children follow 3 step instructions
	Child could follow directions simply by imitating others. Yes _____ No _____

Materials are presented through (check all that apply)
 	
Lecture_____Direct Instruction _____
Discussion _____ Chalkboard _____
Demonstration _____Reading _____
Film _____
Other Media _____ give examples:
	Children Participate in Discussions (check all that apply):
	
	Raise hand and wait to be called on ___
	Make eye contact with speaker _____
	Answer simple, factual questions _____
	Answer complex, conceptual, or
	  inferential questions _____
	Attend to task with minimal teacher
	  intervention for:
	  10 - 15 minutes _____
	  15 - 20 minutes _____
	  20 - 30 minutes _____
	  more than 30 minutes _____
	Take turn with materials _____
	Initiate interactions with peers _____
	Give examples of how children initiate
	  interactions with peers:

The teacher gets children's attention by (check all that apply): Nonverbal Signals _____, such as: Repeated Phrases _____, such as: Calling Children by Name _____	
For inappropriate behaviors, the teacher uses: (check all that apply) Reprimands _____ Ignoring _____ Removing Child _____ Other _____ give examples:	Notes:
For appropriate behaviors, the teacher uses: (check all that apply) Free Time _____ Praise _____ Edibles _____ Earned Privileges _____ Other _____ give examples:	

Appendix 10.C. (continued)

Section 3

Peer Systems and Grouping Techniques

Characteristics of groups in this setting are:

Number of groups used in class _____
Number of children per group _____
Competitive activities commonly
    used _____
Cooperative activities commonly
    used _____
Individualized activities commonly
    used _____
Independent work commonly
    used _____

Notes:

Classroom peers are used for (Check all
    that apply):

Informal academic assistance _____
Formal peer tutoring _____
Other _____

Notes:

Section 4

Resources

Personnel

How many adults work in the classroom? _____
How many children are in the classroom? _____
What ages are the children? _____

Physical Arrangement

Child sit:
    in circle on floor_____
    at tables _____
    at individual desks _____

For children in wheelchairs or with motor difficulties,
note limitations for going to, using, and returning from:

Bathroom (location, size of door, angle of entry way,
    size of stalls, etc.)

Cafeteria (location, width of ordering line, seating
    arrangements, etc.)

Library (location, height of shelves, accessible
    tables, etc.)

Gym/Playground (location, supervision, equipment,
    fencing, etc.)

Assembly/Auditorium (location, seating, etc.)

Fire Exits (location, accessibility, ramps, etc.)

Appendix 10.C. (continued)

Section 5
Curriculum

Indicate (a) curriculum used in each subject area.
(b) teacher instructions commonly used in that subject area.
(c) time of day when subject is taught.

Reading	Social Studies
(a)	(a)
(b)	(b)
(c)	(c)
Math	Science
(a)	(a)
(b)	(b)
(c)	(c)
Spelling	Other
(a)	(a)
(b)	(b)
(c)	(c)

Additional Curriculum Notes:

Section 6
Draw Classroom Diagram

Note width of aisles, spaces between seats, lighting, and any potential barriers. Also note presence of wall rails, etc., to assist students in wheelchairs.

Chapter 11

• • •

Program and Child Progress Evaluation

Successful programs are based on a process that recognizes the usefulness of feedback obtained from program and child progress evaluations. The essential components for conducting both types of evaluations are discussed in this chapter, along with information on how to use the date obtained to improve the program. The future of preschool integration as a permanent part of the education system is also discussed.

Multiple Indices of Impact

The integration of children with and without handicaps in a preschool program has been presented as a multifaceted process. This process involves people (children, their families, teachers, specialists, and administrators) as well as material resources (e.g., physical plant, money). A system that involves this complex interplay of variables can easily drift away from the original goals of the program, unless methods for evaluating the progress and impact of the various components are in place and utilized. Only through ongoing evaluation can a system be assured of remaining focused on meeting the needs of the children in the program.

Evaluation of an integrated program is conducted to accomplish three main objectives: (a) to assess child progress, (b) to identify parts

285

of the program that may need modification, and (c) to implement informed changes that maximize the benefits of a program for the amount of money expended. These objectives depend on information regarding children, parents, staff, and material resources. Information may be collected through formal methods or through informal chan-nels. Formal methods include standardized instruments, such as tests, as well as other inventories or measures on various indices. Informal channels depend on unplanned or unstructured observations, retro-spective analyses, self-reports, and other indicators of feedback. Table 11.1 summarizes a variety of methods for evaluating the impact of inte-gration on children, parents, staff, material, resources, and time.

Although each of the procedures outlined in Table 11.1 provides valuable information concerning the success or failure of an integration effort, it is not implied that an evaluation program must contain all of these measures. Every integrated program is unique, and evaluation should be designed to meet the specific needs of each program.

Evaluation of Impact on Children

Formal Measures. An IEP for a child with handicaps lists those skills deemed necessary for that child to function more successfully in his or her environment. The goals and objectives that are delineated for the child may be roughly categorized into five areas: cognitive skills, communication skills, self-help skills, gross and fine motor skills, and social skills. The child's IEP team should closely evaluate progress toward these goals and objectives and, if the child was previously not in an integrated setting, contrast the progress previously shown in these areas to expectations of progress before placement occurred. Progress on goals and objectives can be determined only by collecting ongoing samples of a child's performance on the skills being taught. The ongoing collection of data in the classroom was discussed in detail in Chapter 8 in relation to the training of skills in various group settings and in microsessions. As this information is gathered, the trainer must decide whether the child's performance is indicative of learning (progress), remains unchanged, or indicates loss of skills (regression). Evidence of learning is clear when the child's data reflect an increas-ing number of correct responses during training. No changes or regres-sion, however, can be more difficult to interpret. It is not unusual for data to remain unchanged or even to show a slight regression as a child adjusts to a new environment, trainer, or task. Additionally, external factors such as health or family changes can slow a child's progress. The trainer must observe the child very carefully for evidence that

Table 11.1. Methods for Evaluation

Target Area	Formal Measures	Informal Measures
Children	IEP	Informal Observation
	Test Scores	Parent Report of Generalization
	Formal Observation	Child's Self-Report
	Number of Microsessions	
	MESA-PK	
	Social Interaction System	
Parents	Pre/Post Opinionnaire	Informal Communication
	Written Program Evaluation	Word of Mouth Recruitment
Staff	Written Program Evaluation	Informal Communication
	(Teachers and Administrators)	Cooperative Teacher Projects
	TEAM-PK	Teacher-Initiated Contributions
Materials/Time	Additional funds required for equipment, materials, and staff unique to integration	Unaccounted Staff Time
	Funds to modify the integrated environment	
	Staff time devoted to implementing integration procedures	
	Cost of substitutes used during training	

may suggest that lack of progress could be transitory (e.g., attributable to normal adjustment to the task) versus evidence that other steps must be taken (e.g., child shows increasing discomfort or disruptive behaviors; regression persists beyond 2 weeks).

It cannot be assumed that a child will make strides toward meeting his or her goals in all areas; however, evaluation should indicate success in some of the areas. The first course of action when progress does not occur is to look at aspects of the program to see if the program is being conducted as designed, if functional reinforcers are available, if the child possesses the requisite skills, if the goal or objective needs further task analysis, if a small group or a microsession is needed, and if progress is different from when the child was not mainstreamed (Striefel & Cadez, 1983a). In some cases, the services provided in the integrated setting will need to be changed several times for child progress to occur, including providing the same services in the same way they would be provided in a nonintegrated setting.

An additional index of the impact of integration on a child with handicaps is a reduction or increase in the number of microsessions needed to address goals and objectives. In a successfully integrated program, the number of microsessions may be expected to decrease as a child learns new skills and the training can be incorporated into integrated activities. Keep in mind, however, that even microsessions can use peer models.

Formal tests and other instruments of pre-/postskill assessments may be used to evaluate impact on children with and without handicaps. There are many standardized tests that may be used; however, consideration should be given to the sensitivity of the test and the purpose for its use. For example, a measure of intelligence may yield interesting and informative data about a child's cognitive functioning. However, such a test may not be appropriate for assessing changes within a 6- or 12-month period. A more desirable instrument may be a developmental scale, such as the *Battelle Developmental Inventory* (Newborg, Stock, Wnek, Guidubaldi, & Svinicki, 1984). Other instruments such as the MESA-PK (see Chapter 8) or criterion-referenced measures such as the *Program Assessment and Planning Guide for Developmentally Disabled and Preschool Children* (Striefel & Cadez, 1983b) can demonstrate the acquisition or loss of specific skills.

The development and practice of social skills is a major objective of integrated preschool services. Formal measures of the development and use of social skills can be obtained through direct observation of children during play activities. The FMS Social Interaction Coding System (Appendix 11.A) outlines one way of formally observing behaviors of children at play. The system tracks different forms of inter-action, but particularly focuses on reciprocal positive exchanges between children. Reciprocal interactions are considered more indica-tive of social skills development than the more traditional, cooper-ative play, because a reciprocal interaction demands that children establish physical or verbal contact with one another in a request or exchange. Cooperative play, however, can occur in a group without children necessarily having to establish physical or verbal contact with a peer.

Informal Measures. Teacher and parent observations of a child can yield valuable information about that child's adjustment to, and benefit from, participation in an integrated program. Observations about a child's response to school (e.g., Does the child appear happy, smiling, eager to go see his friends?) can reveal much about the child's opinion of a program. Direct child feedback can also be obtained by asking children how they like school and/or their friends. Responses obtained directly from preschoolers must be interpreted very cautiously, however, since self-reports of preschoolers can be unreliable and unstable from one day to another (Rule et al., 1990). Young children may report "hating" a playmate because he or she took away a desired toy. Shortly thereafter, the same child may categorize the playmate as a "best friend" because they collaborated successfully on another activity. The value of direct inquiry, however, is that the child's responses may reflect how the child feels from day to day or within specific activities.

More information may be gleaned from informal observations of children during relatively unstructured times, such as free play, arrival in the mornings, lining up, and preparation for going home. A teacher might observe for unprompted situations where children with and without handicaps approach and interact with one another. Positive or inappropriate behaviors observed at these times may signal success-ful integration or may suggest areas where more skill development or prompting and praising are needed.

Another method of informal evaluation involves how many and what types of interactions children have outside of the program. For example, a child with handicaps visiting, by invitation, the home of a child without handicaps for an afternoon of play, or vice versa, may be an indicator that community acceptance and inclusion beyond the confines of the preschool setting have been achieved. Ultimately, this level of acceptance and inclusion defines true community inte-gration.

Evaluation of Impact on Parents

Formal Measures. Parents of children in an integrated program are consumers of a product, their child's preschool education. As consumers, they should be given an opportunity to express satisfaction/dissatisfaction with the program, and to offer suggestions for improvements. Appendix 11.B shows a sample parent satisfaction questionnaire that may be used with parents.

In developing a parent questionnaire, items should be kept simple and short. A questionnaire that does not exceed one page in length is also more easily completed and more likely to be returned than longer ones.

In Chapter 5, the Parent Integration Opinionnaire (Appendix 5.A) was discussed as a measure for designing parent preparation activities. This opinionnaire can also be used as a pre-post measure to assess parents' knowledge about and general support for integration.

Informal Measures. Valuable parent feedback can often be obtained from the brief, daily exchanges between parents and teachers when children are brought to or picked up at school. Teachers should remain alert to subtle messages of concern and to indicators of success that can be logged for future reference. A log or notebook for entering statements as they arise is a useful mechanism for recalling informal exchanges.

Another indicator of impact is the recruitment of new children through word-of-mouth information passed from one parent to another. The best endorsement that a program can receive is a recommendation from a participating parent to another family in the community.

Evaluation of Impact on Staff

Formal Measures. The staff who implement the day-to-day activities of an integrated preschool program are critical to the program's outcome. The impressions, opinions, and satisfaction of staff should be sampled regularly, and close attention should be directed at recommendations or concerns raised. It is critical that staff see that their suggestions are genuinely considered, and that changes occur based on their input whenever possible. One version of a staff satisfaction form is shown in Appendix 11.C.

A similar feedback form can be utilized to obtain administrator feedback by modifying question number 2 to assess the reaction of staff in the school or program, instead of the reactions of children.

The TEAM-PK (Appendix 3.D) and General Teacher Needs Assessment (Appendix 3.C) were discussed in Chapter 3 as instruments for identifying inservice needs of teachers. The same instrument can also serve as pre-post measures to evaluate the self-reported acquisition of skills by teachers. It is expected that a successful training program, in conjunction with successful integration activities, will result in an increase in the number of responses of teachers indicating self-perceived adequacy of skills related to integration. Administrators and/or program evaluators could also use the TEAM-PK as a guide for conducting direct observations of staff skills. This procedure is time-consuming, but may be a viable option if the development of teacher skills is a primary goal of the integration effort. Too often, teacher skills are taken for granted with no effort made to increase them. Failure to consider teacher skills and their improvement can result in extensive dissatisfaction with integration efforts.

Informal Measures. Casual statements and observations outside the settings of structured classrooms (e.g., teacher lounges, playground) can reveal information about staff's adjustment to integration. While a certain amount of negative opinions about a program may be a common and, in fact, healthy outlet for the stress of day-to-day problems, excessive negative statements or negative reflections on recurring issues can signal areas that demand attention. These negative behaviors may also signal personnel concerns that might require administrative intervention before other staff are negatively affected by the feelings of pervasive gloom created by one individual.

Another informal index of impact is the number and quality of ideas and suggestions initiated by participating teachers as the program evolves. Individuals proceed through levels of use in the process of adopting a new program (Hall & Loucks, 1978; Hall, Loucks, Rutherford, & Newlove, 1975; Loucks, 1983). Initially, individuals engage in *awareness* and *informational* phases during which they acquire knowledge about the innovation. In the next phases, *personal, management*, and *consequence*, individuals study how the innovation will affect them personally, how the system can be managed, and how the target population will be affected. After implementation, ideas from other sources are incorporated in the *collaboration* phase. Finally, when a system is successfully adopted and becomes accepted, *refocusing* occurs as individuals begin to add new ideas and modify the innovation as part of the permanent, greater structure. As teachers become comfortable with integration, refocusing may be observed and can be a sign of successful incorporation of integrated classes into the larger school system. The use of an integration task force makes incorporation into the larger system more likely and establishes it earlier than it might otherwise occur.

As an integrated classroom becomes accepted as part of the greater agency, teachers of nonintegrated, regular classes and teachers in integrated classes may begin to cooperate on teacher projects, such as organizing assemblies, fairs, and sports events; sponsoring extra-curricular activities; and developing common curriculum plans and/or materials. The emergence of cooperative teacher behavior is another index of acceptance of integration as a part of the larger system. This type of acceptance reduces the possibility that an integrated program will dissolve or be discontinued as a result of staff changes.

Evaluation of Materials/Time

Formal Measures.   The integration of an existing regular classroom or the reverse integration of a special education classroom may require commitment of new material resources and, during start-up, usually requires a considerable expenditure of time. To accurately determine costs, the administrator or program evaluator must consider additional expenses for building modifications, additional materials, and staff required by integration. These costs should be separated from costs that would already be expected in a program (e.g., adaptive equipment will be needed regardless of where a child with handicaps is served and, thus, cannot be considered an expense unique to integration). Generally, the desegregation of a special education program may have lower start-up costs than the integration of a regular preschool, because the setting already can accommodate wheelchairs and usually contains adaptive equipment. Additionally, consultants typically are already accessible for serving children with special needs. Table 11.2 lists items to consider as potential expenses in an integrated program.

In desegregating a special education program, additional staff to cover the extra children entering the program will be a major consideration. This additional cost of integration can be offset by income from tuition for children without handicaps. Since these families would pay for preschool services in the community, tuition payments are not unexpected for this group.

In integrating a regular preschool program, extra staff would typically accompany the pool of children with handicaps who were formerly served in a segregated setting. Primary expenses may involve modifications of the environment and purchase of materials that may not already accompany specific children when they enter the program.

Table 11.2. Resources Needed for Integrating Special Education or Regular Education Preschool Programs

	Special Education Program	Regular Preschool Program
Building Modifications		X
Additional Staff	X	X
Additional Materials	X	X
(consumables,		
furniture, meals, etc.)		
Adaptive Equipment		X
Consultants		X
Staff Trainers	X	X

Regardless of whether a special education setting or a regular preschool is integrated, time and expense must be planned for staff training concerning integration. The amount of training required will vary, depending on the familiarity of staff with integration. Additionally, training would be expected to be less involved in future years if staff turnover is not great. Administrators or the integration task force can keep a log of time devoted to integration activities such as inservice training, materials preparation, individual study of teaching materials or child information, and organization or planning meetings. An estimate of the personnel costs of integration can be obtained by multiplying hourly rate by amount of time reported. If additional staff were hired or part-time staff were reassigned to full-time status, the cost of personnel would need to include additional items such as benefits for the increased work force.

Informal Measures. Some amount of staff time will remain undocumented. This situation may arise when staff interact in spontaneous meetings or passing conversation, when they fail to report take-home activities and work "after hours," or as they begin to lose a clear distinction of activities performed as part of the integration effort versus activities that they would normally do as part of their traditional duties.

Although these situations may yield an underestimate of the actual personnel costs of integration, they also signal that the integration effort is becoming a routine activity and, as such, is no longer salient as an extra burden or responsibility.

Timing and Frequency

The frequency at which measures of impact may be sampled is an individual decision for each program. This decision must consider the questions that need to be answered regarding impact, the measures necessary to determine if the program's goals were attained, and the disruption of ongoing activities that may result from stopping to sample impact.

In the initial stages of implementation, frequent and detailed feedback is critical for a program to be successful. The information provided through ongoing evaluation is used to modify procedures, prepare further training, and/or identify needed resources to support the new program. It is important to have identified the indices that will be used for evaluation of impact and to have established an initial baseline measure for each. As the program is implemented, indices of impact may be sampled quarterly. A quarterly measure, however, should be quick to complete and relatively unobtrusive, so that participants will not be overwhelmed by the requirements of the evaluation as well as the requirements of the new program. Consequently, although several indices may be selected for evaluation, only some may be sampled quarterly. For example, evaluation of impact upon children may involve standardized testing, criterion-referenced testing, IEP progress on goals and objectives, parent reports, and child reports; however, quarterly evaluation in this area may only consist of reviewing IEP progress and obtaining parent and child reports.

Who Conducts the Evaluation?

When the impact of integration is evaluated, three points should be considered:

1. All indices are unlikely to reflect success or gains. Some may reflect no changes, and some may reflect losses.

2. Supporters of integration may be inclined to emphasize measures of successful outcome.

3. Detractors of integration may be inclined to emphasize measures that do not demonstrate benefits of integrated versus segregated education.

These three points would support a position that an integrated program might best be evaluated by an objective third party. However, few programs can afford the luxury of an external consultant to conduct evaluations. Most programs conduct internal evaluations and must depend on internal checks and balances to gather reliable data.

One option for distributing the responsibility of assessment is to assign different components to various participants from the integration task force. For example, a parent representative may organize formal parent feedback measures while one teacher organizes teacher feedback. Typically, all teachers and parents will share the responsibility of measuring child impact, and administrators or program coordinators will compile data on material resources and time allocation. At some point, however, all of the information must be centralized, reviewed, analyzed, and interpreted. A program administrator can execute this task; however, few administrators can devote the time to this duty. Additionally, participants may wish to comment on the administrator's role in the integration effort, and knowing that this person will receive and process the feedback could affect the content of the responses given. The integration task force is another option for organizing this information.

The members of the integration task force provide a format in which several viewpoints can be considered in addressing concerns. Additionally, having been instrumental in establishing the integrated program, they are knowledgeable of the program and are in a unique position to recommend modifications that are more likely to be realistic and more easily incorporated.

The Future of Preschool Integration

Integration is here to stay. The implementation of P.L. 99-457 provides each school district with a mandate to educate preschoolers who have handicaps in the least restrictive environment that will meet their needs. We believe this is a totally integrated preschool.

Each state education agency has a legal, ethical, and professional responsibility to enforce compliance with the intent and spirit of the law. Program audits should be rigorous, so noncompliance is identified and corrective action applied until compliance occurs. Those preschools implementing exemplary programs should be reinforced for exceeding minimal standards. Some methods for reinforcing districts are to provide additional resources through discretionary funding, to publish newspaper articles, to identify those programs publicly as models, and to write letters to school boards. States must set an expectation of total compliance with the intent of the law and must assist local areas in accessing the training, staffing, and financial resources needed to make statewide integrated preschools a reality. For example, the State of Utah, Office of Special Education, has cooperated in several federal grant activities that have been funded to provide needed training. The Integrated Outreach of Utah Project is one such project, and one portion of its focus is to train school personnel to implement the FMS model.

All of the statements made about the state education agency apply equally to local education agencies. Local education agencies must also expect maximal compliance with the intent of P.L. 99-457, and must reinforce and support efforts to do so. Parent involvement in groups such as the integration task force, when set up by the local board of education or superintendent, can provide the emphasis, leadership, and creditability needed to make integrated preschools a reality. The FMS procedures and materials provide one model for implementing such efforts.

Appendix 11.A.

SOCIAL INTERACTION CODING SYSTEM

Thornburg, M., Striefel, S., Nelke, C., Quintero, M., & Killoran, J.

Purpose: The purpose of this social interaction scoring system is to identify reciprocal social interactions and cooperative play between children with and without handicaps.

Target Behavior: The target behavior throughout the observation time is Social Behavior which is defined as a directed vocalization and/or motor gesture made to another child. Vocalizations and motor gestures are defined as follows:

Directed Vocalization. A vocalization is directed at another child. The first child calls a second child by name, or clearly indicates by gesture that the vocalization is directed to the second child (e.g., establishes eye contact). Interactions with classroom adults are not recorded.

Motor Gestures. A movement causes a child's head, arms, or feet to come into direct contact with the body of another child; there is waving or extending of a child's arms toward another child; one child hands an object to another child, or adds an object to a structure that received attention from another child earlier in the interval; one child smiles directly at another child; one child imitates or follows another child.

A social behavior can also be negative, defined as follows:

Negative Behavior. A negative behavior is an initiation or reciprocation that consists of an aggressive verbalization (e.g., threatens, calls another child names, or vocalizes a refusal to play with others, such as, "No, go away!") and/or an aggressive act (e.g., hits, pinches, bites, exhibits nonplay pushing or pulling, grabs objects without permission, destroys the construction of another child, or indicates by gesture a refusal to play with others through actions such as pushing others away). If an initiation or a reciprocation consists of negative behavior, cooperative play is not recorded, even if other cooperative play is seen during the interval.

Observation Procedure: Each target child is observed for 12 intervals (10 seconds per interval) with five seconds for recording at the end of each interval. An audiotape with verbal cues at the beginning of each observe and record interval is needed. The child is

Appendix 11.A. (continued)

observed for a total of three minutes at a time. Observer should be no more than 20 feet away from target child.

The observation period begins when an audiotaped voice finishes saying, "Begin observation" and ends when the voice starts to say, "Record data." As each new interval begins, observe the <u>first</u> social behavior exhibited. If social behavior is seen, watch to see if interacting parties reciprocate within the 10-second interval. Record which party made an initiation and which party made a reciprocation by circling the appropriate letter (S=subject being observed; H=handicapped peer; N=nonhandicapped peer). If interacting parties do not reciprocate within the 10-second interval, either because they did not have time or just did not respond, record no reciprocation with a dash below party (e.g., <u>N</u>). Additionally, circle (C) if cooperative play was observed during the interval. During group play (e.g., children playing a structured game with three or more individuals), a distinction is made between target child and the group. Record prompts by adults by placing a slash (/) through (P) indicating that a prompt set the occasion for the initiation or reciprocation, and to whom the prompt was directed (S, H, or N). "Imitating" or "following" counts as I=initiation or R=reciprocation only if indicated by a gesture or verbalization organizing the activity, otherwise it is cooperative play. An example of four 10-second intervals making up a one-minute interval, and the definitions for initiations, reciprocations, cooperative play, and prompts, are listed below:

INITIATION	INITIATION	INITIATION	INITIATION
(P) S H N	(P) S H N	(P) S H N	(P) S H N
RECIPROCATION	RECIPROCATION	RECIPROCATION	RECIPROCATION
(P) S H N	(P) S H N	(P) S H N	(P) S H N
COOP. PLAY	COOP. PLAY	COOP. PLAY	COOP. PLAY
C	C	C	C
NEG. BEHAV.	NEG. BEHAV.	NEG. BEHAV.	NEG. BEHAV.
S H N	S H N	S H N	S H N

Social Initiation. The first social behavior exhibited either by the target child or by another child to the target child during a specific interval is a social initiation. The social behavior must be directed to a specific child or group of children.

Appendix 11.A. (continued)

Social Reciprocation. A response made within the 10-second interval by a second child to the initiation made by the first child is a social reciprocation. The return interaction must be directed specifically to the child who made the initiation or to another member of the group if child is involved in group play. If no response is seen within the 10-second interval, reciprocation is marked as no reciprocation.

Reciprocations may also be acts of compliance. For example, if one child says, "Put the block over there," and another child complies within five seconds, reciprocation is coded. In this case, reciprocation is coded even if there is an absence of a vocalization or motor gesture directed specifically to the initiating child.

Cooperative Play. Some reciprocal social interactions may be additionally characterized as cooperative play. The reciprocal social interaction may then be coded as cooperative play if the interaction included any of the following:

A)   Activity involving a common moveable object or objects (e.g., both children add blocks to the same structure).

B)   Activity involving an exchange of objects.

C)   "Unified" or "organized" activity involving common movements or gestures or common vocalizations (e.g., children crawling on ground and roaring like lions, a "game").

D)   Shared-play activity identified as such through verbal approach and response between children (e.g., one child says, "Let's build a house," and the other child answers, "O.K.," or starts building).

E)   The target child and another child move together from one area to another following an initiation by a third child to do so.

F)   The target child waits for and takes a turn with other children during an activity (e.g., children on the slide).

Prompt. A teacher or classroom worker proposes a social exchange between the subject child and other children, or gives attention to ongoing social behavior between the children. If there is no ongoing social behavior and the classroom worker attempts to stimulate such behavior on the part of the interacting child, then a prompt for an initiation is scored. If one of the interacting children has already exhibited social behavior in the current interval, and the classroom worker gives attention to the ongoing interaction, then a prompt for a reciprocation is scored. Continued social behaviors emitted in intervals following the prompted interval are NOT marked as prompted.

Appendix 11.A. (continued)

Peer Interaction Data Collection System

#HC _____

#NHC _____

Observer _____

Date _____
Experimental Condition _____

Target Student _____
Play Activity _____

Initiation	Initiation	Initiation	Initiation
(P) S H N	(P) S H N	(P) S H N	(P) S H N
Reciprocation	Reciprocation	Reciprocation	Reciprocation
(P) S H N	(P) S H N	(P) S H N	(P) S H N
Coop. Play	Coop. Play	Coop. Play	Coop. Play
C	C	C	C
Neg. Beh.	Neg. Beh.	Neg. Beh.	Neg. Beh.
S H N	S H N	S H N	S H N
Initiation	Initiation	Initiation	Initiation
(P) S H N	(P) S H N	(P) S H N	(P) S H N
Reciprocation	Reciprocation	Reciprocation	Reciprocation
(P) S H N	(P) S H N	(P) S H N	(P) S H N
Coop. Play	Coop. Play	Coop. Play	Coop. Play
C	C	C	C
Neg. Beh.	Neg. Beh.	Neg. Beh.	Neg. Beh.
S H N	S H N	S H N	S H N
Initiation	Initiation	Initiation	Initiation
(P) S H N	(P) S H N	(P) S H N	(P) S H N
Reciprocation	Reciprocation	Reciprocation	Reciprocation
(P) S H N	(P) S H N	(P) S H N	(P) S H N
Coop. Play	Coop. Play	Coop. Play	Coop. Play
C	C	C	C
Neg. Beh.	Neg. Beh.	Neg. Beh.	Neg. Beh.
S H N	S H N	S H N	S H N
Initiation	Initiation	Initiation	Initiation
(P) S H N	(P) S H N	(P) S H N	(P) S H N
Reciprocation	Reciprocation	Reciprocation	Reciprocation
(P) S H N	(P) S H N	(P) S H N	(P) S H N
Coop. Play	Coop. Play	Coop. Play	Coop. Play
C	C	C	C
Neg. Beh.	Neg. Beh.	Neg. Beh.	Neg. Beh.
S H N	S H N	S H N	S H N

Appendix 11.B.

Parent Satisfaction Form

Your feedback is critical to the success of future integrated activities. Please take a moment to complete this form about the integrated activities in which your child is participating. Please indicate your response to each item by circling one choice:

1. Generally, I feel positive about the integrated activities in which my child is participating.

Agree	Agree	Disagree	Disagree
Strongly	Somewhat	Somewhat	Strongly

2. I understand the purpose(s) for integrating children with handicaps into classes with their non-handicapped peers.

Agree	Agree	Disagree	Disagree
Strongly	Somewhat	Somewhat	Strongly

3. I think the benefits significantly outweigh any inconveniences of integrated activities.

Agree	Agree	Disagree	Disagree
Strongly	Somewhat	Somewhat	Strongly

4. I have been given the opportunity to be as involved as I wish to be in the I.E.P. decisions regarding the integration of my child.

Agree	Agree	Disagree	Disagree
Strongly	Somewhat	Somewhat	Strongly

5. Regarding my involvement in the decisions to integrate my child I have been: (circle one)

Extremely	Very	Somewhat	Barely	Not
involved	involved	involved	involved	involved
1	2	3	4	5

6. I feel that the interactions that resulted from these activities between children with and without handicaps, were positive and beneficial to all the children.

Agree	Agree	Disagree	Disagree
Strongly	Somewhat	Somewhat	Strongly

7. Your child has been involved in mainstreaming for the past year. During that time, have there been any changes in the amount of social interaction between your child and other children at:

    If yes, then is the amount:

Church	Yes	No	increasing	decreasing
Neighborhood	Yes	No	increasing	decreasing
After school home visiting	Yes	No	increasing	decreasing
Invitations (birthday parties, sleep-overs, etc.)	Yes	No	increasing	decreasing
_____ (other activity)	Yes	No	increasing	decreasing

8. As a result of mainstreaming, has your child made any friends who regularly play with him/her and who themselves are not handicapped?

9. In future integration activities, I would change or recommend the following:

    Any other comments are welcome. Thank you!

Appendix 11.C.

Staff Satisfaction Form

Your feedback is critical to the success of future mainstreaming activities. Please take a moment to complete this form about the mainstreaming activities in which your students are participating. Please indicate your response to each item by circling one choice:

1. Generally, I feel positive about the mainstreaming activities in which we are participating.

   Agree   *Agree*   *Disagree*   *Disagree*
   Strongly   *Somewhat*   *Somewhat*   *Strongly*

2. The children in my classroom/program reacted positively to the mainstreaming activities.

   Agree   *Agree*   *Disagree*   *Disagree*
   Strongly   *Somewhat*   *Somewhat*   *Strongly*

3. I understand the purpose(s) for integrating children with handicaps into classes with their non-handicapped peers.

   Agree   *Agree*   *Disagree*   *Disagree*
   Strongly   *Somewhat*   *Somewhat*   *Strongly*

4. I think the benefits significantly outweigh any inconveniences of mainstreaming activities.

   Agree   *Agree*   *Disagree*   *Disagree*
   Strongly   *Somewhat*   *Somewhat*   *Strongly*

5. I have been given the opportunity to be as involved as I wish to be, in planning and carrying out this mainstreaming.

   Agree   *Agree*   *Disagree*   *Disagree*
   Strongly   *Somewhat*   *Somewhat*   *Strongly*

6. I feel that the interactions that resulted from the activities between children with and without handicaps were positive and beneficial to all the children.

   Agree   *Agree*   *Disagree*   *Disagree*
   Strongly   *Somewhat*   *Somewhat*   *Strongly*

7. In future mainstreaming activities, I would change or recommend the following:

Any other comments are welcome. Thank you!

References

Adams, P., Striefel, S., Frede, E., Quintero, M., & Killoran, J. (1985). *Successful mainstreaming: The elimination of common barriers.* Logan: Utah State University, Developmental Center for Handicapped Persons.

Arick, J. R., Almond, P. J., Young, C., & Krug, D. A. (1983). *Effective mainstreaming in the schools.* Portland, OR: ASIEP Education.

Asper, A. L. (1973). The effects of cross-age tutoring on the frequency of social contacts initiated by withdrawn elementary school children. *Dissertation Abstracts International, 35,* 02–A, 878.

Ballard, J., Ramirez, B., & Zantal-Wiener, K. (1987). *Public Law 94-142, Section 504, and Public Law 99-457: Understanding what they are and are not.* Department of Government Relations. Reston, VA: The Council for Exceptional Children.

Bauer, A., & Shea, T. (1985). Parent involvement: The development of capital in special education. *Techniques: A Journal for Remedial Education and Counseling, 1*(3), 239–244.

Bayley, N. (1969). *Bayley Scales of Infant Development.* New York: Psychological Corp.

Beery, K. E. (1977). *Models for mainstreaming.* San Raphael, CA: Dimensions.

Behl, D. (1988). *Assessment of young children with handicaps.* Paper presented at Utah State Office of Education Preschool Training Conference, Salt Lake City.

Berres, M. S., & Knoblock, P. (1987). Introduction and perspective. In M. S. Berres & P. Knoblock (Eds.), *Program models for mainstreaming: Integrating students with moderate to severe disabilities* (pp. 1–18). Austin, TX: PRO-ED.

Birch, J. M. (1974). *Mainstreaming educable mentally retarded regular classes.* Reston, VA: The Council for Exceptional Children.

Bloom, M., & Garfunkel, F. (1981). Least restrictive environments and parent-child rights: A paradox. *Urban Education, 15*(4), 379–401.

Brigance, A. (1978). *Brigance Diagnostic Inventory of Early Development.* Woburn, MA: Curriculum Associates.

Brown, L., Branston, M. B., Hamre-Nietupski, S., Johnson, F., Wilcox, B., & Gruenewald, L. (1979). A rationale for comprehensive longitudinal interactions between severely handicapped students and nonhandicapped students and other citizens. *AAESPH Review, 4*(1), 3–14.

Brown, L., Branston, M. B., Hamre-Nietupski, S., Pumpian, I., Certo, N., & Gruenewald, L. (1979). A strategy for developing chronological age appropriate and functional curricular content for severely handicapped adolescents and young adults. *The Journal of Special Education, 13*(1), 81–90.

Brown, L., Ford, A., Nisbet, J., Sweet, M., Donnellan, A., & Gruenewald, L. (1983). Opportunities available when severely handicapped students attend chronological age appropriate regular schools. *Journal of the Association for the Severely Handicapped, 8*(1), 16–24.

Brown, L., Nietupski, J., & Hamre-Nietupski, S. (1976). The criterion of ultimate functioning. In M. A. Thomas (Ed.), *Hey, don't forget about me! Education's investment in the severely and profoundly handicapped*. Reston, VA: The Council for Exceptional Children.

Brown, L., Nisbet, J., Ford, A., Sweet, M., Shiraga, B., York, J., & Loomis, R. (1983). The critical need for nonschool instruction in educational programs for severely handicapped students. *Journal of the Association for the Severely Handicapped, 8*(3), 71–77.

Bzoch, K. R., & League, R. (1971). *Receptive Expressive Emergent Language Scale*. Gainesville, FL: Tree of Life Press.

Cansler, D. P., & Winton, P. (1983). Parents and preschool mainstreaming. In I. Anderson & T. Black (Eds.), *Mainstreaming in early education* (pp. 65–83). Chapel Hill: University of North Carolina, TADS Publications.

Carlberg, C., & Kavale, K. (1980). Efficacy of special versus regular class placement for exceptional children: A meta-analysis. *The Journal of Special Education, 14*(3), 295–309.

Carta, J., Sainato, D. M., & Greenwood, C. R. (1988). Advances in the ecological assessment of classroom instruction of young children with handicaps. In S. L. Odom & M. V. Karnes (Eds.), *Early intervention for infants and children with handicaps* (pp. 217–239). Baltimore: Brookes.

Casto, G., & Mastropieri, M. (1986). Strain & Smith do protest too much: A response. *Exceptional Children, 53*(3), 266–268.

Cooke, T. P., Ruskus, J. A., Appolloni, T., & Peck, C. A. (1981). Handicapped preschool children in the mainstream: Background, outcomes and clinical suggestions. *Topics in Early Childhood Special Education, 1*(1), 73–83.

Crisci, P. E. (1981). Competencies for integration: Problems and issues. *Education and Training of the Mentally Retarded, 16*, 175–182.

Danielson, E.B., Lynch, E.C., Monyano, A., Johnson, B., & Bettenburg, A. (1988). *Assessment: Best practices for assessing young children*. Saint Paul: Minnesota Department of Education.

Demerest, E., & Vuoulo, P. (1983). Perspectives of mainstreaming: A parent's view, a teacher's view. *Children Today, 18*(1), 26–28.

DeWulf, M. J., Biery, T. M., & Stowitschek, J. J. (1987). Modifying preschool teaching behavior through telecommunications and graphic feedback. *Teacher Education and Special Education, 10*(4), 171–179.

Donaldson, J. (1980). Changing attitudes toward handicapped persons: A review and analysis of research. *Exceptional Children, 46*(7), 504–513.

Donder, J., & York, R. (1984). Integration of students with severe handicaps. In N. Certo, N. Haring, & R. York (Eds.), *Integration of severely handicapped students* (pp. 1–14). Baltimore: Brookes.

Dunn, L. M., Chun, L. T., Crowell, D. C., Dunn, L. M., Alevy, L. G., & Yackel, E. R. (1976). *PEEK (Peabody Early Experiences Kit)*. Circle Pines, MN: American Guidance Service.

Education of Handicapped Amendment of 1986 (Public Law 99-457). (1986). *Education of the Handicapped*. Alexandria, VA: CRR

Elbaum, L. (1981). *Working with schools: For parents of children in need of exceptional education*. Madison: Wisconsin Coalition for Advocacy.

Englemann, S. A., Osborn, J. (1976). *DISTAR Language I*. Chicago: Science Research Associates.

Fiechtl, B., Innocenti, M., & Rule, S. (1987). *Skills for school success*. Logan: Utah State University.

Findlay, J., Miller, P., Pegram, A., Richey, L., Sanford, A., & Semrau, B. (1976). *A planning guide to the preschool curriculum: The child, the process, the day*. Chapel Hill: University of North Carolina, Chapel Hill Training–Outreach Project.

Folio, M. R., & Fewell, R. R. (1983). *Peabody Developmental Motor Scales and Activity Cards*. New York: Teaching Resources.

Gaylord-Ross, R. (1988). *Integration strategies for students with handicaps*. Baltimore: Brookes.

Greer, J. G., Anderson, R. M., & Odle, S. J. (1982). *Strategies for helping severely and multiply handicapped citizens*. Austin, TX: PRO-ED.

Gresham, F. M. (1982). Misguided mainstreaming: The case for social skills training with handicapped children. *Exceptional Children, 48*(5), 422–433.

Guralnick, M. J. (1983). Fundamental issues in preschool mainstreaming. In J. Anderson & T. Black (Eds.), *Mainstreaming in early education* (pp. 1–20). Chapel Hill: University of North Carolina, Technical Assistance Development System.

Guralnick, M. J., & Bennett, F. C. (1987). *The effectiveness of early intervention for at-risk and handicapped children*. San Diego: Academic Press.

Hains, A. H., Fowler, S. A., & Chandler, L. K. (1988). Planning school transitions: Family and professional collaboration. *Journal of the Division for Early Childhood, 12*(2), 108–115.

Hall, G. E., & Loucks, S. F. (1978). *Innovation configurations: Analyzing the adaptations of innovations*. Austin: Research and Development Center for Teacher Education, University of Texas.

Hall, G. E., Loucks, S., Rutherford, W., & Newlove, B. (1975). Levels of use of the innovation: A framework for analyzing innovation adoption. *The Journal of Teacher Education, 26*(1), 52–56.

Hamre-Nietupski, S., Nietupski, J., Stainback, W., & Stainback, S. (1984). Preparing school systems for longitudinal integration efforts. In N. Certo, N. Haring, & R. Yonk (Eds.), *Public school integration of severely handicapped students* (pp. 107–142). Baltimore: Brookes.

Hanline, M. F. (1985). Integrating disabled children. *Young Children, 40*(2), 45–48.

Hannah, M. E., & Pliner, S. (1983). Teacher attitudes toward handicapped children: A review and synthesis. *School Psychology Review, 12*(1), 12–25.

Hanson, M. J., & Hanline, M. F. (1989). Integration options for the very young child. In R. Gaylord-Ross (Ed.), *Integration strategies for students with handicaps* (pp. 177–194). Baltimore: Brookes.

Heekin, S., & Mengel, P. (Eds.). (1983). *New friends.* Chapel Hill: University of North Carolina, Chapel Hill Training–Outreach Project.

Horner, R. (1989). *Social support: Measurement and assistance procedures.* Paper presented at Office of Special Education Programs, Research Project Directors' Conference, Washington, DC.

Hughes, J. H., & Hurth, J. L. (1984). *Handicapped children and mainstreaming: A mental health perspective.* Rockville, MD: U.S. Department of Health and Human Services.

Jenkins, J. R., & Jenkins, L. M. (1981). *Cross-age and peer tutoring: Help for children with learning problems.* Reston, VA: The Council for Exceptional Children.

Jenkins, J. R., & Jenkins, L. M. (1982). *Peer and cross-age tutoring.* Washington, DC: American Association of Colleges for Teacher Education.

Johnson, D. W., & Johnson, R. T. (1981). Organizing the school's social structure for mainstreaming. In P. Bates (Ed.), *Mainstreaming: Our current knowledge base* (pp. 141–160). Minneapolis: University of Minnesota.

Johnson, D. W., & Johnson, R. T. (1986). Mainstreaming and cooperative learning strategies. *Exceptional Children, 52*(6), 553–561.

Karnes, M. B. (1980). Mainstreaming parents of the handicapped. In H. D. Burbach (Ed.), *Mainstreaming: A book of readings and resources for the classroom teachers* (pp. 68–70). Dubuque, IA: Kendall-Hunt.

Karnes, M. B., & Lee, R. C. (1978). *Early childhood.* Reston, VA: The Council for Exceptional Children.

Kaufman, M., Gottlieb, J., Agard, J., & Kukic, M. (1975). Mainstreaming: Toward an explication of the construct. In E. L. Meyer, G. A. Vergason, & R. J. Whelan (Eds.), *Alternatives for teaching exceptional children* (pp. 40–41). Denver: Love.

Killoran, J. (1988a). Characteristics of effective early intervention models: What we should strive for. *The Special Educator, 8*(5), 2–3.

Killoran, J. (1988b). Transition in transition. *Special Educator, 8*(6), 2–3.

Killoran, P. M., Killoran, J., Rule, S., Innocenti, M., Morgan, J., & Stowitschek, J. (1987). *Microsession training and transfer procedural manual (revised).* Logan: Utah State University, Developmental Center for Handicapped Persons.

Killoran, J., Striefel, S., Quintero, M., & Yanito, T. (1986). *The mainstreaming expectations and skills assessment–Preschool and kindergarten.* Curriculum product, Utah State University, Developmental Center for Handicapped Persons, Logan.

Killoran, J., Striefel, S., Stowitschek, J., Rule, S., Innocenti, M., & Boswell, C. (1983). Prompting and praising social interactions: Teaching basic skills to handicapped preschoolers in integrated settings. In C. Mason (Ed.), *Early education and the exceptional child: Early impact and long term gains.* Billings: Institute for Habilitative Services, Eastern Montana College.

Knoll, J. A., & Meyer, L. H. (1986). Integrated schooling and educational quality: Principles and effective practices. In M. S. Berres & P. Knoblock (Eds.), *Program models for mainstreaming* (pp. 41–59). Austin, TX: PRO-ED.

Krehbiel, R., & Sheldon, P. (1985). *Family involvement and the preschool program.* Albuquerque: Albuquerque Special Preschool.

Kroth, R. L. (1980). The mirror model of parental involvement. *Pointer, 25*(1), 18–22.

Kroth, R., & Krehbiel, R. (1982). *Parent-teacher interaction.* Washington, DC: American Association of Colleges for Teacher Education.

Krouse, J., Gerber, M., & Kauffman, J. (1981). Peer tutoring: Procedures, promises and unresolved issues. *Exceptional Education Quarterly, 1*(4), 107–115.

Larrivee, B. (1981, September). Effect of inservice training intensity on teacher's attitudes toward mainstreaming. *Exceptional Children, 48*(1), 34–40.

Larrivee, B. (1982). Identifying effective teaching behaviors for mainstreaming. *Teacher Education and Special Education, 5*(3), 2–6.

Leiberman, L. M. (1986). *Special educator's guide to regular education.* Newtonville, MA: Glo Worm.

Lombardi, T., Meadowcroft, P., & Strasburger, R. (1982). Modifying teacher trainers' attitudes toward mainstreaming. *Exceptional Children, 48*(6), 544–545.

Loucks, S. (1983). *Planning for dissemination.* Chapel Hill: Technical University of North Carolina, Assistance Development System.

Madden, N. A., & Slavin, R. E. (1983). Mainstreaming students with mild handicaps: Academic and social outcomes. *Review of Educational Research, 53*(4), 519–569.

Marion, R. L. (1981). *Educators, parents, and exceptional children: A handbook for counselors, teachers, and special children.* Rockville, MD: Aspen.

Masat, L. J., & Schack, F. K. (1981). The mainstream teacher: Training is not enough. *Principal, 61*(2), 28–30.

McClean, M., & Odom, S. (1988, June). Least restrictive environment and social integration. *Division of Early Childhood White Paper,* 1–8.

McCormack, M. (1984). *What they don't teach you at the Harvard Business School.* New York: Bantam.

McCormick, L., & Kawate, J. (1982). Kindergarten survival skills: New directions for preschool special education. *Education and Training of the Mentally Retarded, 17*(3), 247–252.

McDonnell, A., & Hardman, M. (1988). A synthesis of "best practice" guidelines for early childhood services. *Journal of the Division for Early Childhood, 12*(4), 328–341.

McLean, J., & Snyder-McLean, L. (1987). *A transactional approach to language.* Parsons: Parsons Research Center, University of Kansas.

Mlynek, S., Hannah, M. E., & Hamlin, M. A. (1982). Mainstreaming: Parental perceptions. *Psychology in the Schools, 19*(3), 354–359.

Mott, S., Striefel, S., & Quintero, M. (1986). *Preparing nonhandicapped students for mainstreaming: A literature review for school psychologists.* Logan: Developmental Center for Handicapped Persons, Utah State University.

Nash, C. E., & Boileau, J. L. (1980). *The teacher's guide to mainstreaming: A handbook for regular classroom teachers.* Unpublished manuscript.

Newborg, J., Stock, J. R., Wnek, L., Guidubaldi, J., & Svinicki, J. (1984). *Battelle Developmental Inventory.* Allen, TX: Teaching Resources.

Nietupski, J., Hamre-Nietupski, S., Schultz, C., & Oakwood, L. (1980). *Severely handicapped students in regular school: A progress report.* Milwaukee, WI: Milwaukee Public Schools.

Noel, M. (1984). Securing integrated services: Four histories. In N. Certo, N. Haring, & R. York (Eds.), *Public school integration of severely handicapped students* (pp. 43–64). Baltimore: Brookes.

O'Connell, J. C. (1986, Spring). Managing small group instruction in an integrated preschool setting. *Teaching Exceptional Children, 18*(3), 166–172.

O'Conner, R. D. (1972). Relative efficacy of modeling, shaping, and combined procedures for modification of social withdrawal. *Journal of Abnormal Psychology, 79*(3), 327–334.

Odom, S. L., Hoyson, M., Jamieson, B., & Strain, P. S. (1985). Increasing handicapped preschoolers' peer social interactions: Cross-setting and component analysis. *Journal of Applied Behavior Analysis, 18*(1), 3–6.

Odom, S. L., & Karnes, M. (1988). *Early intervention with infants and children with handicaps: An empirical base.* Baltimore: Brookes.

Odom, S. L., & McEvoy, M. A. (1988). Integration of young children with handicaps and normally developing children. In S. L. Odom & M. B. Karnes (Eds.), *Early intervention for infants and children with handicaps* (pp. 241–268). Baltimore: Brookes.

Pasanella, A. L., & Volkmor, C. B. (1981). *Teaching handicapped students in the mainstream: Coming back or never leaving* (2nd ed.). Columbus, OH: Merrill.

Peterson, N. L. (1983). Personnel training for mainstreaming young handicapped children. In J. Anderson & T. Black (Eds.), *Mainstreaming in early education* (pp. 21–44). Chapel Hill, NC: Technical Assistance Development System.

Powers, D. A. (1983). Mainstreaming and the inservice education of teachers. *Exceptional Children, 49*(5), 432–439.

Price, M., & Weinberg, N. (1982). *Making integration work.* Albuquerque: Albuquerque Special Preschool.

Public Law 94-142. (1975). The Education for All Handicapped Children Act, *Federal Register*, November 27th, 1975: Washington, DC.

Public Law 99-457. (1986). The Education for All Handicapped Children Act Amendments of 1986, *Federal Register*, October 8th, 1986: Washington, DC.

Quintero, M., & Striefel, S. (1986). *Creating support for mainstreaming through parent education*. Reston, VA: The Council for Exceptional Children.

Redden, M. R. (1976). *An investigation of mainstreaming competencies of regular elementary teachers*. Unpublished doctoral dissertation, University of Kentucky, Lexington.

Reynolds, M. C. (1988). Past, present, and future of school integration. *Impact, 1*(2), 2.

Reynolds, M. C., & Birch, J. W. (1982). *Teaching exceptional children in all America's schools*. Reston, VA: The Council for Exceptional Children.

Rule, S., Fiechtl, B. J., & Innocenti, M. S. (1990). Preparation for transition to mainstreamed post-preschool environments: Development of a survival skills curriculum. *Topics in Early Childhood Special Education, 9*, 78–90.

Rule, S., Killoran, J., Stowitschek, J., Innocenti, M., Striefel, S., & Boswell, C. (1985). Training and support for mainstream day care staff. *Early Childhood Research Quarterly, 20*(2–3), 99–113.

Rule, S., Stowitschek, J., Innocenti, M., Striefel, S., Killoran, J., Swezey, K., & Boswell, C. (1987). The social integration program: An analysis of the effects of mainstreaming handicapped children into day care centers. *Education and Treatment of Children, 10*(2), 175–192.

Salend, S., & Johns, J. (1983). A tale of two teachers: Changing teacher commitment to mainstreaming. *Teaching Exceptional Children, 15*(2), 82–85.

Sanok, R.L., & Striefel, S. (1979). Elective mutism: Generalization of verbal responding across people and settings. *Behavior Therapy, 10*, 357–371.

Schaefer, D. S., & Moersch, M. S. (Eds.). (1981). *Developmental Programming for Infants and Young Children, Vols. 1, 2, & 3*. Lansing: University of Michigan.

Schanzer, S. S. (1981). When can we justify mainstreaming? *Principal, 61*(2), 31–32.

Schrag, J. (1984). Statewide integration of severely handicapped students: Issues and alternatives for states. In N. Certo, N. Haring, & R. York (Eds.), *Public school integration of severely handicapped students* (pp. 227–292). Baltimore: Brookes.

Schultz, J. B., & Turnbull, A. P. (1983). *Mainstreaming handicapped students: A guide for classroom teachers* (2nd ed.). Boston: Allyn & Bacon.

Schwartz, L. L. (1984). *Exceptional students in the mainstream*. Belmont, CA: Wadsworth.

Scruggs, T. E., Mastropieri, M. A., & Richter, L. (1981). *Tutoring with behaviorally disordered students: Social and academic benefits*. Unpublished manuscript, Utah State University, Developmental Center for Handicapped Persons, Logan.

Sharp, B. L. (1982). Key support personnel: Administrators, counselors, psychologists. In B. L. Sharp (Ed.), *Dean's grants projects: Challenge and change in teacher education* (pp. 117–130). Washington, DC: American Association of Colleges for Teacher Education.

Stainback, W., & Stainback, S. (1981). A review of research on interactions between severely handicapped and nonhandicapped students. *The Journal of the Association for the Severely Handicapped, 6*(3), 23–29.

Stainback, W., & Stainback, S. (1983). A review of research on the educability of profoundly retarded persons. *Education and Training of the Mentally Retarded, 18*(2), 90–100.

Stainback, W., Stainback, S., & Jaben, T. (1981). Providing opportunities for interactions between severely handicapped and nonhandicapped students. *Teaching Exceptional Children, 13*(2), 72–75.

Stetson, F. (1984). Critical factors that facilitate integration. In N. Certo, N. Haring, & R. York (Eds.), *Public school integration of severely handicapped students* (pp. 65–82). Baltimore: Brookes.

Stokes, T. F., & Baer, D. M. (1977). An implicit technology of generalization. *Journal of Applied Behavior Analysis, 10*(2), 349–369.

Stowitschek, J., Striefel, S., & Boswell, C. (1981). *A social integration model for young handicapped children* (U.S. Department of Special Education Grant No. G008100249). Logan: Utah State University.

Strain, P. S., Hoyson, M., & Jamieson, B. (1985). Normally developing preschoolers as intervention agents for autistic-like children: Effects on class department and social interaction. *Journal of the Division for Early Childhood Education, 9*(2), 105–112.

Strain, P., & Smith, B. (1986). A counter interpretation of early intervention effects: A response to Casto and Mastropieri. *Exceptional Children, 53*(3), 260–265.

Stremel-Campbell, K., Moore, W., Johnson-Dorn, N., Clark, J., & Toews, J. (1983). Integration for severely handicapped children and youth. *Teaching Research Infant and Child Center Newsletter, 12*(1), 1–6.

Striefel, S., & Cadez, M. J. (1983a). *Serving children and adolescents with developmental disabilities in the special education classroom: Proven methods.* Baltimore: Brookes.

Striefel, S., & Cadez, M. (1983b). *The program assessment and planning guide for developmentally disabled and preschool children.* Springfield, IL: Charles C Thomas.

Striefel, S., & Killoran, J. (1984a). *Research and validation of procedures and materials for enhancing mainstreaming* (U.S. Department of Special Education Grant No. G008430088). Logan: Utah State University.

Striefel, S., & Killoran, J. (1984b). *Grouping handicapped and nonhandicapped children in mainstream settings* (HCEEP Grant No. G008401757). Logan: Utah State University.

Striefel, S., Killoran J., & Quintero, M. (1984). *Grouping handicapped and nonhandicapped students in mainstream settings.* Paper presented at American Association on Mental Deficiency, Region IV Conference, Salt Lake City.

Striefel, S., Killoran, J., & Quintero, M. (1985a). *Research and validation of procedure and materials for enhancing mainstreaming* (U.S. Department of Special Education Grant No. G008430088). Logan: Utah State University.

Striefel, S., Killoran, J., & Quintero, M. (1985b). *Grouping handicapped and non-handicapped children in mainstream settings* (HCEEP Grant No. G008401757). Logan: Utah State University.

Striefel, S., Killoran, J., & Quintero, M. (1986). *Research and validation of procedures and materials for enhancing mainstreaming* (U.S. Department of Special Education Grant No. G00840088). Logan: Utah State University.

Striefel, S., Killoran, J., & Quintero, M. (1987). *Functional Mainstreaming for Success project final report.* Logan: Utah State University.

Taylor, S. J. (1982, Fall). From segregation to integration: Strategies for integrating severely handicapped students in normal school and community settings. *Journal of the Association for the Severely Handicapped, 7*(3), 42–49.

Thomason, J., & Arkell, C. (1980). Educating the severely/profoundly handicapped in the public schools: A side-by-side approach. *Exceptional Children, 47*(2), 114–122.

Turnbull, A. P., & Blacher-Dixon, J. (1980). Preschool mainstreaming: Impact on parents. In J. J. Gallagher (Ed.), *New directions for exceptional children, 1* (pp. 71–99). San Francisco: Jossey-Bass.

Turnbull, A. P., & Schultz, J. B. (1979). *Mainstreaming handicapped students: A guide for the classroom teacher.* Boston: Allyn & Bacon.

Turnbull, A. P., Winton, P. J., Blacher, J., & Salkind, N. (1982, December). Mainstreaming in the kindergarten classroom: Perspectives of parents of handicapped and nonhandicapped children. *Journal of the Division for Early Childhood, 6*, 14–20.

Vergon, C., & Ross, J. (1981). Educating handicapped with nonhandicapped children: The legal foundation for the least restrictive environment concept. In P. Bates (Ed.), *Mainstreaming: Our current knowledge base* (pp. 35–58). Minneapolis: University of Minnesota National Support Systems Project.

Voeltz, L. (1984). Program and curriculum innovations to prepare children for integration. In N. Certo, N. Haring, & R. York (Eds.), *Public school integration of severely handicapped students* (pp. 155–184). Baltimore: Brookes.

Voeltz, L., Keshi, G., Brown, S., & Kube, C. (1980). *Special friends training manual: Starting a project in your school.* Honolulu: University of Hawaii.

Walker, H. M. (1983). *A systematic approach to the integration of handicapped children into less restrictive settings.* Eugene: University of Oregon, College of Education.

Walter, G., & Vincent, L. (1982, December). The handicapped child in the regular kindergarten classroom. *Journal of the Division for Early Childhood, 6*, 84–95.

Weintraub, F. (1979). Professional responsibilities in personnel preparation. In P. O'Brian (Ed.), *Proceedings of the Dean's Grants Northeast Regional Meeting* (pp. 112–130). College Park: University of Maryland.

Weisenstein, G. R., & Pelz, R. (1986). *Administrator's desk reference on special education.* Rockville, MD: Aspen.

White, K., & Mott, S. (1987). Conducting longitudinal research on the efficacy of early intervention with handicapped children. *Journal of the Division for Early Childhood, 12*(1), 13–22.

Whitney, R., & Striefel, S. (1981). Functionality and generalization in training the severely and profoundly handicapped. *Journal of Special Education Technology, 4*(3), 33–39.

Widerstrom, A. (1982). Mainstreaming preschoolers: Should we or shouldn't we? *Childhood Education, 58*(3), 172–174.

Wilcox, B., & Bellamy, G. T. (1982). *Design of high school programs of severely handicapped students*. Baltimore: Brookes.

Wilson, W.C. (1988). Administrative strategies for integration. In R. Gaylord-Ross, *Integration strategies for students with handicaps* (pp. 299–350). Baltimore: Brookes.

Winton, P. J., & Turnbull, A. P. (1981). Parent involvement as viewed by parents of handicapped children. *Topics in Early Childhood Special Education, 1*(1), 11–20.

Winton, P. J., Turnbull, A. P., & Blacher, J. (1983). *Selecting a preschool: A guide for parents of handicapped children*. Baltimore, MD: University Park Press.

Zigmond, N., & Sansone, J. (1981). What we know about mainstreaming from experience. In P. Bates (Ed.), *Mainstreaming: Our current knowledge base* (pp. 97–111). Minneapolis: University of Minnesota, National Support Systems Project.

Zimmerman, I. L., Steiner, V. G., & Pond, R. E. (1979). *Preschool Language Scale*. Columbus, OH: Merrill.

Author Index

Subject Index